LOS PRIMEROS POBLADORES

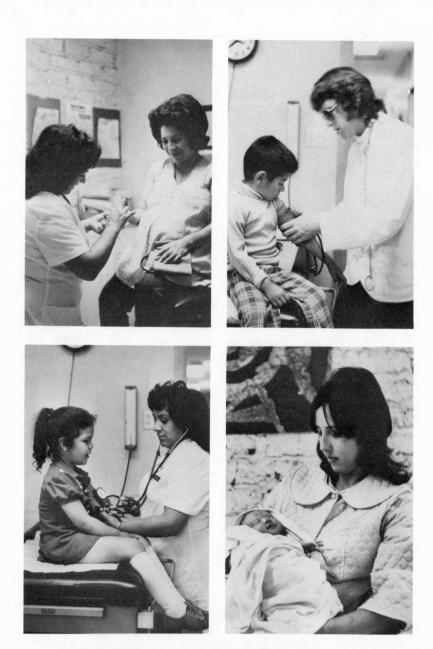

**THE CLINICA DEL PUEBLO DE RIO ARRIBA,
TIERRA AMARILLA, NEW MEXICO**

"The vitality of the descendants of Hispano frontiersmen will find
many new forms of expression" (p. 132).

Photos by J. H. Holliday, D.D.S.

Los Prímeros Pobladores

HISPANIC AMERICANS OF THE UTE FRONTIER

Frances Leon Swadesh

UNIVERSITY   OF   NOTRE   DAME   PRESS
NOTRE DAME   LONDON

Library of Congress Cataloging in Publication Data

Swadesh, Frances Leon.
  Los primeros pobladores.

  Bibliography: p.
  1. Spanish-Americans in New Mexico.   2. Spanish-
Americans in Colorado.   I. Title.   II. Title:
Hispanic Americans of the Ute frontier.
F805.S75S92 1974   917.89'06'68   73-11566
ISBN 0-268-00505-2
ISBN 0-268-00511-7 (pbk.)

Manufactured in the United States of America

To

MANUELITA AND FABIAN

A Fond Salute

The publication of this book was made possible through Ford Foundation Grant No. 710-0372, designed to develop scholars and scholarly materials in the field of Mexican-American studies.

The grant is under the general direction of Julian Samora, University of Notre Dame.

The opinions expressed in the book do not necessarily represent the views of the Ford Foundation.

Contents

Acknowledgments

The research on which this book is based was originally undertaken as background for a doctoral dissertation ("Hispanic Americans of the Ute Frontier," University of Colorado, 1966). It was funded under National Institute of Mental Health Grant No. 3M-9156, Tri-Ethnic Project, Professors Omer C. Stewart and Richard Jessor, co-directors. During the summer of 1963, research was also funded by a grant from the University of Colorado Committee on Research and Creative Work, for the intensive study of historical documents. Research has continued since then, largely on the author's own initiative or as an activity peripheral to other work.

Many thanks are due to the institutions and people who aided in the production of the original work. Professor Stewart, my faculty advisor, and other members of the thesis committee, Professors Gordon Hewes and C. P. Westermeier, were helpful in many ways. Dr. Myra Ellen Jenkins, archivist of the state of New Mexico, gave welcome assistance in the early stages of archival research. In the intervening years, many experts with or without academic degrees have helped and enlightened me. Special thanks go to Eastburn R. Smith for his

careful proofreading, and also to Dr. Anne M. Smith for
her help and counsel in revising the manuscript. They, as
well as Gilbert Benito Cordova, the "Genízaro" scholar
of Abiquiu, have been for years my constant mentors.
Thanks are also due to my son Joel Swadesh for his
patience with me and sometimes cooking dinner during
the writing of this book.

My deepest debt, though, is to the wonderful people
of the San Juan Basin who first guided me toward an
understanding of their cultural and social life and
whetted my curiosity about their history. The accuracy
of their traditional and largely unrecorded historical
recollection was confirmed again and again as long-for-
gotten documents came to light. They and hundreds of
other people of northern New Mexico have generously
given me of their time and knowledge over the years,
asking in return only that *I tell the truth.*

This is exactly what I have tried to do, to the best of
my ability and with many qualms, for Spanish-speaking
people of the Southwest have ample reason to complain
about many interpretations of their history and culture
in the writings of Anglo-American social scientists. Such
errors and misinterpretations as have crept into this
work are deeply regretted. They are entirely my own
responsibility and do not reflect upon informants, advisors, or even written sources.

In order to protect the privacy of individuals, no
name of a living person is mentioned in this book.
Names from previous generations are frequently mentioned, however, especially in the extensive chapter
footnotes at the back. This is for the benefit of mod-
ern-day descendants of *los primeros pobladores* (the
first settlers) who may want to explore their genealogical roots. May they and their children feel as I did while
assembling this record of the living past: that the simple
truth about the people who are the subject of this book
could only shed upon them the honor they merit.

Glossary

Acequia: irrigation ditch.

Alabado: praise-song, hymn.

Alcalde: magistrate; civil and judicial leader of a town or municipality. *Alcalde Mayor:* chief magistrate. *Alcalde Ordinario:* assistant magistrate.

Alferez: standard bearer, ensign, an officer of Colonial troops or militia.

Alianza Federal de los Pueblos Libres: Federated Alliance of Free Communities, an organization of land grant heirs with headquarters in Albuquerque, New Mexico.

Ancón: bend of a river, sheltered cove.

Arroyo: streambed, normally dry, cut into a hillside by runoff from sudden rains.

Arroz: literally, rice; tiny pebbles collected from anthills by Penitentes and strewn over the ground on which they knelt to pray.

Asesor: legal advisor

Atole: gruel of pulverized, dried corn.

Ayuntamiento: town or municipal council.

Barrio: district or suburb of a town.

Bastonero: official at a dance who kept order and called the dances.

Belduque: long hunting knife, a standard item of trade with nomadic Indians.

Bizcocho: hard, sweetened biscuit; a standard item of trade with nomadic Indians.

Caballada: string or herd of horses.

Caciquismo: bossism in political and economic life.

Cambalache: barter trade.

Camino Real: King's Highway, a wagon trail with extensions and alternate routes, running between Santa Fe and Chihuahua. One of its extensions went north to Ojo Caliente.

Campanilismo: literally, support of one's church bells; attachment to the home village.

Cantor: religious song leader.

Capote: division of Utes who, in colonial times, ranged the basin of the San Juan River and its tributary valleys and who traded at Abiquiu. Their descendants are a component of the Southern Utes.

Carne Seca: dried meat, jerky.

Casa: house. *Casa Fuerte:* strong house, fort. *Casita:* small house. *Caseta:* sentry house.

Casta: person of mixed ancestry, whose rights were limited in early colonial times. Castas included Coyotes, Mestizos, Mulatos and Sambos. *Casticismo:* value system of an elite caste.

Chamiso: rabbit brush; in the San Juan Basin, sagebrush. Often pronounced *chamisa.*

Chaqueue: blue corn atole; a dish adopted, like the word itself, from the Tewa Pueblos.

Charolita: casserole, general term used for Lenten foods which are contributed to participants in prayer vigils and are shared in the community.

Chicano: Spanish-speaking person of the Southwest, a term current among people active in the political and cultural movement that stresses historical and cultural ties with Mexico. The term is a contracted form of *Mexicano.*

Cibolero: buffalo hunter.

Coa: digging stick used in planting corn.

Cofradía: religious lay brotherhood. The official title of the Penitente Brotherhood was *La Cofradía de Nuestro Padre Jesús Nazareno* (Brotherhood of Our Father Jesus the Nazarene).

Cojones: literally, testicles. Popular term in Spain and Mexico, but not New Mexico, to connote all aspects of virility and male dominance.

Comanchero: trader, licensed or unlicensed, who traveled out on the buffalo plains to trade with Comanches and other nomadic tribes. After New Mexico was incorporated into the United States, Texas Rangers and vigilante groups sent raiders and lynching parties deep into New Mexico on the claim that the Comancheros were dealing in stolen cattle they had obtained from the Comanches.

Comisionado: deputy, civil leader of a small community.

Compadre: ritual co-parent ("gossip"). *Compadrazgo:* the relationship between the parents and godparents of a child.

Consuegro: co-parents-in-law, a relationship equated with compadrazgo.

Corrida de Gallo: rooster pull, a competitive game played on horseback, especially on the feast day of Santiago (Saint James Major).

Cortes: Spanish parliament.

Coyote, (-a): individual of mixed European and New Mexico Indian or Hispanic parentage.

Criado, (-a): one who has been reared or educated; servant.

Dehesa: community irrigated pasture.

Dieta: forty-day period of rest and seclusion observed by postpartum mothers in New Mexico in emulation of the Virgin Mary.

Ejido: community land.

Encomienda: assignment to a Spanish conqueror of supervision over land near an Indian community whose population was required to perform *repartimiento* labor on these lands for the benefit of the assignee.

Encomendero: recipient of an encomienda grant.

Eriazo: (often written as *hiriazas* in colonial documents): uncultivated lands. At times, the term is used to refer to stubble fields.

Español: Spaniard; New World colonist whose culture was Hispanic and whose ancestry was not obviously of recent Indian origin. *Español Mexicano:* person of Hispanic culture born in Mexico, in many instances a descendant of the soldiers of Hernán Cortés and the Indian women they married. The bulk of the volunteers who colonized New Mexico with Diego de Vargas were members of this group.

Extranjero: stranger, a term usually applied to a Spanish-speaking villager from a community some distance away from the village of the speaker.

Flojo: lax, lazy.

Fortaleza: fortitude.

Fragua: forge, a favorite place-name due to the importance of metal-working and repair of metal tools in the colonial period, since metals were in short supply. In the villages, blacksmiths enjoyed and still enjoy high social status.

Gamuza: dressed hide, chamois leather.

Genízaro: detribalized Christian Indian living under control of colonial authorities. The term was primarily used to apply to Indians of various tribes not native to New Mexico who had been ransomed from captivity among the nomadic tribes and placed as servants in settler households. In practice, many Genízaros were Pueblo Indians who had been expelled from the home village for being overly adaptive to Hispanic culture. They asked for and received rights on Genízaro grants.

Gente de Razón: literally, reasonable people, meaning Christian, settled people of Hispanic culture, regardless of ancestry. Castas and Genízaros were included in this category but often not the Pueblos, because they resisted assimilation into the Hispanic culture.

Gentil: Indian of a nomadic tribe, unconverted to Christianity. The term nomadic is used loosely, since the Navajos after becoming herders abandoned nomadism and had only seasonal shifts of residence.

Gorra Blanca: "White Hood," member of an Hispano vigilante organization which was formed in San Miguel County to combat Anglo usurpation of community range and terrorist tactics in politics in the 1880's.

Hacienda: literally, holding or property, usually meaning real property. In Mexico, this term generally refers to a large ranch community owned by a wealthy landlord who commanded the labor of many peons (landless farmworkers). Haciendas in New Mexico were on a more modest scale.

Hermano, (-a): brother, sister. *Hermano Mayor:* literally, older brother, the principal leader of a Penitente chapter. *Hermano de la Luz:* brother of light, one of the officers of a Penitente chapter.

Hidalgo de Solar Conocido: literally, gentleman of known abode; landed gentleman.

Hispano: Spanish-speaking person. In the Southwest, descen-

dant of seventeenth and eighteenth century colonial settlers of the area.

Hombría: manliness, fulfillment of an adult man's social roles.

Indio: individual born into and still a member of an Indian
tribe.

Indirecta: innuendo, a term rarely heard in New Mexico, where
maliciada is the term used. Innuendoes are used as a gadfly
form of social control over their targets, who can never be
quite sure if the subtle insinuation was intentional or not.

Indo-Hispano: individual of a blend of Indian and Hispanic
ancestry and culture, a term which in the Southwest
stresses the Indian contribution to the local Hispanic culture.

Jacal: wattle and daub (pole and 'dobe) house, ranging in size
from a hut to a spacious building, depending upon the size
of timber available.

Jefe Político: political chief, the title given to the first governors
of New Mexico after establishment of the Mexican Repub-
lic in 1821.

Kachina: sacred personage of the Pueblos, impersonated by a
masked dancer, only seen by the public in Hopi villages
and in the Zuñi *Shalako* dance.

Kiva: chamber used in Pueblo ceremonial observances, often
built underground.

Latia: ceiling made of rows of poles, often laid in a herringbone
design over the roof beams of a house.

Machismo: maleness; values of the male; a term heard less often
in villages of northern New Mexico than *hombría,* a term
which stresses socially responsible adult behavior rather
than sexual prowess and dominance.

Maleficio: the use of incantations and evil brews to induce
illness or death.

Maliciada: gossip, supposition, hint, innuendo. See *indirecta.*

Mano: hand; the stone muller used to grind grain on a metate.
Mano Negra: "Black Hand" vigilante organization of Rio
Arriba County, active since 1912 in opposing fencing of
the open range and its monopoly by Anglo-American cattlemen.

Maromero: acrobat, traveling performer.

Matachine: dance or dancer of a dance-drama with Hispanic
roots in the conquest of the Moors, adapted for New
World enactment. Matachine dances take place at a num-

ber of Tanoan Pueblos, especially at Christmas time, and
are also enacted in some Hispano villages. The San Juan
Basin descendants of Abiquiu settlers have completely lost
knowledge of the Matachines, but some people who were
born in villages neighboring the Pueblos are familiar with
the steps and the music.

Matraca: wooden noisemaker which is whirled by Penitentes
during Holy Week to symbolize the mockery of Jews who
witnessed the Passion of Jesus.

Mayordomo: foreman, supervisor.

Metate: grinding stone with a slight hollow in the center, used
by Indians of the Southwest and Mesoamerica in general to
grind seeds and grains, especially corn.

Mexicano: Mexican or person of southwestern Hispanic culture.

Moache: division of Utes who ranged the eastern portion of the
San Luis Valley of southern Colorado, trading often at
Taos and moving eastward each summer to hunt buffalo
on the Plains. Their descendants are a component of the
Southern Utes of Ignacio, Colorado.

Morada: Penitente chapter house or chapel, often used for
social as well as religious purposes.

Mujerota: "a lot of woman"; woman who fulfills the ideal of
womanhood by her industry, tenderness, and religious
devotion.

Mulato: person of mixed Hispanic and African ancestry.

Panocha: baked, sweetened, sprouted wheat; a favorite Lenten
dish.

Paraje: encampment, location.

Partido: (1) small community within a larger district; (2) shares
agreement between an owner and a contractor to raise
crops or livestock for a fixed percentage of the yield.
Partidario: sharecropper or shareherder.

Patrón: literally, patron, in a protective and paternalistic sense.
Often used in New Mexico to mean employer or boss
without the connotation of protectiveness or paternalism.
People of the San Juan Basin deny that a patrón system
operated in their community, since the status of *rico* was,
and always had been, unstable.

Penitente: member of a religious confraternity, *La Cofradía de
Nuestro Padre Jesús Nazareno* (Brotherhood of Our Father
Jesus the Nazarene), devoted to religious and practical
assistance to the families of those who are sick or dying

and to ritual, penitential activities during Lent and Holy Week.

Pedernal: mountain or knife of flintstone.

Perezoso: lazy.

Piedra Imana: lodestone. Some people of Abiquiu still believe that possession of such a stone imbues its owner with power to attract to himself love and riches.

Piedra Lumbre: alum stone, name of a land grant.

Plaza: in colonial usage, a townsite laid out on a grid-plan, with the church, government buildings, and market fronting on the central square. In New Mexico, many plazas and *placitas* (small plazas) developed in a far less precise and concentrated pattern, and in later times such descriptive terms as "Five Mile Plaza" were used.

Plazuela: house built around one or more patios, forming a maniature plaza, with solid outer walls and all windows facing into the patio. A plazuela structure was built for defensive purposes and often had towers for lookout and defense. Its entry was a *zaguán* (covered entry hall) with a massive gate opening to the outside.

Portal: covered, colonnaded porch.

Primer Poblador: first settler; pioneer.

Puesto: outpost settlement.

Punche: semidomesticated tobacco raised by New Mexico settlers for their own use and for trade with nomadic tribes, without paying the legal tax. Also called "tabaco zimarrón."

Quedirán: literally, "what will they say"; fear of gossip.

Ramada: brush-covered shelter, used for various purposes. Ramadas are still used by some villagers for outdoor cooking in the summertime. Some ramadas are built to provide shade for livestock.

Raza: literally, race, a term used to refer to all Spanish-speaking people of the New World without regard to racial antecedents, blending to varying degrees Old World and New World culture.

Realengo: royal forfeiture, referring especially to land grants. Realengo was often threatened but rarely applied in New Mexico.

Reducción: literally, reduction; a mission center for the conversion of nomadic Indians.

Regidor: councilman of the *ayuntamiento* (town or municipal council).

Repartimiento: apportionment of labor required from the Indian population living near an encomienda.

Resolanero: idle.

Rezador, (-a): prayer leader.

Rico: rich man.

Río Abajo: The Río Grande Valley and its tributary valleys south of Santa Fe County.

Río Arriba: (1) the Río Grande Valley and its tributary valleys from Santa Fe northward; (2) a county of northern New Mexico; (3) an early eighteenth century settlement near present-day Alcalde founded by Sebastian Martín.

Sabuagana: division of Utes, later known as the White Rivers, who traded with Abiquiu settlers. Now a component of the Northern Utes.

Saguarichi: division of Utes ranging central Utah, now a component of the Northern Utes.

Sampuchi: "Sanpete" Utes of Central Utah, now a component of the Northern Utes.

Sobrenombre: nickname.

Socoyote, (-a): youngest child in a family.

Tabewache: divison of Uncompahgre Utes, living in the Uncompahgre and San Luis Valleys of western and southern Colorado, later pushed northwestward and now a component of the Northern Utes.

Tata: literally, grandfather; elder, community leader.

Tegua: moccasin.

Teniente: lieutenant, aide.

Terrón: solid block of adobe soil dug out of the earth with its grass cover intact and used in housebuilding.

Timpanago: division of Utes ranging the Utah Lake area of Central Utah. Their descendants are a component of the Northern Utes.

Tinieblas: Tenebrae or "darkening" ceremony recalling the moment of Jesus' death. Observed on Good Friday in village churches and moradas.

Unión Protectiva: Protective Union, a lay Catholic burial society which has developed in a number of communities of New Mexico, apparently without Church sponsorship or a single center of propagation.

Vara: measure, approximately 33 inches, roughly comparable to a yard.

Vecino: literally, neighbor; tithes-paying settler of *español* or *casta* status.

Vendido: sold out; collaborator.

Vergüenza: literally, shame; the Mediterranean code of modesty, purity, and reserve by which women uphold the system of honor of which their fathers, brothers, and husbands are the custodians. In New Mexico, the term is most often heard in its negative form, *sin vergüenza* (shameless) referring in jocular tones to the deportment of young children. More rarely, the term *sin vergüenza* is applied to local businessmen who have abandoned the Hispanic code of familial solidarity in favor of Anglo "business as usual" business ethics.

Viga: roof beam, generally consisting of the peeled bole of a large conifer, cut to a six to eight inch top diameter (minimum).

Wiminuche: division of Utes who ranged southwestern Colorado and southeastern Utah. Their descendants form the nucleus of the Ute Mountain Utes of southwestern Colorado.

Zaguán: enclosed entry of a plazuela residence, fronted by a massive gate.

Zambo: individual of mixed Indian and African ancestry.

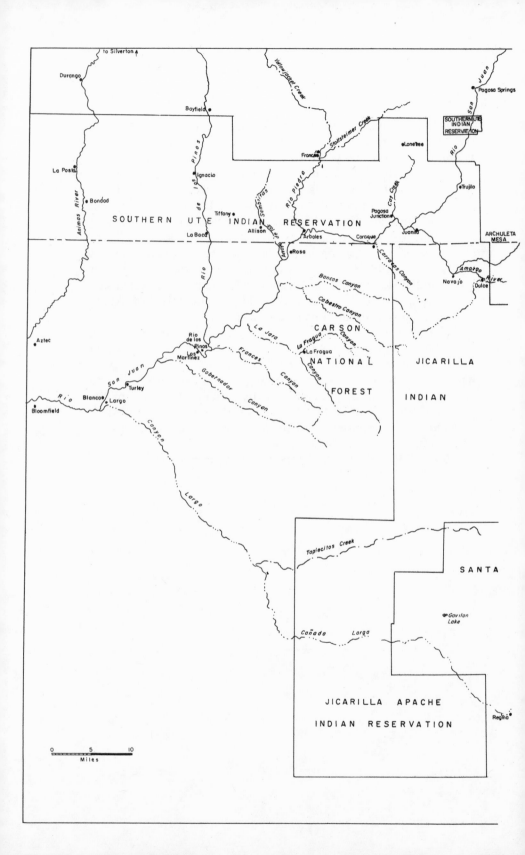

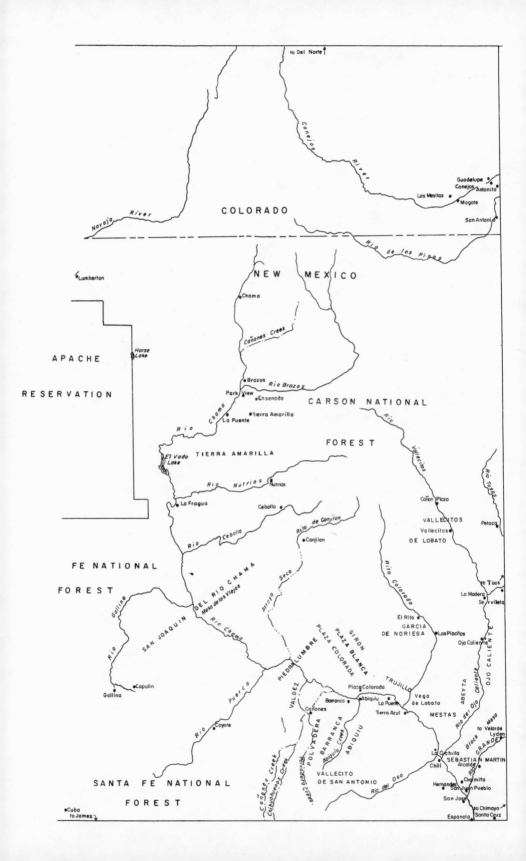

Introduction

This is an historical study of the first eighteenth century Spanish-speaking pioneers of the Chama Valley of north central New Mexico. They first settled Abiquiu, Ojo Caliente, and El Rito, and their descendants spread northward to the San Luis Valley of southern Colorado and the San Juan Basin in the New Mexico-Colorado borderlands. Most of the present-day Spanish-speaking population from Abiquiu north into Colorado is descended from those early settlers and shares much of the history which will be here recounted.

The study commenced in 1960 with a series of interviews with some two hundred Hispano[1] families of the San Juan Basin, whose natal communities were about to be displaced by construction of the Navajo Reservoir. Moving backward in historical time, one family after another traced its forebears to Chama Valley communities with deep roots in the colonial past.

Chama Valley families had moved to the San Luis Valley in the late 1840's. They moved to the San Juan Basin along the New Mexico-Colorado border shortly after the founding of the Southern Ute Agency in 1877 at Ignacio, Colorado. Many had worked with and for the Utes and had benefited from the use of the tribal livestock range. Utes, on their side, had enjoyed economic, religious, recreational, and educational relations with

1

their Hispano neighbors. During the first half-century of reservation life, the Hispanos had functioned as a buffer against domination by the Bureau of Indian Affairs and by Anglo-American neighbors intolerant of Indian ways. In the truest sense, the Ute-Hispano relationship had been free of dominance by either side.

The Hispano population of the San Juan Basin lives within the boundaries of what the *Chicano*[2] political movement calls "Occupied Mexico." During colonial times, this area was part of New Spain; after Mexican independence in 1821, it became a part of the Republic of Mexico. The population in question is part of *La Raza*, a Latin-American expression covering the entire Spanish-speaking New World population, regardless of racial antecedents and varying blends of Old and New World cultures.

Regional differences are pronounced, however, within the overall unity of La Raza, and the villagers of the San Juan Basin in the early 1960's were in many ways divergent from Spanish-speaking villagers of Texas, California, other parts of New Mexico, and Mexico itself.

New Mexico diverges regionally from the rest of the Southwest in that its Spanish-speaking population until recent years has been a majority of the state and has been overwhelmingly composed of rural small landowners. Both Texas and California, which have much greater Spanish-speaking populations, have experienced this group as a landless, largely urban minority, among whom recent arrivals from Mexico have until the last two decades outnumbered citizens by birth. In the New World, New Mexico diverges historically from the rest of Latin America in its scattered settlement pattern despite the regulation for fortified "grid-plan" towns; its weak development of structures of subordination, whether of Indians by Spaniards, the poor by the rich, the landless by the landed, or women by men; its *compadrazgo* (ritual co-parent) system based on existing kin ties and subordinate to the kinship system and its development of a *cofradía* (the religious brotherhood known as the *Penitentes*) as the chief extrafamilial institution for social integration and mutual aid.

Whereas most eighteenth century Hispanic settlements were

influenced by their close proximity to Pueblo neighbors, the Chama Valley settlements were in more intimate contact with nomadic Indians, especially Utes. This contact entailed such pervasive risks and potential profit that few Chama Valley settlers acquired a great deal more wealth than their neighbors. As a result, social stratification was less marked in the Chama Valley communities than in Santa Fe or even in lesser mercantile centers such as Manzano until well after 1846.[3]

Any culture is shaped by the individual and group experience of its bearers; historical research shows that symbiotic contact with Ute Indians commenced early in the eighteenth century and shaped in part the founding and growth of the Chama Valley communities. No Indians dwelt in the Chama Valley west of San Juan Pueblo, but the Utes were frequent visitors to the frontier settlements.

Another vital factor shaping present-day San Juan Basin life is the history of man's relation to land in the communities studied. When this study commenced, the Chicano movement was barely nascent in the Southwest. The land grant movement led by the *Alianza Federal de los Pueblos Libres* (Federated Alliance of Free Communities), New Mexico's distinctive contribution to the Chicano movement, had not yet emerged. Yet discussion with San Juan Basin Hispanos had already made it clear that land and its uses had central importance in their society.

Since 1846 the loss of title to community land grants had spelled impoverishment and community disruption to the settlers of the Chama Valley and their descendants in the San Juan Basin. Now the government was about to displace whole communities again and was remunerating people for their condemned lands at a rate that made it impossible for most of them to replace that which they were losing. The tragedy which faced them added a poignant note to the recollections of past losses, especially the loss of the Tierra Amarilla Grant.

The narration of 250 years of frontier experience in New Mexico revealed a pattern of existence with curious parallels in small and isolated Spanish-speaking populations of both the Old World and the New, who have maintained a mixed pastoral-mercantile economy. The small landowners and sheepmen of

the Chama Valley who lived in recurrent contact with Ute
Indians and shared the risks and profits of this contact had
many resemblances to pastoral communities of northwestern
Spain and even more with Hispano frontiersmen of South
America living in direct contact with nomadic Indians. It can be
said, in fact, that the Hispanic frontier produced a pattern at
least as distinctive as that of the Anglo-American frontier.[4]

The history of the pioneers of the Chama Valley and the San
Juan Basin is presented, therefore, from the standpoint of the
adaptations they made to the challenges and opportunities of
the north central New Mexican environment. They bent the
rigid and hierarchical rules of Spanish colonial society to sim-
pler and more egalitarian forms, while maintaining a strong
sense of community and many gracious traditions in the face of
hardships.

The way of life they evolved was tough, resilient, and survives
today—at least in part. Its setting is in the small and isolated
mountain villages where many people still own some land and
livestock, and it withers as poverty forces families to splinter
and move into urban slums. Applied social scientists may well
ask themselves not only whether it is possible for a culture to
survive under conditions of such traumatic change, but also
whether it is just—or even sensible—to put groups of human
beings through such a cultural wringer.

While the case of the Chama Valley-San Juan Basin frontiersmen is a special one, the same kinds of adaptations and the
same pattern of present-day dilemmas hold in other rural New
Mexican communities that were on the periphery of the frontier
in colonial times and had trading relations with Navajos,
Apaches, Comanches, and other nomadic Indians as their principal means toward economic advancement and social mobility.

Presently exposed to the forces of destruction as it is, the
culture of these frontiersmen shows little disposition to die. A
rich tradition persists under siege, fighting against extinction.
The growth of the Chicano movement and the Alianza has
brought to public attention the vitality of the culture and its
appeal to the hearts of Spanish-speaking southwesterners.[5]

Countrywide, the Anglo-American myth of the melting pot is
giving ground, as the Black, Indian, and Chicano movements

assert their right to equal American citizenship in a context of cultural pluralism. This trend grows as the Anglo-American culture faces an internal crisis brought on by some of its less flexible customs.

It is extraordinarily difficult to change sets of habits that are sanctified by tradition. As we begin to face the economic and environmental dilemmas to which our own cultural biases have brought us, it seems altogether senseless to continue insisting that cultural minorities in the United States put aside their own traditions to conform to the "American Way of Life." As we seek out a more adaptive American Way for the majority of the nation, we would do well to learn about other existing American ways, the ways of Indians and Hispanos, long tested in this land. Having survived in the face of adversity, including that which our dominance has imposed upon them, they can teach us a great deal about cultural survival and social adaptation.

New Mexico's Cultural Sequences[1]

PREHISTORIC INDIANS

Human settlement began in the Southwest some twenty thousand years ago. Since no human skeletal remains have been found, we can only guess that the first inhabitants of the Southwest were the ancestors of today's New Mexico Pueblo Indians and of other groups of Indians with a record of early residence in various parts of the Southwest. Paleo-Indians, who hunted big game, lived east of the Rocky Mountains and continued to hunt mammoths, giant bison, mastodons, and other huge Pleistocene mammals until some nine thousand years ago, when a drier climate set in and the big mammals gradually became extinct.

From west of the Rocky Mountains to the California coast, early populations lived by hunting small animals and gathering wild plant foods. They ground seeds on stone mortars (*metates*) with handheld stones (*manos*). In some parts of New Mexico, Paleo-Indians and Archaic-Desert food gatherers appear to have occupied the same sites simultaneously, especially during the period when big game was growing scarce.[2] This suggests that the Paleo-Indians did not leave with the big game but adapted to the changing environment by following the subsistence methods of the food gatherers. From then until now, adaptation in

7

New Mexico primarily has meant learning how to live in an arid environment.

As early as 3,000 B.C., the presence of corncobs in eastern Arizona and western New Mexico shows that maize cultivation had come from Mexico to the Southwest. Not for another thousand years, however, did cultivation of beans and squash enter the area, and the Archaic-Desert culture lingered as a way of life in New Mexico for another two thousand years. In Utah, Nevada, and parts of California this way of life continued into modern times as a technologically simple but viable adaptation to a harsh environment.

About 300 B.C. a new way of life emerged in southwestern New Mexico, with the pit-house villages of the Mogollon farmers, the first potters of New Mexico. A few hundred years later in the Four Corners area, where Arizona, Utah, Colorado, and New Mexico meet, the first Basketmaker phase of the Anasazi culture began to develop. The art of pottery-making was transmitted, perhaps directly, from the Mogollon to the Anasazi villages.

At some time between 300 B.C. and 700 A.D., cotton was introduced from Mexico to the Southwest. By 700 A.D. cotton cloth was woven in the farming villages, which increasingly showed characteristics directly ancestral to the Pueblo villages of today. By 1100 A.D. the village populations were becoming concentrated in multiple dwelling units. This concentration was made possible by improved agricultural methods.

During the first millenium of the present era, the Hohokam culture of irrigation farmers—under direct influence from urbanized centers of Mexico—emerged in southern Arizona; subsequently, Hohokam influence diffused into New Mexico.[3]

Late in the thirteenth century at the very peak of the prehistoric Pueblo cultures, the large Mogollon, Anasazi, and Hohokam communities were suddenly abandoned, and the main center of Pueblo population shifted eastward to smaller villages in the Rio Grande and Pecos drainages. Scholars believe this was caused by a severe dry cycle, arroyo cutting, and a reduced growing season. As the population of the Eastern Pueblos grew, irrigation farming methods of Hohokam origin solved the problem of subsistence in an increasingly arid climate.

THE PUEBLOS AT TIME OF
FIRST SPANISH CONTACT

By the end of the fourteenth century, the New Mexico Pueblos had occupied the villages that the first Spanish explorers of the mid-sixteenth century described in their travel journals. At the time of contact there were an estimated forty thousand Pueblo Indians, compared with fewer than twenty-six thousand in 1960; and Pueblo villages were more numerous than they are today.

The Pueblos were divided into an eastern and a western branch, distinguished by the fact that the Eastern Pueblos practiced irrigation farming, while the Western Pueblos (Acoma, Zuñi, and—in eastern Arizona—the Hopi villages) continued to rely on floodplain farming. They also had to depend more on wild plants and hunting than did the Eastern Pueblos.

The Pueblos were further subdivided by language. The Tiwas, Tewas, Towas, and Piros of the East all spoke Tanoan languages, a group related to the Uto-Aztecan family. Hopi belongs to the Shoshonean branch of Uto-Aztecan, to which Ute and Comanche also belong, and hence is remotely related to the Tanoan languages. The Keresan Pueblos, both on the Rio Grande and farther west, are thought to be linguistically related to the Caddoans, while the Zuñi language has been variously linked with Uto-Aztecan, Penutian, or Macro-Quechuan, whose main nucleus is in South America.

Each pueblo was an independent, self-governing entity with a primarily religious leadership. The Tanoans had a bilateral kinship system and a dual (moiety) division of the entire village with membership in one's father's moiety. Community structure was tightly organized for ritual purposes and for tasks connected with irrigation farming.

The Western Pueblos were subdivided into matrilineages grouped into clans. Organization was less centralized, and women had important functions in home ownership, care of ceremonial paraphernalia, and control of land. The Rio Grande Keresan Pueblos (Cochití, Santo Domingo, San Felipe and, on the Jemez River, Santa Ana and Zía) practiced irrigation farming and had an intermediate organizational structure, with clans and moieties combined. Jemez, northwest of Zía, was Tanoan in speech but shared the social organization of the Eastern Keresan Pueblos.

Religion in all pueblos was highly ritualized and permeated everyday life. In the West, the dominant concern of religion was weather control, while in the East there was more diversified concern both for other aspects of man's relation with nature and for maintenance of health.

NOMADIC INDIANS OF THE SOUTHWEST

Late in the fifteenth century, bands of Indians whose speech and lifeways were different from the Pueblos' began to drift down from the North. These were the Athapaskan-speaking ancestors of today's Navajos and Apaches. When first they reached New Mexico they were nomadic hunters and food gatherers, but all except the Mescalero Apaches eventually adopted some farming practices, learned directly or indirectly from the Pueblos.

When the Spaniards arrived, some Eastern Pueblos complained that for over half a century Apaches had raided their crops. Relations between the Pueblos and Athapaskans were, however, usually more cordial. Some eastern bands of Apaches traded deer and buffalo meat for vegetable foods and cotton cloth at the pueblos. Groups of Apaches set up their winter camps near certain Tanoan pueblos, sometimes even within the pueblo walls. Possibly the Apache men went off to hunt as they did in colonial times, leaving their women and children in the protection of the pueblo. Had the Spaniards not entered New Mexico when they did, further accommodation of the two cultural types might have occurred, and New Mexico's history might have been very different.[4]

HISPANIC EXPLORATION AND SETTLEMENT OF NEW MEXICO

The first Spanish explorer to set foot in New Mexico was Fray Marcos de Niza in search of the fabled cities of Cíbola. All that Fray Marcos saw of the Pueblos in 1539 was a distant, twilight view of the Zuñi pueblo of Hawikuh, where his guide Estevanico was put to death. The friar's accounts of what had looked like a great city led to authorization of a conquest expedition of several hundred armed horsemen led by Francisco Vasquez de Coronado in 1540.

Coronado sent reconnoitering parties as far west as the Grand Canyon and as far east as the buffalo plains. Supplies for his men were exacted as tribute from the Tiwa Pueblos near Albuquerque. When the Pueblo of Tiguex rebelled against arbitrary demands, the Spaniards put down the uprising by slaughtering hundreds of Indians.

The surviving Tiguex Indians took refuge on the mesa tops, and resistance began to spread among the Pueblos. When Coronado returned to Mexico in 1542, he reported that the Pueblos were neither as wealthy nor as easy to conquer as had been expected. For twenty-nine years there were no further expeditions into New Mexico.

Meanwhile the great silver strikes in Zacatecas in the 1550's moved the perimeter of Spanish settlement northward and reopened the question of potential mineral wealth in New Mexico. In the 1580's and 1590's several expeditions reached New Mexico, attempting conquest and/or conversion, and prospecting for minerals.

The Pueblos had become suspicious of the Spaniards, and whenever force was exerted on them, they resorted to counterforce and flight. Their ability to revert to a life of hunting and food-gathering in times of crisis frustrated a full-scale conquest. They began to select better defensive locations for their villages.[5] When Juan de Oñate brought the first colonists in 1598, the southern Tiwa Pueblos had already regrouped into a few large villages with better defenses than their previous communities.

Oñate's group crossed the Rio Grande at Paso del Norte, the present location of Ciudad Juarez, Chihuahua. The party then traveled up the Rio Grande, passing southern pueblos which had never before been visited by Spaniards. At each pueblo a ceremony was performed, exacting of the pueblo leaders fealty to the King of Spain, a ceremony probably entirely meaningless to the Indians. Reaching the Española Valley, Oñate occupied the pueblo of Okeh, which he renamed San Juan de los Caballeros in honor of his troops. Shortly thereafter, the Spaniards settled in the pueblo of Yuquequnque across the Rio Grande from Okeh near the mouth of the Chama. This pueblo was renamed San Gabriel, and a chapel honoring that saint was soon built.

Oñate brought with him 130 soldiers, many of whom traveled from Mexico with their wives and Indian servants. It is likely that Mexican Indians, both servants and soldiers, outnumbered the Spaniards. In 1610, when the capital villa of Santa Fé was built as the main population nucleus of the colony, a special *barrio* (district) was set aside for these Indian colonists, who were referred to as *Tlaxcalan*.

Tlaxcala is the Nahua-speaking town which allied itself with Cortés in the conquest of the Aztecs. As a reward, the Tlaxcalans were offered the opportunity to participate in further conquests and to receive lands for settlement in conquered territories. Thus, in Santa Fé, the Barrio de Analco was supposedly settled by Tlaxcalans, and the San Miguel Chapel, first built in the seventeenth century, was known as the Chapel of the Indians.

Tlaxcalans and other Indian allies of the Spaniards were Christian converts and spoke Spanish, but their cultural roots were in Mexico, as was true of many other colonists who, though considered Spaniards, were Mexican-born, descendants of Cortés' soldiers and the Indian women they married.[6] The culturally Spanish portion of the population of seventeenth century New Mexico apparently never exceeded three thousand, and its cultural impact on the Indians of New Mexico was slight.

The history of the seventeenth century is one of gross oppression and of rising Indian rebellion, culminating in the 1680 Pueblo Revolt. Although the New Laws of the Indies, promulgated by the Spanish crown in 1540 at the insistence of Fray Bartolomé de las Casas, forbade the imposition of slavery and forced personal service upon Indians, the very nature of colonial rule made the Pueblo Indians unwilling targets of several kinds of exploitation.

In addition to the capital of San Gabriel, which transferred to Santa Fé in 1610, six civil and religious divisions were established near the pueblos, each controlled by a Franciscan missionary, a civil magistrate or *alcalde*, and a military leader. Oñate's principal soldiers were rewarded with *encomiendas*, assigned lands near the pueblos, whose population could be required to furnish tribute in goods and labor, called *repartimiento*. Although the recipients of encomiendas were not supposed to live on their assigned lands, this rule was violated in New Mexico, making it possible for the encomenderos to exploit Indian labor without cease.

The encomienda system did not affect nomadic Indians, who could not be brought under control. Raiding for captives among the nomads, however, brought on counterraids from which the Pueblos suffered no less than the colonists. Indian captives were kept as servants or were sold in the mining communities of northern Mexico.

The Pueblo Indians were obliged to labor for the Franciscan missionaries, building the mission churches, cultivating mission crops, and tending mission livestock. Despite the sincerity of the Franciscans' effort "to save the souls of the Indians," they failed dismally in the seventeenth century. They made little effort to learn the diverse Indian languages or to understand Pueblo religious values. Forcible efforts were made to extirpate the native religion by destroying *kivas* (chambers for religious activities, largely built underground), by burning the masks of *kachinas* (sacred personages impersonated by religious dancers), and by subjecting religious leaders to corporal punishment or even putting them to death. The overriding cause of the 1680 revolt was the series of atrocities perpetrated to suppress Pueblo religion.

The colonial governors, who served without salary, also oppressed the Pueblos by requiring goods and labor, ostensibly for royal tribute but more often for personal profit. Mutual recriminations by settlers, missionaries, and governors fill the meager records of the seventeenth century, as they competed for the services of the Pueblo Indians. There can be no doubt about the Indians' acute suffering, even though some factional accusations may have been exaggerated.[7]

The Pueblos had never really been conquered but had acceded to colonization because the Spaniards promised to protect them from Apache raids, to share their hitherto unknown plants (both food and medicinal) and their domestic animals, and to provide formal education. During the seventeenth century, however, the Apache raids intensified, and the colonists, too few to repel them, began to demand militia service of the Pueblos. The Pueblos received little livestock and were forbidden to ride horses, a mark of aristocracy. Few Pueblos learned to read, although many learned to speak some Spanish.

THE PUEBLO REVOLT

At the time of the Pueblo Revolt of 1680, there were fewer than twenty-five hundred colonists and more than twenty-four thousand Pueblo Indians in New Mexico. Unaccustomed as the Pueblo autonomous villages were to alliances for social action, a joint plan was devised with—as the Spaniards later thought—Apache involvement. Some of the Mexican Indian, mestizo, and mulatto members of the colony certainly did aid the revolt and brought to it their knowledge of Spanish battle tactics and horsemanship. Positive details on this involvement are few, but we know that in both the seventeenth and the eighteenth centuries some deserters from the colony fully assimilated into an Indian way of life.[8]

Acting in unison, the Pueblos put to death twenty-one of the thirty-three Franciscan missionary fathers as well as some 380 settlers in the province. Many women and children were taken captive. The death toll would have been higher had not the Pueblos refrained from further attack during the desperate retreat of the survivors to Paso del Norte. Most of the slain settlers had lived near the Pueblos and were probably encomenderos.

Many Indians of Isleta Pueblo who had not taken part in the uprising were forced to join the retreat, and Indians from the Piro Pueblos near Socorro, decimated by Apache raids in previous years, also joined the retreat. Ysleta del Sur and San Antonio de Senecú are communities near present-day Ciudad Juarez founded by these Indians, who have largely assimilated the Hispanic culture.

In the next twelve years, repeated efforts were made to

reconquer New Mexico. The Indians of several pueblos sustained terrible massacres and some capitulated. Others held out, even though the inter-Pueblo alliance had crumbled shortly after the expulsion of the Spaniards, and Apache raids had resumed on a massive scale.[9]

HISPANIC RESETTLEMENT OF
NEW MEXICO

In 1692 Diego de Vargas was appointed governor of New Mexico and leader of the reconquest. In the late summer and early fall of 1692 he entered New Mexico with a military contingent and traveled from one pueblo to another to secure consent to a new colony. De Vargas took with him Pueblo interpreters and through them made a number of promises which were relayed from pueblo to pueblo. Pursuant to the Laws of the Indies, there were to be no more encomiendas or forced labor. The missionaries were to refrain from forcible evangelization and no one was to violate the privacy of the pueblos. Settlers of the previous colony whose cruelty had aroused Pueblo resentment were to be banned from returning to New Mexico.[10]

When de Vargas restored the colony in the winter of 1693-1694, his proudest boast was that he had made a bloodless reconquest. He spoke too soon, however; a bloody battle took place before the Villa of Santa Fé was recaptured, and in the aftermath of the battle seventy Pueblo leaders were executed. Many of the surviving Tano Indians who had built their pueblo in the Santa Fé plaza were distributed among the colonists and soldiers to serve as slaves and servants.

Pueblo resistance to the reconquest flared sporadically from 1693 to 1696. For many years thereafter, some pueblos were deserted as Indians fled to the mesa tops or went to live with the nomadic tribes. The Picurís Indians went to live with Apaches at Cuartelejo on the Plains. The Towas of Jemez and some Keresans and Tewas lived for years with Navajos of northwestern New Mexico, profoundly influencing Navajo material culture, social organization, and religious symbolism. Many Tanos (southern Tewas) fled to the Hopi villages, where they founded the village of Hano. Some Pueblos decided to live permanently with the nomads, whose numbers from that time rose, while the Pueblo population sharply dwindled.

EIGHTEENTH CENTURY CHANGES

Even during the early troubled years of the eighteenth century, however, the new colony avoided repeating the tragic errors of the seventeenth century. In the first place, the encomienda system disappeared, the settlers instead receiving outright grants for settlement and subsistence on lands not claimed by Indians. These grants were of several kinds, beginning with the town grants for such communities as Santa Fe. Comparable to the town grants, but different from them because no portion could be sold, were the grants confirmed to the Pueblo Indians. Each town and pueblo had a central site for its residential, administrative, and religious buildings, with all irrigable lands divided as agricultural allotments or set aside as community orchard or pasture. An area four leagues square, measuring from the village church, completed the area of a pueblo or town grant. The unsettled lands were the inalienable property of the community, open to all residents for grazing, for collecting firewood, and, when necessary, for cutting timber.

Land grants were also made to individuals, although in New Mexico the large hacienda grant was not characteristic of the eighteenth century. Often a series of adjacent grants of moderate size would be made to a series of families, and if Indian attack forced them to evacuate, efforts would be made to resettle them in one community, much like a town grant. Particularly after the Mexican Republic was established in 1821, the size of grants was increased because the new government desired to colonize all the territory it had inherited from Spain. It feared the expansionist policies of the United States and wanted to establish buffer settlements to defend the territory against raiding Indians.

Many grants were made to groups of petitioners who promised to establish one or more communities on a grant. These grants differed from the town grants because after the first settlement had been made, new settlements could be opened on the grant on petition of the heirs. As long as unused arable lands continued to exist, the population remained there, but as arable land became scarce or was worn out, petitions for new lands went to the authorities. Although these grants were made in the name of the king of Spain from whose royal domain they were bestowed, grantees were generally placed in possession by the nearest town magistrate at the request of the governor. By the mid-eighteenth century, grant documents were sent to Guadalajara for judicial inspection and filing.

Whether a grant was made to a single individual, a group of petitioners, or a town, the grant was conditional until it had been settled for at least three or four years. To earn full title to their grant, the petitioners had to build dwellings, clear fields, dig irrigation ditches, and cultivate crops. As time went on and it became clear that the few presidial troops assigned to the colony would be unable to defend the multiplying communities against the raids of the nomadic Indians, a further condition was established for grantees: they had to provide militia service, not only for the defense of their own communities, but for the whole province as necessary.

Due to recurrent attacks, many grant settlements were periodically abandoned. The settlers would move back to live with relatives in the communities where they had lived before bestowal of the grant. Thus, people of the New Villa of Santa Cruz de la Cañada had to receive their refugee relatives from all the settlements of the Chama Valley. At such times, the governors would try to press for early resettlement by threatening to revoke the grants; nonetheless, grants which were frequently deserted for long periods were not revoked unless it became clear that their grantees had no intention of returning. During the colonial period, virtually all settlers held title on some grant.

When grantees were put into possession of their lands, the governor himself or an alcalde delegated by him would place the grantees in possession. Each grantee would receive a private allotment for a homesite and a strip of agricultural land adequate for raising crops for himself and his family. These strips were usually one hundred fifty *varas* wide, a vara being approximately thirty-three inches. The length of the strip extended from the irrigation ditch at the high end of the field to an area as close to the riverbank as cultivation could be done, since short irrigation ditches were dug upstream of the fields and ran roughly parallel to the stream from which they obtained their water. As the population grew, ditches were sometimes many miles long and brought water, by means of log flumes, to fields distant from the river bank. Despite the shortage of even the simplest tools, irrigation ditches were at times so well engineered that they could carry water over hills. Often, a ditch line was run to the center of a settlement, providing water for a community or church orchard.

At first, control of the flow of a ditch and its maintenance rested with single families or with whichever groups of families had jointly constructed the ditch and used its waters. As the population grew, as the irrigation systems became more complex, and as a series of settlements along a single stream began to experience shortage of irrigation water in a dry year, overall organization of the use of water and maintenance of ditches became increasingly necessary on both a community level and an intercommunity level. Each *acequia madre* (mother ditch) shared by a group of families or an entire community had to be maintained by the able-bodied men of every family that took water from it. In a dry season each family had assigned times to take water from the ditch. Use of water and work on the ditch was supervised by an elected *mayordomo de acequia* (ditch supervisor) who understood the provisions of colonial law governing the use of water and whose authority was great. In years when several *placitas* (plazas) taking water from the same stream were suffering from shortage of water, the communities upstream were not allowed to appropriate all the flow. The mayordomos of all the communities involved met to divide the waters so that all would share equally. Those villages located near Indian pueblos included the pueblo mayordomo in their deliberations, since the priority of rights of the pueblos settled prior to colonial times was recognized by law.

The rationing of water in times of need and the reconciliation of differences between different communities sharing the use of the same stream required the guidance of prudent and strong leaders, knowledgeable in law and precedent. Leadership in managing the irrigation water and in bringing the population together seasonally to clean the ditches and repair the gates was developed over centuries. It continues to operate in northern New Mexican communities as the most respected and unifying force outside the kin group.

Although settlers originally tended to seek lands close to the Pueblos for the protection they afforded, the population increasingly began to fan out along all the watercourses of central New Mexico. The Pueblos were also gradually relieved of the violent interventions against their religious practices which had characterized the seventeenth century, although some settlers and missionaries persisted in accusing individual Indians of witchcraft. Investigations often proved such charges false, and the weight of religious oppression was increasingly lifted.[11]

HORSE AND BUFFALO ON THE PLAINS

On the plains east of the colony, the Eastern Apaches, the Kiowas, and other tribes of the western Plains who hunted the buffalo, learned horsemanship from the Spaniards in the seventeenth century. The way of life that they evolved had revolutionary effects on the whole colony: they became more mobile, more affluent, and more aggressive. Now they had the means to acquire a year-round supply of buffalo for their meat, their hides which provided material for tipis, implements, and warm robes for bedding and winter cloaks. Their sinews provided strings for bows and their hooves provided glue. Horse-drawn travois could carry a great deal more household gear over longer distances than the dog-drawn travois. With horses, these tribes could raid the Pueblos and Spanish settlements and flee with their booty beyond the reach of punitive avengers.

The Plains way of life attracted more and more Indians. Early in the eighteenth century, the Comanches moved southeast to displace the Kiowas and Lipan Apaches; presently they became the supreme horsemen of the Plains and the principal scourge of the New Mexico settlements. During the late eighteenth and early nineteenth centuries, tribes such as the Sioux and Cheyenne, forced westward by Anglo-American settlers, also adopted the equestrian, buffalo-hunting way of life.

Equestrian buffalo hunting required knowing the habits of

the buffalo, knowledge which the Spaniards had to learn from hunting tribes. It also involved a hunting method introduced to Spain by the Visigoths who established kingdoms there early in the Christian Era. This was the technique of riding into a herd of milling buffalo, moving ahead of the selected prey, and taking it with a backward thrust of the spear—the "Parthian Shot."

The effect of the Plains culture on New Mexico was twofold: raids and counterraids between the Plains horsemen and the colonial and Pueblo militia became frequent, while at the same time trading and hunting with the nomads became a highly profitable activity.[12]

The Navajos, pushed southward by the Utes early in the eighteenth century, lived west of the Pueblo and Spanish settlements, from which they acquired both horses and sheep. By the late eighteenth century some Navajos owned large flocks and had adopted a yearly round, adapted to grazing needs. The majority of Navajos probably owned few sheep until chronic warfare with the settlers erupted early in the nineteenth century. In later years the Navajos would quip that they allowed the settlers to remain as the herders of their future sheep.

In sum, during the later colonial period the Pueblos and settlers of New Mexico became surrounded at ever closer range by nomadic Indians who represented both a threat and an opportunity as they expanded in their new lifeways.

THE NEW SETTLERS OF NEW MEXICO

The very nature of the Hispanic settlement underwent drastic change in the eighteenth century. A fundamental difference between the colonists of the seventeenth century and those of the eighteenth century lay in the identity and outlook of the settlers themselves. Fewer than forty families returned with de Vargas from exile in Paso Del Norte, and the selected groups of new colonists he brought in were different in important ways.

Sixty-seven families of Españoles Mexicanos were selected from volunteers who came forward in the city and valley of Mexico. Some accompanied de Vargas in the reentry of 1693, while others came in 1694. Twenty-seven more families were brought in from the Zacatecas area in 1695. The fact that these people were called *Españoles Mexicanos* indicates that all were born in Mexico, that many if not all were partly descended from Mexican Indians, and that they were the cultural product of several generations of Hispanic adaptation to a New World environment in which the Spaniards constituted a small minority of the population.

The rosters of these new colonists listed skills which emphasize that they were expected to fend for themselves rather than depend upon the convoys from the urban centers of New Spain. There were weavers, blacksmiths, hatmakers, leatherworkers, and other artisans. Most were apparently experienced in irrigation farming and care of livestock. No doubt many from the Zacatecas area were skilled in mining techniques, since prospecting for New Mexico's elusive mineral wealth continued in the eighteenth century, as it had during the previous two centuries.

The settlers were informed that they could not look to the Pueblo Indians for uncompensated or forced labor and that even the nomadic Indians had rights which must be respected. The history of the eighteenth century gives many instances of violations of these standards but also shows that the government made a consistent effort to uphold the Laws of the Indies. It also shows that the Indians were aware of their rights. An advocate was selected as protector of the Indians and spokesman of the frequent grievances which they submitted.

In the spring of 1695 the new settlers were granted lands at La Cañada, where Tano Indians from Galisteo had built two pueblos after the revolt in an area previously occupied by settlers. The Tanos were obliged to resettle on lands granted to them near Chimayó, leaving the houses they had occupied to the settlers. The Tanos were indignant, and only a year later, they were active in the final Pueblo uprising of 1696. The area they had been forced to vacate was renamed La Nueva Villa de los Españoles Mexicanos, now Santa Cruz de la Cañada.

After the critical period of resettlement passed, the new colonial settlers began to relate to the Pueblo Indians in a manner less autocratic than before. The settlers were forbidden to live in the pueblos, both to prevent exploitation of the Indians and also to prevent assimilation of so-called "Spaniards" to an

Indian culture. From time to time assimilation of a partial nature actually occurred, as when a settler lived in the pueblo with the family of his wife. The Pueblos provided housing for such families but denied membership in the pueblo to the offspring of a non-Pueblo man, since affiliation in the village moieties (dual divisions with social and ceremonial functions) passed from father to child.[13]

During the eighteenth century, the Pueblo Indians adopted the Catholic faith; however, they did not relinquish their traditional faith and practice. Many settlers who lived in communities adjacent to Pueblo lands served as baptismal and confirmation sponsors to the "neophytes" and developed cordial relations of *compadrazgo* (the ceremonial and personal relationship between the parents and godparents of a child). Few of these settlers seem to have worried about their compadres' simultaneous practice of a religion other than that prescribed by Catholic doctrine. Settlers were excluded from witnessing most Pueblo ceremonials and were not overly inquisitive about them.

DECENTRALIZATION OF THE COLONY

Early in the eighteenth century, settlers began to apply for land grants at increasing distances from the pueblos. As the century wore on, the grantees moved to new lands distant not only from the pueblos but also from the churches, administrative centers, and protection of the Santa Fe garrison. This decentralization of the settler population served the needs of a growing population, but growth was slow until late in the century. It also met the needs for fresh agricultural and grazing lands and for buffer populations to protect the main population centers, the Villas of Santa Fe, Santa Cruz, and Albuquerque from the raids of nomadic Indians.

Decentralization was a stimulant to extralegal activity which greatly benefited the settlers who practiced it. The secret raising of a semidomesticated tobacco called *punche,* which was sold to the Indians without paying legal taxes levied by the colonial government, was one activity which disturbed the authorities. Unauthorized trading expeditions siphoned off horses, often stolen, and placed them in the hands of equestrian Ute bands in exchange for dressed hides or captive women and children. The latter traffic was strictly illegal but was popular among settlers and Indians alike. The nomadic bands raided other bands for children, and in times of economic scarcity, they even traded their own children for much-needed mounts.

The settlers either sold their captives at prices which made them affluent or, because of the great population shortage, they raised the children in their own homes. A child raised in such a household became fully assimilated to the culture of the settler community and often married into it. These were not hereditary chattel slaves.

The peripheral community served another purpose in the eighteenth century New Mexican colony. The Pueblos were at great pains to keep down outside cultural influences, and from time to time the religious leaders expelled community members who had become overly assimilated into the settler culture. These outcasts sought refuge with the settlers of peripheral communities, especially with those detribalized Indian communities called *Genízaro,* which will be described later in detail.

INTERGROUP RELATIONS

The process of reconciliation between the settlers and the Pueblos, which began in the eighteenth century, continued into the nineteenth century. When Mexico achieved her independence from Spain in 1821, the settled Christian Indians were proclaimed citizens. The extent to which the Pueblos exercised their right of manhood suffrage is uncertain, but the detribalized Genízaros participated to the fullest extent. As outcast Pueblos lived in Genízaro communities, they, too, were probably active in political life. The Pueblos did participate in some crucial political movements in which Genízaros took leading roles. This included the 1837 uprising and the widespread resistance to conquest by the United States during 1847, misnamed the "Taos Uprising." Clearly, Pueblos, Genízaros, and Hispanic settlers could communicate effectively in times of crisis.

Between the settlers and the nomads, relations of peace and trade alternated with periods of intensive raiding and counter-raiding. A period of peace with one group often meant a period of warfare with another, since viceregal policy favored keeping the Indians at odds with one another.[14]

Early in the eighteenth century, the Apache bands which had most harassed the settlers of the seventeenth century were pushed southward by the Comanches—an emerging power on the Plains. At the same time, the Navajos were being pushed southward from the Four Corners area of northwestern New Mexico and eastern Arizona by the pressure of Ute expansionism.

This movement of tribes brought into play new intertribal contact and influence. A band of Apaches joined the Sun Dance celebration of the Kiowas of the Oklahoma Panhandle. Taos Pueblo developed a close relationship with the Comanches, and Picurís Pueblo was particularly friendly with the Jicarilla Apaches. The Faraon Apaches visited regularly at Pecos Pueblo. Throughout most of the eighteenth century Jemez Pueblo was on very friendly terms with the Navajos.[15]

Some segments of the settler population, including entire communities, courted contact with particular nomadic tribes. Taos held an annual trade fair for the Comanches, and Abiquiu maintained for some years a similar fair for the Utes. Official fairs under the scrutiny of the authorities, however, were less profitable than direct barter with the Indians for contraband goods.

Each of the settlements yearly sent out a group of men to hunt buffalo on the plains, dry the meat and bones, and bring them back for a longlasting meat supply. The buffalo hunters, known as *ciboleros,* could survive on the plains only to the extent that the Plains Indians accepted them. Therefore, close acquaintance with the Indians was not only profitable but necessary. Parties of traders called *Comancheros* were soon going out on the buffalo plains. For every party that was licensed by the colonial government, there must have been many traveling with no more license than the goodwill of the Indians. While the Comanches were favorite customers, other Plains Indians participated in the trading, and trading parties to the Utes traveled northwestward to Colorado and Utah.

An important aspect of Spanish colonial policy covered relationships with nomadic tribes. In addition to the tactic already mentioned of setting tribes against one another, efforts were made to establish official ties with tribal leaders by offering peace treaties and gifts. Officialdom was forever seeking "principal leaders" among Indians whose band organization did not provide for centralized leadership. In some of these bands a temporary war leader might attract a following of young braves from his own and neighboring bands. His authority, however, was limited only to these individuals and to the business of raiding. The history of reprisals against whole tribes for breaking treaties made with a single war leader is a history of unrealistic perceptions on the part of treaty makers.[16]

On the other hand, the contraband traders dealt with Indians on a more intimate basis and knew the yearly round and camp groups of the bands with which they traded. Relationships tended to last from one generation to the next and to provide better protection than treaties for the individuals and communities involved. The colonial government could only react to these private understandings with suspicion and alarm.

Throughout the colonial period, New Mexico was administered by religious, civil, and military leaders, many of them Spanish-born. Since most of them spent few years in the province, they neither became intimately acquainted with Indian lifeways nor understood the increasing extent of compatibility between the settlers and their Indian neighbors. As the years passed, official reports increasingly characterized the settlers as "rustic," "uncouth," and "obstinate": a measure of the growing cultural gap between the administrators and the administered, both Indian and Hispanic.[17]

The caste system, a strong institution of New Spain, broke down in New Mexico with the passage of time. This process will be shown in detail in later sections dealing with ethnic labels and their changes over the years. Between the polar extremes of *Indio* and *Español,* intermediate categories of *coyote, mulato, zambo, mestizo,* and *genízaro* were recognized, but an individual might shift from one caste to another in the course of several years.

THE UNITED STATES TAKEOVER

By the time the Mexican Republic with its constitutional form of government and egalitarian ideals was proclaimed in New Mexico, the advance forces of another nation of profoundly different culture had already begun to extend their influence in the Southwest. The secret reconnoitering journey into the San Luis Valley of New Mexico (now southern Colorado), led by Major Zebulon Pike in 1806-1807, put the Spanish colonial government on notice that the Louisiana Purchase had provided them with an intrusive, new neighbor. The Spanish authorities arrested and deported Pike but could not effectively patrol their long northern boundary against all intruders.

The expansiveness of the United States was expressed informally by the journeys of trappers and traders into lands bordering on New Mexico. Long before trade with New Mexico was legally possible, informal transactions took place. Baptiste La Lande, representing William Morrison of Kaskaskia, Illinois, reached Santa Fe with a small stock of goods in 1804, and the following year an American trapper, James Purcell of Bardstown, Kentucky, arrived. After Major Pike published an account of his journey and capture by Spanish colonial authorities, trapping, hunting, and trading parties began to travel to the borders of New Mexico from the Missouri outposts.[18]

Some traders fell afoul of Indian war parties and colonial troops. But by 1821, when William Becknell's party made the first official crossing from the United States to Santa Fe along the Santa Fe Trail, a great deal of informal interaction had already taken place. According to traditional accounts in northern New Mexico, herds of sheep were grazed eastward over two-year periods across the Plains to Missouri to provide meat and wool for St. Louis and Independence, long before the opening of the Santa Fe Trail.[19]

Trade with the United States brought about a series of internal changes in New Mexico. These changes were already in motion before the United States conquest and they continued to unfold through the territorial years. From the early years of the nineteenth century, a mercantile group began to develop in New Mexico. Engaging in commerce in a series of communities on the Trail, this group emerged as a class of dominant *ricos* (rich men). They established stores and within a few years acquired considerable lands from their indebted neighbors. As their businesses expanded in cooperation with the traders from the United States, their interests began to merge with those of the apostles of "Manifest Destiny." They had little attachment to the young and unstable government of Mexico, which was unable to defend its northern frontiers either from the depredations of nomadic Indians or from the expansionism of the United States.

The easy conquest of New Mexico by General Kearny's forces in 1846 was largely due to the influence of these ricos, some of whom were active allies in the conquest. That their views were not shared by the majority of Spanish-speaking and Indian New Mexicans is demonstrated by the flurry of uprisings which took place some months after the conquest. It was too late for resistance, however, as New Mexico was strongly controlled by United States military forces.[20] Even after the establishment of a nominally civilian government of New Mexico in 1851, the power of the military, with large contingents of troops, continued dominant until the 1880's. The troops' presence was justified by campaigns against the Utes, Navajos, and Apaches and by New Mexico's vulnerable position during the Civil War.

As General Kearny marched through New Mexico in 1846, he issued reassuring proclamations to the Mexican citizenry, promising them protection if they laid down their arms voluntarily. The United States government would furthermore protect their persons, property, and religion; would defend them against the raids of the nomadic Indians; and would treat them as friends rather than as a conquered people. Shortly after arriving in Santa Fe, Kearny proclaimed a "Bill of Rights," later called the Kearny Code, defining the rights of individuals under the interim military government. Provisions of this code included the statement that "no private property shall be taken for public use without compensation."[21] As territorial government took over in New Mexico, each governor appointed by the federal government reiterated Kearny's promises to the New Mexicans; i.e., that their personal and property rights would be held inviolate until they had been admitted to the Union as full-fledged citizens.

THE TREATY OF GUADALUPE HIDALGO

Official hostilities between the governments of the United States and Mexico were terminated in 1848 by the Treaty of Guadalupe Hidalgo, whose provisions extended to all the residents of the conquered territories. For two reasons Congress refused to ratify Article X of the treaty, despite the insistence of the Mexican negotiators: (1) because it would have provided a clearcut procedure for confirming Southwest land grants whose documentation was as yet incomplete; and (2) because so many of the Texas grants had already been forcibly expropriated by Anglo-Americans. Attorney General Nathan Clifford, however, was sent to Mexico with Senator Ambrose Sevier, chairman of the Foreign Relations Committee. They were to draw up a protocol explaining to the Mexican government that land grants in territories other than Texas would be protected.

The Mexican government, deeply concerned about the fate of its former citizens, was reassured by the envoys that the protocol, along with the guarantees of Articles VIII and IX, would guarantee the freedom and protection of rights and interests of the New Mexicans and Californians. Article VIII stated that "in the said territories, property of every kind now belonging to Mexicans now established there, shall be inviolably respected. The present owners, the heirs of these, and all Mexicans who may hereafter acquire said property by contract, shall enjoy with respect to it guaranties equally ample as if the same belonged to citizens of the United States." Article IX stated that the former Mexican citizens of the ceded territories "shall be incorporated in the Union of the United States and shall be admitted at the proper time (to be judged by the congress of the United States) to the enjoyment of all the rights of citizens of the United States, according to the principles of the Constitution; and in the meantime shall be protected in the free enjoyment of their liberty and property and secured in the free exercise of their religion without restriction."[22]

The provisions of the Treaty of Guadalupe Hidalgo, ratified by the Congresses of both the United States and Mexico, have been repeatedly invoked as binding and have been incorporated into the Constitution of the state of New Mexico. Nonetheless, these provisions have been cynically violated from the first. In

Texas and, immediately following the 1849 gold rush, in California the personal and property rights of all but a few wealthy collaborators with the United States authorities fell under violent assault. Within a few years, the status of some ten thousand Spanish-speaking people within each state had taken on the characteristics of semicolonial oppression. The Anglo-American population, which outnumbered the Spanish-speakers by about ten to one, took over family and community landholdings, leaving the former Mexican citizens and grant heirs no choice but to work as low-paid hands on their former ranches.

The pattern of Yankee colonialism in New Mexico was not as strong. For many years the large majority of the population continued to be Spanish-speaking. Also, the territory was too arid, too poor in known mineral resources, and too beset by troubles with nomadic Indians to attract a heavy influx of immigrants from the United States. The Pueblo Indians and Spanish-speaking villagers continued to live in their traditional communities, usually quite unaware either that a handful of land speculators from the United States, Great Britain, and Holland were deeply involved in maneuvers to gain control of the grant papers or that millions of acres of grant lands were being assigned to the public domain, later to be incorporated into national forests.

The *pattern* of colonialism was present in New Mexico, however. Those Indians and Hispanos who were most eager to accommodate the new rulers became prosperous; those who were not became impoverished. By the early years of the twentieth century, many Spanish-speaking villagers had been altogether displaced from their grants, in a process of land loss which continues today. The industries which developed in New Mexico were largely extractive and owned by large out-of-state concerns. New Mexico was denied statehood until a system of controls was established to keep the Indian and Spanish-speaking New Mexicans well in hand through a system of patronage and threats of sanctions against resisters. In many respects, New Mexico has never emerged from colonial status.

2

Early Chama Valley Settlers

THE FIRST CHAMA VALLEY SETTLEMENTS

When Diego de Vargas restored the New Mexico Colony in 1692-1695, some of the families who had fled to El Paso in 1680 accompanied him to reclaim ancestral lands north of Santa Fe. They were reinstated on royal grants with no encomienda privileges. In addition to these descendants of earlier settlers, the new colonists, described as *Españoles Mexicanos,* were settled at the New Villa of Santa Cruz de la Cañada.

Among the families returning from exile were a number of related people surnamed Martín Serrano. Their most prominent member was Sebastian Martín, who returned with his father, Pedro Martín Serrano de Salazar, and many other relatives to their ancestral lands near Santa Cruz. By 1714, Sebastian Martín had become alcalde of Santa Cruz. In later years, he built the chapel of Our Lady of Solitude on his grant at Río Arriba, populated by a small cluster of ranches about a league north of San Juan Pueblo on the east bank of the Río Grande.[1]

The Martín Serranos continued to constitute a large segment of the population of the Río Arriba country and were prominent among the first settlers of grants west of the Río Grande. From the eighteenth century to the present about twenty percent of all families descended from Chama Valley pioneers

31

have carried the Martín surname. Early in the nineteenth century the name was changed to Martinez and a separate surname of Serrano later appeared. Virtually the entire population can trace ancestry to a Martín Serrano descended from the followers of de Vargas.

Another descendant of seventeenth century settlers was Antonio de Salazar, who petitioned in 1714 for return of the lands of his grandfather, Alonso Martín Barba. These lands were west of the Rio Grande and for some miles along the southwest bank of the Chama.[2] Other settlers petitioned for lands near the abandoned first capital of San Gabriel and westward along both banks of the Chama. These grants were encroachments on lands belonging to the pueblo of San Juan but formed the nuclei for present-day Chamita, Wache, Hernandez, Chile, and other tiny villages.

Early settlement of the Chama Valley and its tributary streams (the Rio del Ojo Caliente, the Oso, the Rito Colorado, Abiquiu Creek, Frijoles Creek and the Polvadera-Chihua-hueños-Cañones Creek drainage) produced a pattern of scattered ranches inhabited by expanded family groups. They generally built their dwellings on the high ground overlooking their small fields in the river bottomlands. But more often in the early days, they built a single multiroom house around a square patio which served as a center of economic and social activity for the joint families.

Corn, wheat, frijoles, and a few vegetables were the principal crops for subsistence. Irrigation ditches were dug, generally one to a ranch, along the slopes above the bottomland fields—their laterals watering the crops. As the population grew, these individual ditches often caused conflict between older and newer settlers. The ditches either drained into fields which the newer families wanted to plant, or they caused flooding of fields below.

Because Utes and Comanches frequently visited the area, often to raid, dwellings were built with windows facing in one direction only, small and secured against forced entry by wooden shutters or iron grills. The outer walls of a house built around a patio were generally windowless, and entry to the house was theoretically possible only through a single heavy entry gate. Some ranches had a defensive watchtower built apart or into a corner of the wall. Corrals for the livestock adjoined the house and a separate patio might accommodate an outdoor kitchen with a brush-sheltered hearth and adobe baking ovens.

Where stream flow permitted, a millstone might be established for grinding wheat. On the hills and mesa tops above the ranches, domestic animals were grazed on open range. Only milk cows and mares with their colts were kept in irrigated pastures close to the ranch house. A few fruit trees were often planted in the irrigated pastures.

The nearest neighbors were usually at least several miles away, and the nearest church was at a much greater distance. Some of the early settlers built chapels, although they had no regularly assigned priest to conduct services for them.

FOUNDING FAMILIES OF THE CHAMA VALLEY

Juan de Mestas received a grant at La Cuchilla, west of the confluence of the Rio del Ojo Caliente with the Chama. North of him, Antonio de Beytia (Abeyta) built a ten-room house on his grant. A number of other families were allotted land in severalty along both banks of the Chama, beginning in the 1730's. In 1734 Bartolomé Trujillo was settled on the north bank of the Chama, west of the mouth of the Rito Colorado. To his west, Vincente Girón had a grant. On the south bank of the Chama, from east to west starting near the present location of La Puente, lands were granted to Francisco Trujillo, Miguel Martín Serrano, Juan Trujillo, Miguel Montoya (below the ruins of the prehistoric pueblo of Abiquiu), Jose de la Serda (later written Serna), Josefa de Torres, Cristobal Tafoya, and Salvador de Torres.[3]

In the following year the acting governor, Juan Paez Hurtado, made a number of grants in the Chama watershed. These were challenged by Governor Gervasio Cruzat y Góngora upon his return to New Mexico, but most of them appear to have continued operative. A joint grant to Gerónimo and Ignacio Martín Serrano, Pascual and Tomás Manzanares, and Juan de Gamboa (all with families) was made at the present location of

San José del Barranco. Juan Esteban García de Noriega and Antonio de Ulibarrí received grants along the Rito Colorado. Jose Antonio Torres and Francisco Trujillo received land at the mouth of the Rito Colorado south of Antonio de Ulibarrí.[4]

The Rio del Oso flows into the chama from the west, its headwaters trickling down from the flanks of Tsicoma peak. Near its headwaters in the 1730's lived Roque Jacinto Jaramillo, Juan Manuel de Herrera, and Rosalía Valdez with her two sons, Ygnacio and Juan Lorenzo. A few miles from the mouth of the Rio del Oso was the settlement of Pueblo Quemado.[5]

Southwest of Abiquiu, facing toward Pedernal Peak, was a ranch on a large grant owned by José de Riaño, one of the richest men in New Mexico in the mid-eighteenth century. His 1743 will listed an inventory of 1,027 breeding ewes, 1,298 wethers, 74 bulls, 26 steers, 207 breeding cows, 46 heifers, 47 calves, and a fair number of horses. In addition, he owned a mulatto slave, 150 pesos worth of pelts, and other valuables. The Spanish-born José de Riaño owned a splendid house near Santa Fe and apparently did not reside at his ranch which comprised the lands later divided into the Polvadera and Piedra Lumbre Grants. In the 1740's the Montoyas and their sheep herders had permission to use the wooden ranch house, corrals, and rangelands of José de Riaño for their livestock operations. In a sudden Indian attack in 1745, one of the sons of Miguel Montoya was killed and the remaining members of that family were forced to flee to the Rio Abajo country, where they remained.[6]

During the 1730's and 1740's and into the early 1750's the settlements in the Chama watershed were frequently displaced by Indian attacks. When the Rio del Oso settlement was attacked, the Valdez family left for good and in 1737 received the grant along the Chama which came to be known as the Plaza Colorada. At the same time Manuel Bustos received the Plaza Blanca Grant. Both were narrow strips facing Abiquiu from the north bank of the Rio Chama.[7]

In 1744 Father Miguel de Menchero reported that the Spanish settlers of the Abiquiu area totaled twenty scattered families, while the Ojo Caliente area had forty-six Spanish families plus some Indian residents. We lack a roster of names of the

Ranch country of the Lower Chama Valley. From Museum of New Mexico Photoarchives.

East Morada at Abiquiu, New Mexico. From Museum of New Mexico Photoarchives.

An adobe ranch in the Lower Chama Valley. F. Swadesh, 1970.

early settlers along the Rio del Ojo Caliente, other than Antonio de Beytia, Ventura Mestas, Lázaro de Atienza (Atencio), Antonio Martín, Nicholás Martín, and Blas Martín Serrano, son of Domingo.[8]

INDIAN RAIDS AND EVACUATION OF SETTLEMENTS

In August 1747 all settlements west of the Rio Grande were attacked by nomadic Indians. Twenty-three women and children were carried off and a girl and an old woman were killed on the spot for "having defended themselves." The settlers followed the tracks of the raiders and came upon the bodies of three women and a newborn child. Seven years later, one of the captives was returned. Meanwhile a punitive expedition pursued and fell upon the Utes who were thought to have instigated the attacks. Only much later was it established that the raiders were mainly Comanches with a few Moache Ute allies.[9]

In March 1748 the Abiquiu, Ojo Caliente, and Pueblo Quemado settlers asked permission to withdraw from their exposed settlements to a safer community. Permission was withheld until the summer, when the settlers were ordered to vacate within eight days, abandoning their growing crops and ranging livestock. They withdrew to live with relatives at Santa Cruz.[10]

After this retreat the settlers were reluctant to return to their frontier settlements. Consequently, in early 1750 Governor Thomas Veles Cachupin instructed the alcalde mayor of Santa Cruz, Juan José Lobato, to order the fugitives from Abiquiu and Ojo Caliente to resettle in time for the spring planting or forfeit their titles. He expressed disgust that their houses and lands stood intact, while they continued to live at the expense of their relatives. The governor instructed the alcalde to make the resettlement around a square plaza, with the houses built in a solid row and gates for entry and exit. This defensive town design on a grid-plan was actually required by colonial regulations. Veles Cachupin promised an escort from the Santa Fe presidio to protect the settlers while they reestablished themselves.

The governor predicted that the Comanches would be impressed by a bold face if the settlers followed the example of others in the kingdom who daily risked their lives to protect the "Royal Domain." This was a pointed reference to the grants which were subject to forfeiture (*realengo*) if settlers failed to maintain residence. The governor proposed that mutual protection be sought by working the fields in teams, rotating from one field to the next and always keeping firearms at hand.

When the governor's decree was read aloud in Santa Cruz, some of the fugitives raised a sharp protest. Juan Lorenzo Valdez, on behalf of his brother Ygnacio and his mother Rosalía, wrote a fiery indictment of the policies of former Governor Juan Codallos y Rabel, by whose "great omission" disaster had befallen the settlers. The Comanches had given advance warning of their August 1, 1747 raid and local scouts were tracking them, but no presidio troops were dispatched to the area. The task of defense, therefore, fell to "six to eight Indians and four or five residents and these so poor that to do their guard duty they had to use their little jack mules, and this was for a week only, our settlers being again left to themselves and it was our misfortune that at this time the Comanches fell upon us."

The burden of the Valdez complaint was that (1) the 1747 attacks and subsequent forced withdrawal had worked great hardships and loss upon all settlers; (2) the Comanches had become more aggressive since 1747; (3) only six families were planning seriously to return—an insufficient number to hold the area secure; (4) no amount of defense *at* the settlement could effectively protect the population "because the farmers and shepherds are compelled to go out in order to attend to their business," indicating that the proposal for reciprocal labor teams was rejected; (5) in order for a priest to visit the settlements, there was need for a stronger escort with more horses than appeared to be presently available; (6) it was unjust to threaten the settlers with realengo if they did not return by the date ordered, since they had validated their titles by many years' residence and intended to return as soon as "there is security and safety from the enemy as there was at the time when we took possession"; (7) resettlement should take place only on one side of the Chama, since the river was impassable when running high; the houses, lots, and chapel should be laid out on the north bank, where the Valdezes had their lands, rather than on the south bank, where Miguel Martín Serrano and his son-in-law Francisco Quintana had already built a chapel in honor of Saint Rose of Lima up to the entablature. The Valdezes objected that this chapel stood right under a hillside in the fields, leaving no space to set up a closed plaza. The final complaint was that although Governor Veles Cachupin's campaign had resulted in a peace treaty with the Utes, the Valdezes feared the "faithlessness" of "so cruel an enemy" and asked that orders for resettlement be deferred until such time as persons and property could be secure.[11]

Other documents show that the Valdez family had a quarrel with Miguel Martín Serrano in 1746 over a diversion of the Rio Chama that they had planned to build to prevent flooding. At that time Martín Serrano claimed that the settlers on the south bank of the Chama had avoided settling on the north bank because of the flooding. He also claimed that when the Valdezes had come from the Rio del Oso to settle on the Chama, they should have settled at a better spot; they should not subject the crops of neighbors on the south bank to the danger of being washed away. Juan de Beytia, *teniente* (assistant to alcalde) of the Villa of Santa Cruz, investigated Martín Serrano's allegations and said he thought they might be entirely false. Martín faced down the threat of a fifty peso fine if his claim was found to be unjust with renewed charges corroborated by his neighbors. This was only the first of many disputes between settlers of the north and south banks of the Chama over the effects of diverting its waters.[12]

RESETTLEMENT IN 1750

Resettlement along the Chama was made on April 16, 1750 under the supervision of Alcalde Mayor Lobato in an atmosphere of mutual recrimination, fear, and discord. Miguel Martín Serrano, Juan José de la Cerda, Gerónimo Martín, Ignacio and Juan Lorenzo Valdez, representing their mother who did not appear, and Manuel de la Rosa "made the resettlement at the place where the chapel is situated, which remained in the center" with the plaza laid out in a square. This settlement on the lands of Miguel Martín is the location known in later times as La Puente, three miles east of Abiquiu on the south bank of the Chama.[13]

This first chapel, dedicated to Saint Rose of Lima, was destroyed a short time later in another Indian raid which once more displaced the settlements on the Chama. Another Chapel of Saint Rose of Lima was built some years later on the south bank of the Chama, about a mile upstream from the one at La Puente. Its crumbling remains are still visible from Highway 84. For awhile the title of Santa Rosa was applied to both locations. In the 1789 census the old site was called La Plaza de Santa Rosa, and the new site was called La Plaza de la Capilla.

The 1750 resettlement included thirteen Genízaros who were assigned by Alcalde Lobato to the former house of Miguel de Montoya, located on the present townsite of Abiquiu, "temporarily until his Excellency shall dispose of them." No names were given for this group of Genízaros, but in view of the fact that they were assigned to the Montoya house, it may be significant that in 1743 the Montoyas had brought to Santa Clara for baptism seventeen Indians identified as *Moquis* (Hopis).[14] We can conjecture that since the Genízaros who set up housekeeping at the Montoya homestead were considered residents of the area, perhaps they were detribalized Hopis, former servants of the Montoyas, who had chosen not to follow them in flight to the Rio Abajo.

Despite the difficulties of maintaining settlements in the peripheral areas of the colony, the government was eager to keep these settlements occupied because of mineral finds in the mountains. In April 1750 the Marqués of Altamira, counsellor general of war for New Spain, praised Governor Veles Cachupin's policy of trying to protect the New Mexico settlements from attack by the Comanches and the "other three nations, the Yutas, Chaguaguas and Moaches." The latter names refer to two regional divisions of Utes: the Sabuaganas of the Western Slope of Colorado and the Moaches north of Taos. Altamira suggested that "flattery, caresses . . . and reasonable terms" be used to persuade the Comanches and Utes to settle at a mission site of their own selection. They should be promised a livelihood, clothing, farm implements, and sufficient food until they could raise enough crops for their own needs "without being compelled, obliged, or teased to be Christians, if they voluntarily would not desire to be." If the Comanches and Utes continued to resist, Altamira suggested putting them down once and for all by calling together the Texas garrison troops of San Antonio de Bexar, the Bahía del Espíritu Santo and Adais, and all the Indians hostile to the Comanches and Apaches.

Governor Veles Cachupin decreed on September 4, 1750 that the deserted settlements, apparently all those north of Santa Fe, be repopulated. It was the official opinion that if miners were to enjoy "the greatest freedom, immunities, privileges, and exemptions that may be possible," they would be willing to resettle. But Veles Cachupin advised that if the nomadic Indians attacked again, troops from Texas would immediately be needed.[15]

THE GENIZARO SETTLEMENTS

In 1754 Genízaro pueblo land grants were established in Abiquiu and Ojo Caliente, and Governor Veles Cachupin founded a Franciscan mission at Abiquiu.[16] Such land grants had already been made at other peripheral settlements of the colony. They provided detribalized Indians who desired freedom from servitude in settlers' homes with the means for an independent life—in exchange for the promise of active militia service. Each Genízaro pueblo had a military captain, often selected from Genízaro ranks, sometimes from the settler population. The land grants were in the corporate pattern of the colonial grants, recognizing the land rights of each community of Pueblo Indians. The pueblo grants were supposed to be square blocks of land extending a league (somewhat under three miles) along lines running north, south, east, and west of the pueblo mission church. Within this area the community leaders assigned the house lots and agricultural plots for families, transferable from one generation to the next but not saleable to outsiders.[17]

There is no list of the first Genízaros who settled at Abiquiu, nor even the number involved. But it is clear that from the start, their presence helped maintain the population in the area and reduce periods of abandonment, following the attacks of Indian

nomads. The Abiquiu mission records, incomplete though they
may be, include entries for every year from 1754 through 1769
from the Chama Valley settlements, but provide a less complete
record for the communities along the Río del Ojo Caliente. The
latter communities were laid out along a favorite raiding corridor of the Kiowas and Comanches. Again and again, Genízaros
received grants along the Ojo Caliente, only to be dislodged. In
1768, thirteen landless Genízaros received land downstream
from the Ojo Caliente plaza; in the following year, twenty-two
Genízaros received land upstream from the plaza, six of them
being grantees from the previous year. At that time, ten settler
families occupied the plaza, while eight families lived downstream.[18]

In 1779, however, when Governor Juan Bautista de Anza was
on the homeward trail from his campaign against the Comanches, he passed the "deserted" settlement of Ojo Caliente. In
1790 José Manuel Velarde of Bernalillo petitioned for permission to settle with eighteen other families at Ojo Caliente, where
he owned land. He wanted to build a fortified settlement at the
location of the old plaza. In 1793, fifty-three settlers of Ojo
Caliente who had been living there without confirmed titles
received formal apportionment of lands. This was but a meager
increase over the forty-six Spanish families and "some" Indians
who inhabited Ojo Caliente in 1744.[19] Abiquiu fared much
better.

The word "Genízaro" supposedly refers to detribalized, nomadic Indians, often of mixed ancestry, who came from areas
both east and west of New Mexico and who had been ransomed
from captivity among the nomadic tribes. In Abiquiu the
church records tell a somewhat different story. In addition to
the record of Hopis settled at the Montoya homestead in 1750,
records of later years show that people from the Hopi Villages,
Zuñis, Isletas, Santa Claras, and other Pueblo Indians continued
to come to Abiquiu throughout the eighteenth century, apparently forming the majority of the local Genízaro population.
Those Genízaros identified as of nomadic or non-New Mexican
origin were the minority, most being purchased as children from
Ute or Comanche captors.

Most Genízaros acquired surnames in the proportion of their

occurrence among the settlers, with a preponderance of Martins and Trujillos. The surname Tagle, bestowed by José de Riaño Tagle Bustamante, survived only among the Genízaros; and such surnames as Borja, Chino, Pineda, Quiros, Telles, Gutierrez, and Trébol were limited to Genízaros in the eighteenth century Abiquiu records. Coruna and Tágueda may have been surnames of Indian origin.[20]

THE GENIZARO WAY OF LIFE

Life as it was lived in a multicultural frontier community such as Abiquiu in the late eighteenth century was described by Fray José de la Prada in his 1793-1794 census report of the New Mexico custody. The father custodian had been in charge of the mission at Abiquiu since 1789, and since he signed the report in Abiquiu, we can be sure he had the Abiquiu Genízaros in mind when he reported that in general the Genízaros were more of a hindrance than a help to the conversions of the nomadic Indians who frequented the *reducciones* (mission centers for the conversion of nomadic Indians). Father Prada wrote that the Genízaros not only tended to be religious backsliders but also were fond of dressing like the nomads, as was also the case with some of the *vecinos* (settler-citizens). He also wrote that the Indians of the Genízaro reductions were too lazy to weave, although some knew the art of weaving. Here, Father Prada used the masculine gender, indicating that the weavers he knew were men. Among the Pueblos all weaving is done by men; among the Navajos, the women are the weavers.

The Genízaros, Prada wrote, raised a little corn, wheat, and vegetables—but not enough to avert starvation for their families. Their women made pottery, which was sold to the vecinos for food supplies. The Indians of the reductions cultivated only a portion of their arable lands, leaving part in *hiriazas* (*eriazo* means "uncultivated") and leasing the rest to vecinos at an excessive rate. They provided for themselves by hunting deer and selling the dressed hides; they also raised sheep, cows, and a few horses.[21]

The population identified as Genízaro was at all times a minority of the Abiquiu population and tended from early times to dwindle, despite fresh recruits to the Genízaro ranks. This atrophy was partially due to an excessive military casualty rate among Genízaro men, since more of them apparently were foot soldiers than were their fellow militiamen. When fighting with the mounted braves of the nomadic tribes, being afoot was a disadvantage. The decline of Genízaro identity was mainly due, however, to the assimilation process, as individual Genízaros adopted Hispanic culture, purchased worldly goods and private lands with the booty of war, and married into vecino families.

There are well-known Genízaro individuals who acquired vecino status. For example, Andrés and Lucrecio Munís were brothers who accompanied the Dominguez-Escalante expedition to Utah in 1775-1776. Andrés had been hired as the Ute interpreter and Lucrecio came along, uninvited. The brothers were from Ojo Caliente, where Juan Munís had reoccupied his settler grant in 1752 to avoid forfeiting it and being sued for desertion. Governor Veles Cachupin was pressuring the vecinos at the time to resettle their grants, but he had not yet established a Genízaro grant at Ojo Caliente. Juan Munís may have been one of the Indians mentioned by Menchero in 1744, but it is more likely that he was a vecino, since he had a settler grant. Andrés and Lucrecio may have been either his sons by an Indian woman, or his servants acquired by purchase or capture from Indians. In 1757 Andrés Munís married María Chaves at Ojo Caliente. Both were described in the church records as "Spaniards," but a year later when the marriage vows were repeated Andrés was listed as a "mulatto" and María was listed as a "coyota." In 1769 both brothers were listed as vecinos of the Ojo Caliente settlement at the "town and river," although a Genízaro grant had been made on the Juana de Herrera lands a year before, and in 1769 another Genízaro grant was made above the hot springs.

Fathers Francisco Atanacio Dominguez and José Velez Escalante, however, unhesitatingly described the Munís brothers as Genízaros. They equated their attitudes with those of the "coyote" Felipe and the Abiquiu Genízaro Juan Domingo who overtook the party on the trail, apparently by prearrangement with the brothers. All wanted to trade with the Utes and eagerly seized the first opportunity to do so. This outraged the missionaries, who had undertaken their arduous journey for "Glory to God and the salvation of souls," not for bartering worldly goods. Escalante commented indignantly in his journal that these Genízaros "manifested little or entire lack of faith and their total unfitness for such enterprises."[22]

Another famous Genízaro who won the status of a vecino was Manuel Mestas. For years he served the Abiquiu settlers as interpreter in their parleys with the Utes. In the 1789 census he was enumerated as a Genízaro of Abiquiu. Several other residents of the same surname, including Guadalupe Mestas, married to "José el Apache," were also listed. These Mestas families may have been relatives of Manuel Mestas, or all may have acquired the surname through service with the Mestas family of La Cuchilla.

Manuel Mestas was recommended in 1805 for the "usual interpreter's pay" by Governor Joaquin del Real Alencaster. On a month-long trip to the Timpanagos Utes of Central Utah, the seventy-year-old Mestas had recovered a number of stolen horses. Three years later the old man was a private landowner at La Cuchilla. He may have purchased the land, but he may also have received a bequest of land from his former master, as did other faithful servants of record.[23]

ASSIMILATION OF GENÍZAROS

In the late eighteenth century, mission entries at Abiquiu refer more frequently to people described as "Genízaro vecino," a term reflecting the assimilative trend. The term occurs earlier and more frequently in reference to residents of the Ojo Caliente communities than to those of the Abiquiu settlements, perhaps because of greater discontinuity of settlement at Ojo Caliente and, consequently, to greater exposure to Hispanic life in the larger settlements of Chamita and Santa Cruz.

In 1789 and 1790 a census was taken at the Abiquiu Pueblo and eight *puestos de españoles* (Spanish outposts) constituting the settlements around Abiquiu. In only one settlement outside the pueblo were many residents identified as Indians or people of mixed ancestry, aside from occasional family servants, often juveniles, who were listed as dependents of the families they served.[24]

The exceptional settlement was called "San Antonio" and listed twelve Spanish households, one Genízaro household, one Indian, and four Coyote. One of the coyote households is further specified as "vecinos del Moqui" (Hopis with vecino status).

It is impossible to be sure where this 1789 plaza of San Antonio was located, but according to other records, one of the residents there lived at the Ranch of Los Frijoles. This was a ranch built by Gerónimo Martín on land immediately west of the Abiquiu Pueblo boundary. In fact, when the Genízaro grant was made in 1754, a slice of Gerónimo Martín's land was included in the pueblo league. By the time of the 1789 census, Gerónimo was dead and his close relative, José Ignacio Martín, who had bought his seven-room house in 1764, was the military leader of the Plaza of San Miguel, near present-day Cañones. A Pedro Martinez and several Martín women, all listed as "Spaniards," and several Martíns listed as "coyotes" did live at San Antonio in 1789.

Although the Plaza of San Antonio cannot be definitely identified as the Frijoles community, it seems plausible that assimilated Genízaros may have acquired land at Los Frijoles by bequest from the Martíns or by purchase from their heirs.

The benevolent paternalism of the Franciscan fathers may have retarded assimilation of the Abiquiu Genízaros compared with those of Ojo Caliente. This may account for the later appearance of Indios Vecinos in the Abiquiu records. A certain amount of social and doctrinal backsliding was expected of them. When vecinos or even priests accused Genízaros of witchcraft, official action was less severe than was customary in those days.

The principal outbreak of witchcraft hysteria at Abiquiu occurred during the 1760's, when an Indian girl claimed that the 1756 death of the first missionary, Father Ordoñez y Machado, was the result of poison given by a Genízaro. The second missionary, Fray Juan José de Toledo, had been suffering from stomach trouble and feared that he might be the second victim. He joined an Indian accuser in advancing charges of *maleficio* (malevolent occult practices).

The alcalde of Santa Cruz took depositions relating to this case in 1763. After the hearings, eight of the Abiquiu Genízaros were ordered to become servants of selected Spanish families, in order to guarantee closer supervision of their actions and to make better Christians of them. Considering the charges, this was a light sentence.

At the same time, troops were dispatched to Abiquiu to destroy the relics of supposed idolatrous worship, including a stone with "hieroglyphics" on it. The stone was not well enough described to determine if it was a figurine from the prehistoric Pueblo ruin above the Abiquiu plaza or, possibly, a *piedra imana* (lodestone), such as some people in Abiquiu still use to attract love and wealth. This kind of magic has its roots in the Old World, not the New.[25]

In the late eighteenth century, more Genízaros of the Abiquiu area began to acquire vecino status in a legal sense but the term *Genízaro* has come down to the present generation of Spanish-speaking New Mexicans with a connotation of social disdain, implying that the vecinos preserved some caste attitudes. Parents of the San Juan Basin used to call their own children Genízaros when rebuking them for bad manners, even though they themselves may have had Genízaro ancestors.

If relations between Genízaros and the settler population were not always fraternal, they appear to have been peaceful enough during the colonial period. During this time the Genízaro segment declined, while the Spanish segment doubled and tripled. In 1821, with the advent of the Mexican Republic, the Indian segment suddenly rose, perhaps in anticipation of the partition of Abiquiu Pueblo lands. In 1821, however, the population total from all ethnic sources was 3,275, whereas a year later it had dropped to 2,342, for reasons unstated by the compiler of the census.[26]

On page 46 is a table of population figures from Abiquiu covering a period of slightly over sixty years.

It is clear from this table that cultural factors rather than ancestry were the determinants of colonial population labels.

TABLE 1

Population Changes in Colonial Abiquiu[27]

Year	Genízaro	Spanish and Castas
1760	166 (57 families)	617 (104 families)
1789	160 (47 families)	992 (203 families)
1798	176	1,573
1808	122	1,816
1821	246 "Indians"	3,029

The term *castas* referred to people of varied mixed ancestry whose cultural identity and civil status approached that of the Spanish settlers. The principal categories of castas were as follows: Mestizos were of mixed Spanish-Indian ancestry; Coyotes in the eighteenth and early nineteenth centuries were children of European non-Spanish fathers and New Mexican mothers who might be Spanish or Mestizo; Mulatos were of mixed Spanish-African ancestry, and Zambos were of mixed Indian-African ancestry. An Indio was a person born into a specific tribe or pueblo, and the Genízaros, regardless of tribal ancestry, were equated with the Pueblos. The nomadic Indians were identified as Gentiles.[28]

Genízaros did not at first have vecino status, nor did the Pueblo Indians. Castas in menial positions were, likewise, not vecinos at the outset. But the baptismal and marriage books of Abiquiu show the gradual acquisition of vecino status in entries like that of the marriage of "Juan Simón, Isleta Indian, and Marta Martín, parents unknown, vecina of Abiquiu, married on June 22, 1777, both vecinos."[29]

Tithable property seems to have been a prerequisite for social upgrading, especially in finding a marriage partner of higher status. An impoverished person of high status might marry a lower status person of means, and their children would inherit the social status of the higher-placed parent. Property considerations kept the marriage of people of vastly different status from becoming the dominant pattern but encouraged an occasional marriage to unite property with status. In this way the formation of rigid castes was prevented.

HISPANIC, GENIZARO, AND UTE RELATIONS

Although the impact of the Genízaro population at Abiquiu may have been weak on settler genealogies and even weaker in terms of cultural impact, their presence affected conditions in the area. People like the Muñis brothers and Manuel Mestas had intimate knowledge of the life of at least one locally important nomadic group, the Utes. Other residents of the Genízaro Pueblo were themselves Apaches, Utes, or Comanches. On the other hand, Abiquiu undoubtedly sustained revenge raids because its own militia forces raided. The Utes who were the closest nomadic neighbors apparently raided least and were themselves infrequent targets.[30]

The Utes most in contact with Abiquiu were the Sabuagana (sometimes called Chaguagua) and Capote bands. Before 1762 they had started making annual trips to the Chama Valley and communities near Santa Cruz to conduct trade and ransom. By 1776 an annual trade fair was held for the Utes at Abiquiu. The Utes brought juvenile captives from the "heathen tribes," as well as deer, buffalo meat, and dressed hides. A fine hide would bring a good horse or two *belduques* (long hunting knives popular as trade items), while the meat was exchanged for maize or flour.[31] The growth of trading partnerships with the Utes made it possible for the settlers to petition for new grants and set up residence in areas remote from administrative, ecclesiastical, and military supervision.

In 1766 Pedro Martín Serrano petitioned for that portion of the abandoned José de Riaño grant called Piedra Lumbre, while his brother Juan Pablo Martín petitioned for the adjacent Polvadera tract. Their purpose in petitioning was to obtain more rangeland. Perhaps they also wanted a better base for informal trade with the Utes, as the location where both grantees settled was ideal for the purpose. This location, called the Plaza de San Miguel, was a short distance below the confluence of Polvadera Creek with what is now written Chihuahueños Creek but old maps show as Chaguaguas (Sabuaganas) Creek. This Creek was also known in later times as Pedernales Creek, the east boundary of the Juan Bautista Valdez Grant, which was made in 1807.[32]

POPULATION GROWTH ALONG THE RITO COLORADO

In the late eighteenth century the grant along the Rito Colorado which had been made to Juan Estevan García de Noriega and which had been revoked but rarely abandoned as the record shows, was the home of Juan's descendant, Joaquin García de Noriega. Several communities were built on this grant. The first, the Poblazón, is the site of present day El Rito, which began to grow after Joaquin García sold land there to Gregorio Quintana in 1808. By 1815 the Chapel of San Juan Nepomuceno had been built. In later years a thinly settled population extended three miles from the Chapel of San Juan Nepomuceno upstream to the family settlement of Los Trujillos below the entrance to El Rito Canyon. South of the Poblazón were the ruins of an older plaza (probably the first settlement made by Juan Esteven García de Noriega); going southward, the Plaza del Medio (possibly the place later called El Llano); the Plaza de los Espinosas (possibly the place now called Placitas); the Plaza de los Atencios, and the Plaza de la Casita. The latter plaza has ruins in the vicinity which date far back into the eighteenth century. Possibly they go back as far as the 1735 grant to Antonio de Torres and Francisco Trujillo, apparently settled for a few years.

By 1820 the combined population of the García or El Rito Grant was some four hundred, each plaza including lands four square leagues from its center. By 1846 the plazas comprising El Rito had their peak population, as follows: sixty to eighty families lived from the Poblazón to the Canyon; thirty to forty families lived at La Casita, and about forty families lived at Espinosas. The other plazas were apparently deserted.[33]

NINETEENTH CENTURY LAND GRANTS

Population growth in the Chama Valley was marked in the 1790's and the first decades of the nineteenth century. Agricultural lands were limited in the Chama and tributary valleys, and new range was needed for growing herds. Petitions for grants in the Upper Chama drainage were submitted starting in the early 1800's.

The first nineteenth century grant was the San Joaquin del Río Chama, for which the *alferez* (standard bearer) Francisco Salazar petitioned in 1806 on behalf of himself, his brothers, and twenty-eight vecinos. In 1808, forty-seven allotments were made on the grant, of which two were in the name of Francisco Salazar. The alcalde mayor of Santa Cruz recited the boundaries of the grant to its recipients: north to the Valley of the Cebolla, east to the Piedra Lumbre boundary, south to the Capulin with headwaters on the slopes of San Pedro Peak, and west to the *cejita blanca* (little white ridge) west of present-day Gallina. The first settlement was in the Chama River Canyon; but by 1832, grantees and their descendants were placed in possession of allotments along the Gallinas River. The San Joaquin Grant has been variously estimated as from 472,000 acres to possibly 750,000 acres. Its agricultural lands, especially in the canyon, were limited; and diversion of water for irrigation was difficult due to the steep canyon walls and the many *ancones* (bends). However, the latter made excellent lambing grounds. To the northeast, the grant stretched into high country near present-day Canjilon, ideal for summer range but with an insufficient growing season for crops other than root and fodder crops.[34]

In 1807 Jose García de la Mora requested for himself and fifteen other individuals lands south of Abiquiu, just west of the Río del Oso. Abiquiu residents complained that the livestock of the new settlement, called Vallecito de San Antonio, wandered into their plantings and caused damage. According to the Abiquiu vecinos, José García de la Mora had had his title separated from that of the other grantees and promptly began to sell off tracts. He was the son of the alcalde of Santa Cruz and in 1824 he became alcalde of Abiquiu. His request for the grant, therefore, was not so much a proposal to settle as it was a business venture to dispose of real estate at a profit, something which rarely occurred in the Abiquiu area. The alcalde of Santa Cruz responded to the complaints from Abiquiu by ordering all settlers of both grants to fence in their croplands and to try to keep their livestock from invading the fields of others. In those days the range was open, and only milk cows and mares with young colts were kept in fenced, irrigated pastures.[35]

In the early nineteenth century the Spanish monarchy was in

a state of crisis and the Spanish empire was toppling. The ideas of the French Revolution entered the colonies of the New World years before Napoleon's armies swept through Spain. During the exile of Fernando VII, the *Cortes* (Parliament) of Spain declared a constitution, which in 1812 granted citizenship to all colonial residents including Indians, and provided for the recognition of their elected representatives in the deliberations of the Cortes. This constitution was repudiated by Fernando VII, when he returned to the throne in 1814, but its ideas were not overthrown. Its main provisions were adopted by the Mexican Constitution.[36]

PETITIONS FOR THE TIERRA AMARILLA GRANT

On February 8, 1814 Marcial Montoya and Pedro Romero petitioned on behalf of themselves and seventy others for a grant on the Brazos del Rio de Chama a few miles north of the present-day Tierra Amarilla. This was the first application for land on what later became known as the Tierra Amarilla Grant. The stated purpose of this petition was "starting and perpetuating a tract of agricultural land, where we will establish ourselves according to the desire of His Majesty (whom may God preserve) and as cited in our wise Constitution . . . to settle all the unappropriated and uncultivated lands . . . to make patriots out of subjects." This petition was recommended for approval by Pedro Ignacio Gallegos, alcalde of Abiquiu. Ironically, the liberal constitution which inspired the wording of the petition was abrogated that same year.

Nothing more was heard about a grant at Tierra Amarilla until 1820, when Manuel Martinez and Juan Pablo Romero, representing themselves and sixty others, presented a new petition. Again, no action was taken. In 1824 Pablo Romero and seventy-six others petitioned once more, on the grounds that most of the petitioners were landless and had large families. Prominent among the names on this list were those of Manuel Martinez, his grown sons, and other well-to-do landowners of the Lower Chama. It appears that the main objective of the many petitioners was to secure the great tract of the Tierra Amarilla as a sheep range for Abiquiu against other possible petitioners. Abiquiu settlers had been grazing their sheep in the area, possibly since before the first petition. Since the Capote Utes hunted in the area, a certain amount of unsupervised trade must also have taken place there.

The final, successful petition of Manuel Martinez on behalf of himself, his children, and all who might care to accompany them was made in 1832. Martinez claimed to be bereft of sufficient agricultural land to bequeath to his ten children, since he had been forced to destroy the reservoir which fed his irrigation ditch—this because of the complaints of the alferez, Mariano Martín, and his son Ramón.

The Committee of the Territorial Deputation consulted with the Abiquiu corporation (town council) concerning Martinez' petition. The corporation replied that the lands of Tierra Amarilla were of excellent quality, capable of supporting a population of five hundred families. It recommended rejection of Martinez' request for limited access for all but the grantees to pastures, roads, and watering places on the grant, recommending that these be left open to all residents of the Abiquiu jurisdiction. The Committee of the Territorial Deputation concurred with the corporation over Manuel Martinez' strenuous protests, leaving the pastures, watering places, and roads "free according to the custom prevailing in all settlements."[37]

CHANGES IN THE LATE COLONIAL PERIOD

From 1780 to 1820, the last four decades of colonial rule in New Mexico, the record provides evidence of substantial changes, heralding the emergence of a new kind of society. The number of people designated as Spaniards and Castas and later as *Gente de Razon* (people of reason) rose from 7,666 in 1760 to 17,153 in 1788, 20,626 in 1805 and some 30,000 in 1822. The Pueblo population remained stable at fewer than 10,000 with a severe dip in 1788 because of an epidemic. Each successive generation after the mid-seventeenth century was more clearly indigenous to New Mexico. Some of the people who accompanied de Vargas in the resettlement of the 1690's returned later to Mexico or Spain, but the later settler generations were New Mexicans to the core.[38]

The rise in the non-Pueblo population with corresponding stable or declining numbers of Pueblos can be partly accounted for by the periodic epidemics which struck the Indian populations even more severely than those of the settlers. In greater part it is symptomatic of the detribalization of many Pueblo Indians assimilating into the non-Pueblo population. In the process of assimilation, however, they may have brought into the ranks of the settlers some remaining Pueblo orientations which were thus adopted into the Hispanic culture. Possible evidences of such cultural transfer will be explored in the concluding chapter.

Despite the colonial government, allegiance to the king of Spain, the nominally Spanish status of the settlers, and the mission system directly exported from Spain and dependent upon royal patronage, the daily lives of the Hispanic settlers and their settled Indian neighbors were largely detached from the administrative superstructure. The Pueblo Indians accepted imposition of new administrative posts to deal with the government and the religion brought in from the outside. But the Indians did not permit these outside influences to encroach upon the functions of their theocratic leadership. The settlers, for their part, paid as little attention as possible to the administrative demands of governors, alcaldes, and priests. They came to depend upon the institutions internal to the immediate community. These trends intensified during subsequent periods, as we shall see in the following chapter.

As for the nomadic Indians of New Mexico, they had been profoundly influenced by the Hispanic colonial culture, but continued to be free of its domination. As the nineteenth century opened, the threat of Apache and Comanche raids was largely replaced by a challenge from the Navajos and a chronic state of hostilities.

3

The Mexican Republic
and United States Conquest
of New Mexico

THE EARLY YEARS OF INDEPENDENCE

Mexico's transition in 1821 from a colony to an independent republic variously affected different regions of the vast country, at that time larger than the rapidly expanding United States. In central Mexico political transition opened decades of turbulence but the remote province of New Mexico at first scarcely felt the transition. Facundo Melgares, the last governor under Spanish rule, served temporarily as the first *jefe politico* (political chief) under the republic. The laws of Spain "to the extent that they are not contrary to the particular conditions of the country" continued in effect. These were the laws of the liberal Constitution, which hitherto had not been systematically followed.

Full citizenship for sedentary Christian Indians with manhood suffrage was one innovation of the Constitution. The special advocate to defend the legal rights of Indians was retained. The Pueblos continued to manage civil affairs which required contact with outsiders through the mediation of the Pueblo governor and other officials, but the Genizaros became active participants in municipal affairs. They lacked the indigenous institutions of social control which the Pueblos had preserved, and certain aspects of citizen status for Indians facilitated their exploitation by non-Indian neighbors.

Land hunger was the most immediate source of conflicting interests between the non-Indian and Indian citizens. This land hunger was manifested in the Abiquiu area not only by the repeated petitions for the huge Tierra Amarilla Grant but by a series of smaller grants made almost immediately following independence. In 1823 a grant was made to fifteen settlers in an area called Cañones de Riaño, said to be two leagues from the Poblazón of El Rito. A year later the settlers complained that rich men who had bought land from Joaquin García at El Rito were claiming the Cañones de Riaño lands and trying to dispossess the settlers or force them to make payment for their own grant. The settlers had already built an acequia (irrigation ditch), but wanted to have their right to the land enforced. Alcalde Francisco Trujillo put them back in possession, but it appears that the grant was later deserted and never confirmed. The chief interest of the Cañones de Riaño record is that it demonstrates the emergence of a group of wealthy men in the Abiquiu area who were seeking to monopolize land and the resistance of the small landowners to such a force.[1]

In 1824 another grant was made above El Rito. This was the Vallecitos de Lobato Grant, requested by José Rafael Zamora and twenty-five companions, but settled by a total of fifty families. Another grant in the same year was that of the Petaca, east of Vallecitos. This was granted to Francisco Vigil, a settler of La Cueva at the north end of the Ojo Caliente Grant, along with some twenty other families. They later deserted and the grant was reassigned in 1836 to new petitioners. Two plazas were settled on this grant: Petaca and La Servilleta to the south.[2]

PARTITION OF GENÍZARO LANDS

During the 1820's lands which had been Genízaro grants were measured, so as to make allotment in severalty to each of the former Genízaro families whose formal citizen status required that they have individual rights to dispose of their lands. Distribution at Ojo Caliente proceeded with little complication, because the lands had been regranted so many times that the special status of the Genízaro grants had been obliterated. The alcalde of Abiquiu, Francisco Trujillo, made the measurements to provide each family an agricultural allotment of exactly 150 varas (a vara is slightly less than a yard).

Trujillo checked the grants made to fifty-three families in the present town of Ojo Caliente, around the Chapel of the Holy Cross, with 350 varas in the center for irrigated orchards. The south boundary of that donation was the tower of José Baca, over three miles downstream from the chapel. North of the plaza were the settlements of the Cañada of the Comanches with fifteen families, La Cueva with fifty-eight landowners, and also some two dozen other landowners in unidentified settlements. Some of the owners had oversize agricultural allotments which were supposed to be reduced to the usual 150 vara width. Clearly the population of Ojo Caliente had greatly increased since the beginning of the nineteenth century.[3]

In Abiquiu the task of partitioning the Genízaro grant proved to be harder than anticipated. In the first place, the lands were partly in very hilly country and of uneven quality. After the first distribution had been made, the governor required that Alcalde Juan Cristobal Quintana make a completely new distribution, giving each grantee an equal amount of desirable and undesirable land.

In the second place, no sooner had the lands been subdivided than some of the former Genízaros began to sell their lands to non-Indian neighbors. Some of the lands of Gerónimo Martín appropriated for the pueblo were sold to a grandson of Gerónimo's, Santiago Salazar. This immediately aroused a challenge from Miguel Velarde, who claimed that as a son of the pueblo, he should not have been excluded from the partition of lands and should have had first choice of the lands in the Ancón Quemado, purchased by Salazar. Final partition of Abiquiu lands was not completed until 1841.

The third problem relating to the subdivision of the Abiquiu lands was the alleged encroachment of the Vallecito de San Antonio Grant upon the *ejído* (common lands) of the pueblo south of the individual allotments. In 1829 Alcalde Miguel Felipe Quintana of Abiquiu reported to Jefe Político Manuel Armijo a situation "which scandalized the public." The south boundary of the grant had been established as "the road of the Teguas which goes to Navajó," but agreement could not be reached as to the exact location of the road, presumably one of many trails. As a result of the altercation, the town council had refused to pay the secretary of the corporation, and he, in turn, had refused to write and publish decrees sent from the governor's office. A few months later the Mexican government appointed José María Alarid as attorney for the Indians to see that the boundaries of their grant were set as stated in the original documents. These documents, however, suddenly disappeared, although they had been used in making the distribution of lands in 1825. Not long after, the Vallecito title papers were also reported missing.

The Vallecito grantees accused the "plenipotentiary of the Indians," José María Alarid, of having plotted with the former alcalde, Miguel Felipe Quintana. He had supposedly permitted the Genízaros to commit stock depredations on the Vallecito lands, pending decision on the case by the Supreme Court of Mexico.

In 1831 the new constitutional alcalde of Abiquiu was José Francisco Vigil, possibly the same man who in 1815 was accused by Abiquiu citizens of intending to pilfer from local contributions to the patriotic war chest. In the litigations between the Genízaro heirs and the Vallecito settlers, Vigil exhibited bias against the former and partiality toward the latter. During this period, Antonio Barreiro, the *asesor* (legal advisor sent from Mexico to establish a judicial system in New Mexico), was in Santa Fe. Vigil directed queries and complaints to him. A Genízaro spokesman, Francisco Marques, had "rashly" initiated litigation against the Vallecito settlers and was being aided by Francisco Trujillo "who has come in to seduce this Pueblo." This may have been the same Trujillo who, as alcalde of Abiquiu in 1824, supervised the partition of lands in Ojo Caliente.

On September 21, 1831, Vigil attempted to measure the distance from the center of Abiquiu to the supposed boundary in the presence of citizens of both Vallecito and Abiquiu. Vallecito had sent its leading citizens to serve as witnesses, but the entire Pueblo of Abiquiu poured into the plaza, calling upon the alcalde to use the same measuring cord he had used for Vallecito.

Pandemonium ensued. The people of the pueblo pressed

forward, trying to halt the measuring with their bodies. Francisco Marques grasped the reins of the mounted alcalde's horse, crying that they might as well die at the hands of the alcalde's henchman as at the hands of the heathens. Alcalde Vigil reported this dramatic scene plaintively: "Tell me, Señor Governor, what remedy can I apply to keep them from being so vicious that a Constitutional Alcalde can be maltreated in public and my person and the men who accompanied me attacked?"

Attorney Barreiro's opinion, when he was consulted on this case, was that no criminal charges should be raised against the Genízaros for their demonstration against the alcalde. He pointed out that the citizens had not taken up arms against constituted authority and that, in fact, the land measures had been completed after everyone quieted down. Secondly, wrote Barreiro, the noisy and threatening demonstration had been stimulated by provocative leadership and the evils of drink. Finally, all eyewitness reports upheld the alcalde's conduct and condemned the demonstrators, so that no outstanding issue remained.

The governor, nonetheless, ordered a hearing on the supposed uprising, to be conducted by the senior *regidor* (councilman) of Abiquiu. The man appointed to this function was thirty-year-old José María Chavez, selected, according to Barreiro, because "by virtue of your knowledge you are the only one who can officiate." Chavez was already renowned as an Indian fighter and later became a general of the territorial militia. He was on his way to becoming a large landowner and was married to a daughter of Manuel Martinez, petitioner for the Tierra Amarilla Grant. He could hardly have been an impartial chairman of the hearings.

Among Chavez' papers, the eyewitness statements of witnesses hostile to the Genízaros later passed into the archives of the state of New Mexico, but no statements by the defendants or their witnesses were found. The depositions singled out Francisco Marques and Francisco, Pedro, Felipe, and Domingo Trujillo as the leaders of the demonstration. Unfilled forms concerning conviction and sentence leave open the possibility that the accused actually were sentenced to labor at public works under the supervision of the alcalde.[4]

THE 1837 REBELLION

This clash of interests, led on one side by representatives of people professing to be poor Indians and on the other side by propertied people professing no Indian affiliations, was a forewarning of greater clashes to come in 1837; namely, the rebellion against Governor Albino Perez and the new system of taxation proposed by the Mexican government under the departmental system.

Rumor had it that traders from the United States stirred up the rebellion in order to reverse a new tax law on imports, but the discontent that led to the uprising was already there. Among the most active rebels were Indians and Genízaros of the Tewa Basin, scene of the main action. José Gonzales, a Genízaro from Taos with relatives in Chimayó, became the insurgent governor. The rebel government was overthrown through the conniving of former and soon-to-be governor Manuel Armijo, who had close business ties with the Americans.

According to the *Illustrated History of New Mexico* by Benjamin Read, one motive for the uprising was that Governor Perez had disbanded the troops because he could no longer pay them. This left the volunteer militia, with its large percentage of Genízaros, completely unsupported in the defense of the frontier at a time when Navajo, Apache, and Ute raids were increasing. The militia of Abiquiu had become more and more unwilling to go on Indian campaigns ever since an 1821 ruling that individuals who took war booty had to turn it over to the commanding officer. The fruits of unlicensed trade and the booty of war had been the main historic factor in the Chama Valley making for social flexibility, since Genízaros shared equal chances with others to better their economic lot through fighting and trade.

The short-lived 1837 Rebellion united Pueblo Indians, Genízaros, and a section of the Hispanic population in an effort to eliminate the new departmental system with its tax burden and to maintain village autonomy. The alcaldes of Santa Cruz and San Juan participated in the new government, as did the governors of at least several pueblos. Popular tradition in the Chama Valley holds that the Abiquiu Genízaros joined the uprising, while the Hispanic population took no action but remained loyal. Even if they may have had something to do with the uprising, U.S. traders cooperated with Manuel Armijo in putting it down. Perhaps they had not anticipated the distinct trend toward social reform to which it would lead.[5]

SOCIAL STRATIFICATION GROWS

The opening of trade with the United States was a principal cause for the increasing stratification of New Mexico society which grew after independence from Spain. The growth of the rico class was most pronounced in the main population centers such as Santa Fé and Albuquerque, but it also developed at a slower pace in the communities surrounding Abiquiu. As a corollary to the enrichment of commercial leaders, indebtedness of their customers led to loss of land in payment of debts.

While it is not certain that any of the local population in Abiquiu was landless in the second quarter of the nineteenth century, we have some data tending to show that those with the least land and property were descendants of Genízaros. A census of 1827, which includes under the Abiquiu demarcation El Rito and all Chama Valley settlements west of Chamita, records a total population of 3,557. It lists 508 heads of household as farmers, 301 as day laborers, 48 as craftsmen, 6 as merchants and, finally, the priest and a school teacher. Many of those listed as day laborers must have been herders and other employees who actually had subsistence farms of their own, since they maintained independent households.

While the 1827 census has no breakdown by plazas, an undated census from the 1820's gives a breakdown for the plaza of Santo Tomás (the still largely Genízaro town of Abiquiu) and three plazas to the west. The town list notes only forty-five houses among seventy-two household heads, indicating either that families employed by the wealthy lived with them or that very poor families lived together. In the other three plazas, there were fifty-five houses for fifty-six families, suggesting less servitude or at least less crowding for non-Genízaro families. In the town of Abiquiu, eight households were headed by widows, compared with only one such household in the other three plazas.[6]

The impression of poverty in the town of Abiquiu is commu-

nicated by reports from the Workman party, which stopped in
Abiquiu in 1841 to secure provisions and employees for their
overland trip to California. Isaac Given, a member of the party,
wrote about one Lorenzo Trujillo of Abiquiu, who said he was a
Comanche. He accompanied the Workman party and helped
found a settlement near Los Angeles. Given wrote: "We found
these people living in a very primitive fashion, footloose and
free, unencumbered with worldly goods and ready, at an hour's
notice, to accompany us in our travels. I remember contracting
with an able-bodied and active man, some forty years of age,
agreeing to pay him all he asked—an advance of two dollars—
and giving him, after reaching California, a hat, a shirt and a pair
of shoes; the negotiation, which was closed on the spot, occupied less time than the writing of this paragraph."[7]

The non-Genízaro families of Abiquiu were not enjoying a
much higher standard of living in those days. Even the sons of
relatively well-to-do families customarily worked as shepherds
or farm laborers before being emancipated and placed in the
"estate of matrimony." Their wages were appropriated by their
fathers and their status was not considered as truly servile but
rather as a temporary condition to accumulate a surplus for the
founding of a new household. The poorer the family, the longer
the marriage had to be deferred.

An undated census of El Rito, taken between the years of
1833 and 1839, identifies only five adults as servants out of a
total population of 1,466. This does not, however, rule out the
possibility that a number of children ten years of age and older,
living with people other than their parents, were actually hired
out or were fosterlings providing extra hands for their foster-
parents. It was taken for granted that children worked as early
as they could and as hard as they could, regardless of family
wealth or ethnic origin. There is no question, however, that
Indian captive children and the children of poor families who
lived as fosterlings of wealthier families, often relatives, worked
the hardest of all.[8]

TRADE AND TRADERS AT ABIQUIU

During the years of the Mexican Republic, Abiquiu's importance as a trading center increased, since this town was the

eastern gateway of the Old Spanish Trail to California, a route first mentioned in the report of the travels of Fathers Dominguez and Escalante in 1776. However, they only got as far as central Utah. The date when traders from Abiquiu first began to travel the full distance to California is uncertain, but by 1835 the trade route was already well established.[9]

Access to California and Sonora expanded the activity in contraband. The trade cycle included exchange of captives obtained from the Utes by Abiquiu settlers for stolen horses obtained from California and Sonora by west coast settlers, often with some Ute assistance. Anglo-American Mountain Men also became involved in this commerce.

During the same period, Abiquiu traders increasingly plied the trade route to Chihuahua along the *Camino Real* (Royal Highway), the rutted track over which wagons had gone for supplies since earliest colonial times. Each year oxcarts assembled near the village of Alcalde to travel for six weeks on the southward journey, reaching Chihuahua for its annual trade fair early in December. Some contingents went further, to Durango and Zacatecas and even Guadalajara. The main exports from Abiquiu were sheep on the hoof, hides, and wool. Products of the Indian trade exported from Abiquiu were fine dressed hides, Indian blankets, and dried buffalo and deer meat. Ojo Caliente was noted for the sacks of piñon nuts gathered from its surrounding hillsides and shipped in quantity.[10]

Some of the men who plied the trade routes out of Abiquiu to Chihuahua, Durango, and California settled at the far end of the trail. They married and in some instances their children and grandchildren returned to the ancestral communities in New Mexico. This explains why some of the Lopez, Lucero, Quintana, Salazar, Martinez, etc., lineages in the San Juan Basin today are descendants of Abiquiu people who had gone to California or Old Mexico for a generation or two.

A DECADE OF UTE HOSTILITIES

The outbreak of chronic hostilities with the Navajos, following the 1805 campaign and massacre in the Cañon de Chelly, brought upon the communities of the Abiquiu area increased demands for militia service, although Abiquiu itself did not come under frequent Navajo attack. The Utes raided settlements on the northern periphery in the 1830's, but no record of fatalities in the Chama Valley resulted until September 1844, when a Ute delegation went to Santa Fe, escorted by Captain José Francisco Vigil and Lieutenant José María Chavez, to negotiate with the governor for compensation of the murder of several tribesmen.

The Utes were also incensed because their annual gifts, provided by the government to keep the peace, had not been delivered. Governor Mariano Martinez de Lejanza, an appointee from Mexico, was as suspicious of the Utes as they were of him and had soldiers stationed behind a drapery. At the first Ute move he considered hostile, he drew his sword, called the soldiers to come out from hiding, and had his guards kill eleven Utes in the palace and the plaza.

The Utes fled back to their encampment on the Vega de Riaño above Abiquiu. In their fury they killed people they met on the way, stopping at Tierra Azul to kill three men and wound a fourth, all of the Vigil family. Among the slain, apparently, was Captain Vigil of their escort to Santa Fe; perhaps because they blamed him for the governor's actions. The former alcalde of Abiquiu, Miguel F. Quintana, went to the Ute encampment with his brother, Juan Cristobal, thinking that out of years of friendship the Utes would listen to reason. Instead, they killed both men on the spot.[11]

Thus was launched a decade of hostility between the Utes and most northern New Mexico settlements. The Utes, however, tended to make exceptions in the case of old friends. While no permanent settlement could be established on the Tierra Amarilla Grant, as Lieutenant J. W. Abert noted in his 1846 reconnaissance report, Abert described the area as a prime stock range and mentioned that it was intersected by the trail between Santa Fe and Los Angeles.[12] His statements tend to support local tradition; i.e., that the Tierra Amarilla Grant was dotted with small summer sheep camps throughout the period of most hostility with the Utes. People say that the sheep were herded in small flocks and were scattered up the canyons when a Ute raid commenced, so that losses would be minimal. This was a period of intensive trade along the Old Spanish Trail, and apparently trading relations between individual settlers and individual Utes were unaffected by the general hostility.

PRELUDE AND AFTERMATH OF CONQUEST

Conquest of New Mexico by the armed forces of the United States occurred in 1846, in the middle of the hostilities with Navajos and Utes. In reality, however, the conquest was the culminating event of a process which began early in the nineteenth century. From the time of the Louisiana Purchase in 1803, the Spanish colonial administration had worried constantly over the expansionist drive of the United States. The northern borders of New Spain were closed off to Yankee travel and trade, as Major Zebulon M. Pike discovered when his reconnoitering—or perhaps spying—trip took him to the headwaters of the Rio Grande, and he was arrested as a trespasser on New Mexico soil. Pike's account of his adventures and observations in New Mexico, *Travels Through the Interior of New Spain,* greatly aroused stateside interest in the remote province.

New Mexicans, for their part, were more interested in their Yankee neighbors than colonial officialdom desired. Trade relations, largely informal, were maintained with New Orleans through French, Spanish, and American administrations. Tradition in the Rio Arriba country holds that early in the nineteenth century people of the northern frontier began to herd sheep eastward toward Saint Louis, making a trip of two years' duration to bring fresh meat, wool, hides, and live sheep to market. From early in the nineteenth century, Mountain Men illegally entered the borders of New Mexico to trap and trade, and they apparently received unofficial encouragement in their activities.

With the victory of Mexican independence, New Mexico welcomed trade with the United States. Santa Fe was not only a center of the commerce but was a stopover on the trail to Chihuahua. This highly profitable trade created a small class of people in New Mexico who were much more affluent than their neighbors and whose commercial ties with the United States caused them to view with equanimity the prospect of being swallowed up by their neighbor to the east. This prospect became a virtual certainty after Texas became an independent republic in 1836, with thinly veiled assistance from the United States government.

During this period the policy of the Mexican federal government to keep United States influence in abeyance in New Mexico was constantly thwarted by the system of bribery and commercial partnership with which the United States traders won the cooperation of New Mexican officials. While New Mexico was delivered over to the United States without firing a shot, due to clandestine agreements between Governor Manuel Armijo and James Magoffin, resistance to conquest did develop within a few months of the takeover. A conspiracy of affluent young Santa Fe citizens to overthrow the military government was discovered and thwarted just before Christmas of 1846. Belated popular uprisings against the occupation occurred in early 1847, bringing together Hispanos, Pueblo Indians, and Genízaros of Taos, Arroyo Hondo, Questa, San Miguel, Pecos, Las Vegas, and Mora. Lacking a centralized leadership, these efforts were foredoomed in the face of a powerful United States Army equipped with the latest weapons and enjoying the aid of Mexican collaborators.[13]

The Abiquiu area, whose only importance in commerce and military maneuvers lay in its access to Navajo and Ute country, did not become involved in either the conspiracy of the Santa Fe Trail merchants with the United States military or the efforts to throw off Yankee control. Following the conquest, however, an outward movement of population reduced the population of the Lower Chama Valley and altered its composition. Some people followed the gold rush to California or, later, to Colorado. Some returned to Old Mexico. The greatest number, however, moved northward into the Upper Chama Valley and the San Luis Valley, occupying grants made in previous years but not permanently settled due to Indian hostilities.

Conquest of New Mexico by the United States unleashed some two decades of furious fighting with various Indian groups, worse than all previous hostilities. The tacticians of this warfare were people who devoutly believed in Indian extermination, and they were able to bring into service weapons much more deadly than had previously been used in New Mexico.

Hispanic New Mexicans, despite General Kearny's promise that the United States government would protect them from Indian raids, were exposed more than ever before and were required to carry the brunt of the fighting in the territorial militia.

Navajo resistance flared to its strongest peak at the outset of the Civil War and was crushed in 1864. From then until 1868, eight thousand Navajos lived in captivity in the Bosque Redondo under the control of the garrison at Fort Sumner, while their fellow Navajos still at large were fair game for raiding parties. During the 1860's and 1870's, the number of Navajo captives in Hispano households of the Chama drainage rose dramatically.

Fighting against certain bands of Utes and the Jicarilla Apaches was most intense in the early and mid-1850's. Thereafter, these Indians raided infrequently, their greatest offense in the eyes of the authorities being their growing addiction to the white man's alcoholic beverages. Both groups went through "removal" ordeals that lasted into the early 1890's. The Jicarillas were shipped in 1880 from agency headquarters they had shared with the Moache Utes at the Maxwell ranch near Cimarron to the newly founded reservation in the Dulce area, where the Gomez family had already settled. In 1883 they were shipped to Fort Sumner and by 1891 they were shipped back to Dulce. The Utes were forced to relinquish their mountain range in Colorado after being engulfed by the gold rush. Eventually they were divided into three reservations, one in northeastern Utah and the other two in southwestern Colorado.

The Capotes and Moaches, who had apparently been the principal victims of the 1844 massacre in Santa Fe, fought hard to hold on to the lands at the northern periphery of New Mexico in the Upper Chama and San Luis Valleys. It is all the more remarkable, therefore, that during the period of the most severe raids some Hispano villagers moved beyond the periphery of non-Indian settlement and directly into areas that were claimed by the very Indians with whom a condition of war existed.

4

Population Shifts in the Territorial Period

THE EARLY TERRITORIAL YEARS

Hispanic population movement during the early decades of United States rule in New Mexico was in part a response to the rapid development of commerce and transportation. Hispanos joined in the expanded wagon trade and during the 1870's helped with the building and maintenance of railroad lines. Already in the 1850's many joined the gold rush to California and the Colorado Rockies.

During the same period, however, there was a very definite Hispano movement to settle beyond the peripheries of the non-Indian population. This was apparently caused by a combination of land loss and the desire to escape direct domination under the new and somewhat oppressive government. In 1852, Richard Weightman, the New Mexico territorial delegate to the House of Representatives, charged that the territorial government was completely controlled by the Army Quartermaster Corps. He claimed that some 150 civil officers, judges, and alcaldes had been handpicked by the corps and that they were blocking statehood for New Mexico. He further stated that they imposed arbitrary taxes, conducted trials without juries, and intervened in Church administration.

Weightman said that some of the wealthiest Hispanos were

allowed to represent their counties in the territorial legislature, but that the bulk of the population was effectively barred from participation in the decisions that most affected them and in which they expressed keen interest:

> I have never met in any part of the United States people more hospitable, more law-abiding, more kind, more generous, more desirous of improvement, more desirous that a general system of education be established among them, more desirous that the many and not the few should govern, more apprehensive of the tendency of power to steal from the many for the few, more desirous of seeing in their own idiom the Declaration of Independence, the Constitution of the United States. . . . Among them I have met men of incorruptible integrity, of honor, refinement, intelligence and information. [1]

Despite this and other flattering statements concerning the readiness of Hispanos for self-government, statehood for New Mexico was deferred until 1912. Even then, citizenship for the Indians was disregarded, and during all the intervening years, Hispanos were gradually stripped of their land grant rights. Chauvinistic and anti-Catholic propaganda was spread to justify discriminatory treatment of the territory and its Hispanic and Indian population, while the record shows that prolongation of territorial status made possible massive alienation of lands in New Mexico. [2]

LAND GRANT ALIENATION

The first of a long line of surveyors-general arrived in New Mexico at the end of 1854. The surveyors-general were to assist the Pueblo Indians and Hispanos to secure confirmation of their land grants, but the procedures followed made this impossible. Claimants had to pay the cost of the investigation and survey of their claims. They were forced to hire lawyers to file the claims, and some lawyers took as much as half the land grant as their fee.

By 1863 only 2,293,142 acres had been surveyed out of a total of 77.5 million acres in New Mexico, of which more than 35 million were claimed under grant titles. The final acreage approved by the Court of Private Land Claims when it adjourned in 1904 was a little over 2 million acres.[3]

Officials appointed by the federal government helped deprive the land grant heirs of their rights. In 1869 Territorial Governor William Pile sold a large number of the colonial and Mexican archives as waste paper. While some claim that these were not land grant documents, virtually all archives were valuable in proving the existence of communities and documenting which families lived in them. At any rate, Pile's action was widely interpreted at the time as being aimed against the land grant heirs and was so reported in 1880 by the famed scientist, Adolph Bandelier. Bandelier also reported that William Arny during a brief tenure as acting governor in 1866 had placed all the archives in an "outhouse," letting the ancient documents rot.[4]

While the rights of land grant heirs were being undermined by New Mexico's new rulers, the federal government consistently neglected its promise to uphold these rights, as provided by the Treaty of Guadalupe Hidalgo. Without a murmur from the administration, Congress confirmed the so-called "Armijo Grants," while deferring or denying the rights of long-established communities.[5] Grant Number One, confirmed to Preston Beck, Jr., was an encroachment on the Anton Chico Grant. Grant Number Fifteen, originally made by Governor Armijo to Narciso Beaubien and Guadalupe Miranda and eventually confirmed to Lucien Maxwell, was more than three times larger than any other grant in New Mexico. John Scolly, Hugh Stephenson, and other Yankees were promptly confirmed as authentic grantees.

More than forty years after the American occupation, most claims were still left pending in the surveyor general's office. The Court of Private Land Claims was established in 1891, and by the time this court's labors were completed in 1904, the work commenced by the surveyors-general, the governors, and the legal vultures of previous decades was fittingly climaxed. Declared invalid were all grants made by colonial officials who had been dismissed from office before signing the grant papers (these officials had left office only after their replacements arrived), even though the Spanish and colonial authorities had officially recognized these grants for generations. Neither the Spanish nor Mexican governments were consulted in making these rulings, nor were they consulted in the court's interpretation concerning title to common lands. This held that title resided in the sovereign, and that the United States, as the new sovereign, held title to all the *ejido* (community lands).[6] Unknown to the heirs, the community lands of many grants were recorded as part of the public domain.

Thousands of grant heirs of the Lower Chama were victims of these arbitrary decisions. Mention has been made (chapter 2, footnote 4) of the decisions which denied recognition to a number of Chama Valley grants in favor of the Juan José Lobato claim, and in 1905, the uncompensated appropriation of most of that land for the Carson National Forest. The Joaquin García (El Rito), Petaca, Vallecitos de Lobato, and several other communities lost all their range to Carson, while the San Joaquin del Rio Chama (again without compensation) lost equally to the Carson and Santa Fe National Forests.

The San Joaquin Grant was the pawn in a speculative game played by William Blackmore, Thomas Catron, Thomas Burns, and others. In the end, 1,422.62 acres of this grant with a total acreage of some half-million acres were finally confirmed by the Court of Private Land Claims, in favor of Thomas Burns. The San Joaquin heirs in Gallina, Capulín, Coyote, and Canjilón had nothing left but their home lots and small irrigated fields. Many heirs had meanwhile left the San Joaquin lands to try their luck in California and the Colorado mines. The strip of land between Nutrias Creek and Cebolla Creek was opened to homesteaders, and San Joaquin heirs who lived on that strip were forced to file homestead claims on land their families had farmed for generations.

When the Court of Private Land Claims was dissolved in 1904, the federal government had acquired control over more than fifty-two million acres of land in New Mexico. Many of these acres, opened for homestead entry, fell into the hands of powerful ranching and mining interests, while nearly nine million acres were set aside for national forests.[7]

Knowingly or unknowingly, some Hispanos were party to the maneuvers that denied grant rights to their fellow grant heirs. A classic instance is that of Sixto Martinez, who went to live in California in 1848 and signed over all his right and title to lands in New Mexico to his brother Francisco. Possibly, Sixto did not realize that this statement, in later years, would serve as evidence that he had signed over to Francisco one-eighth of the entire Tierra Amarilla Grant. Sixto had never settled or received an allotment at Tierra Amarilla and had no valid claim to any part of the grant. When Francisco Martinez petitioned Congress for confirmation of the grant as though ownership were exclusive to the heirs of Manuel Martinez, Congress accepted this fiction, and all the deeds from Francisco's brothers who had never settled the grant were accepted as valid evidence of his sole ownership.[8]

A number of Abiquiu residents had meanwhile become bona fide Tierra Amarilla settlers and did not have the slightest idea that the grant was being taken out from under them. In 1874 Francisco Martinez died, and when President Hayes signed the grant patent to him posthumously in 1881, Martinez' widow and children promptly signed the grant over to Thomas Benton Catron, the notorious lawyer and leader of the Santa Fe Ring. For years past, unknown to the Tierra Amarilla settlers, Catron had been directly or indirectly purchasing deeds and conveyances from the children of Manuel Martinez.[9]

During the early territorial years, the villagers on their scattered land grants did not realize the magnitude of what was taking place: a wholesale violation of their property rights as guaranteed by the Treaty of Guadalupe Hidalgo. In New Mexico there were too few Anglo-American settlers to duplicate the violent dispossession of grant heirs that occurred in Texas and California.[10] On many New Mexico grants, traditional community rights of open pasture and firewood gathering were exercised until recent years, and the social reality of these rights continued alive in the minds of the heirs. In 1935 the legal rights of land grant heirs to use the water that crossed their lands was ably argued. The brief was filed with the Supreme Court of the United States by J. Turley in a dispute between New Mexico and Texas over rights to a certain percentage of the water flowing in the Rio Grande. The Supreme Court, however, refused to examine Turley's brief, and the issues that he raised have never been reviewed by a judicial body.[11] Thus, land loss for New Mexican Hispanos has been a gradual process, reaching critical stages in different regions at different times. The imposition of land taxes in 1895 probably had the broadest impact of any single event in causing widespread loss of land.

NORTHWARD SETTLEMENT TRENDS AND
THE PENITENTE BROTHERHOOD

Hispano settlement of the San Luis Valley, now a part of Colorado, began in the late 1840's, ostensibly an inauspicious time. The Moache Utes and Jicarilla Apaches, who ranged the eastern portion of the Valley, actively opposed settlement and dislodged all those who settled east of the Río Grande until 1851, although a settlement was made without incident in 1849 west of the Río Grande on the Conejos Grant, under an informal agreement with the Tabewache Utes. The Conejos Grant was made in 1832 and several attempted settlements were dislodged. The settlement of Guadalupe near Conejos was nearly dislodged by Ute raids as late as 1854, since nobody had taken the trouble to secure the consent of the Utes.[12]

For three reasons the population was motivated to move northward, despite Indian opposition. They needed new irrigated lands, expanded ranges, and a better corner on the Ute trade. Another motive, never so stated, may have been escape from religious persecution, since a majority of the early settlers of the San Luis Valley were members of the Penitente Brotherhood.

The state of religion in the early territorial years was uncertain. The majority of the conquerors were Protestant, with a pronounced bias against "popery." Furthermore, they feared the influence of the few native priests as potential leaders of rebellion. The presbyter, Father Ramón Ortiz, named by General Kearny as commissioner for the repatriation of Mexican nationals, was so successful in convincing New Mexicans to repatriate that he was summarily banned by territorial authorities from appearing before the people. Ortiz reported that nine hundred families out of a total of one thousand in the San Miguel del Vado area had elected to retain their Mexican citizenship, "willing to lose everything rather than live in a country whose government gave them fewer guarantees than their own and in which they were treated with more disdain than the African race."[13]

Among the native New Mexican priests, the occupation authorities feared none more than Father Antonio José Martinez, a boldly outspoken man, born in the Plaza de la Capilla of the Abiquiu Demarcation. Martinez became parish priest at Taos and was the leader of a prominent family of landowners. He has been represented as a villain in various works purporting to be historical. However, more recent evaluations of his role show him to have been a positive leader.[14]

French-born Father Jean Lamy, consecrated as apostolic vicar of New Mexico in 1850, proceeded to initiate sweeping changes in the New Mexico Church. He overcame the shortage of priests in New Mexico by seeking European priests. In 1867 he requested a Jesuit mission to New Mexico from a Neapolitan province and he placed the Jesuits in charge of an educational campaign centering in the school they established in Las Vegas, New Mexico.[15]

Lamy reacted with disapproval toward the religious practices he observed in the villages of New Mexico. His desire to put an end to them was nourished by the outspoken hostility of anti-Catholic civil leaders in the territory, who circulated blood-curdling stories about the self-mortifications of the Penitente Brotherhood.

This lay brotherhood, the *Cofradía de Nuestro Padre Jesús Nazareno* (Confraternity of Our Father, Jesus the Nazarene), was similar to many secular groups common in medieval Europe. Their practice of expiating sin by corporal penance, their Lenten processions, and reenactment of the Passion of Jesus have not altogether disappeared in modern Europe, although Spain outlawed self-flagellation in 1777.[16]

ORIGINS OF THE PENITENTE BROTHERHOOD

The emergence of the Brotherhood in New Mexico is of uncertain date. The practice of bodily penance was conducted in church under the leadership of the mission father of Abiquiu,

when Fathers Dominguez and Escalante visited there on Good
Friday in 1776. No mention of a New Mexico Penitente Brotherhood exists for this period. It is significant, however, that a
church dedicated to the Nazarene Christ was built in the mid-
eighteenth century at Tepatlcingo, Morelos, Mexico, by the
Cofradía de Nuestro Padre Jesús Nazareno. Thus, we have early
positive documentation for the Brotherhood for at least one
area of colonial New Spain. Furthermore, word of mouth indicates that the Brotherhood has existed from time beyond recall
in mountain communities of northern Mexico and that representatives of the New Mexican Brotherhood periodically visited
the Mexican chapters well into the twentieth century.

In New Mexico the Brotherhood was well developed by the
early nineteenth century. Apparently its developmental period
was stimulated in the late eighteenth century by the extreme
scarcity of priests, due to the nonreplacement of mission fathers
who died or became too old to serve. Fray Angélico Chavez
believes that the Brotherhood, with its cult of the Nazarene
Christ, was introduced at that time by colonists or priests from
Mexico or other regions to the south.[17]

The shortage of priests continued into the first half of the
nineteenth century. In 1827 there were only seventeen priests
in all New Mexico.[18] Many of them were too old to perform
their offices in remote settlements, causing the Mexican legal
adviser Antonio Barreiro to write in 1832:

> Nothing is more common than to see an infinite number of
> the sick die without confession or extreme unction. It is
> indeed unusual to see the eucharist administered to the sick.
> Corpses remain unburied for many days and children are
> baptized at the cost of a thousand hardships. A great many
> unfortunate people spend most of the Sundays of the year
> without hearing mass. Churches are in a state of near ruin,
> and most of them are unworthy of being called the Temple
> of God.[19]

The Brotherhood concerned itself with the problems of the
sick and the dying where priests were unavailable. Through
prayer services to the saints and wakes for the dead, Brothers
brought to sufferers and their loved ones the consolations of
their religion. They also provided material aid by digging graves,

helping bereaved families with their ploughing and heavy tasks, and by organizing food sharing during Lent and Holy Week. These activities were vital to community unity, yet attention and criticism followed the Brotherhood only because of its annual practice of corporal penance.

The first to comment on the Brotherhood was Bishop José Antonio Laureano de Zubiría, when he made an episcopal visit to New Mexico in 1833, the first such visit since Bishop Tamarón's visit of 1760. Zubiría berated "a Brotherhood of Penitentes, already existing for a goodly number of years, but without any authorization or even the knowledge of the bishops who definitely would not have given their consent for such a Brotherhood . . . since the excesses of very indiscreet corporal punishment which they are accustomed to practice on some days of the year, and even publicly, are so contrary to Religion and the regulations of Holy Church." Bishop Zubiría ordered the priests of New Mexico to forbid Penitente gatherings.[20]

SUPPRESSION OF THE PENITENTE BROTHERHOOD

Despite these admonitions, the Brotherhood continued to grow as a village institution, unchecked by parish priests until Bishop Lamy took charge of Church affairs in New Mexico. Knowing nothing of the Spanish cofradía tradition, Lamy assumed that the Penitentes were a degenerate remnant of the Third Order of Franciscans, which had existed in New Mexico in colonial times. Lamy, therefore, tried to impose on the Brotherhood the rules of the Third Order.[21] The Penitentes either ignored his instructions or followed them halfheartedly, and hence were denied the status of a religious society. In 1861 they were incorporated as a benevolent society by the territorial legislature.[22]

After the Civil War, Anglo-Protestant churchmen began to arrive in New Mexico and to take scandalized note of Penitente activities during Lent and Holy Week, much to the embarrassment of the Catholic clergy. Some Protestants claimed that during observation of the *Tinieblas* (the Tenebrae or darkening ceremony which marked the moment of Jesus' death), the Church congregation and priest indulged in orgiastic behavior.

Rumors, especially those regarding the supposed crucifixion of the cross-bearer, so inflamed Anglo-Protestant opinion that Good Friday services were sometimes violently disrupted. In the early 1860's, a troop of cavalry from Fort Garland galloped into the tiny plaza of San Pedro on the Sangre de Cristo Grant to prevent the "murder" of the cross-bearer.[23]

Bishop Lamy instituted the practice of verification before administering the sacraments, in order to screen out Penitentes from receiving these benefits unless they renounced their membership in the Brotherhood. Many priests, however, were lenient in enforcing this rule. A letter written on the eve of the celebration of the Holy Jubilee in 1881 by a man living in Santa Fé informs his close relative in the San Luis Valley that the Jesuit fathers had excused from verification the entire congregation of the church they administered, in order to provide to all the benefits of plenary indulgence. This indulgence extended to all who took Holy Communion on this occasion and to all their departed loved ones.[24]

In the 1870's the Jesuit priests had extended their activities into the San Luis Valley and their leniency toward Penitentes offended Lamy's successor, Jean-Baptiste Salpointe. He became coadjutor in 1884 and bishop after Lamy's death in 1885.[25] Salpointe undertook to tighten the control of the Church over the Brotherhood, first by pressuring the Jesuits to leave New Mexico, in order to prevent them from performing marriages, baptisms, or funeral services "at the request of a parishioner but not always with the permission of the pastor." As a result of Salpointe's pressure, the Jesuits moved their operations to Denver, Colorado, where they founded Regis College.[26]

At the first Synod of the Santa Fe Archdiocese, held in 1888, Salpointe formulated the following regulations by which parish priests were to discourage Penitente affiliation and practices:

1. They were to refuse to celebrate the Mass in the chapels of groups "continuing their abuses."

2. They were to deny the sacraments to those who insisted upon observing their traditional wakes for the dead and those who had opposed his rulings and ignored his threats of the year 1886.

As Fray Angélico Chavez has commented, these rulings had the effect of inflaming controversy between priests and their parishioners, and "the fire was fanned by some Protestant ministers."[27]

THE PRESBYTERIAN INFLUENCE

It was at this time that the Presbyterian evangelizer, Reverend Alexander Darley, "the apostle to the Southwest," was making whirlwind tours of the San Luis Valley and northern New Mexico seeking converts. For years the Presbyterians had been paving the way to conversion by distributing tracts and selling Spanish Bibles. The greater Salpointe's pressure on the Penitentes, the more eager they became to study the Bible for themselves, particularly the Old Testament. People paid the equivalent of one hundred dollars in goods and labor to acquire a Bible for private reading by the Brothers.[28] During those years, many people began to baptize their children with the names of Old Testament patriarchs and prophets.

Soon after Salpointe became bishop many Penitentes, feeling rejected by the Church of their forebears, converted to Presbyterianism. Some went on to become lay or ordained ministers. One convert, Pedro Sanchez of Ceniceros on the New Mexico-Colorado border, made a gift to the Reverend Darley. It was a handwritten copy of "The Rule of Brotherhood of San Buenaventura of Cochití . . . given by the late Bernardo Abeyta, Hermano Mayor Principal." Inscribed on the title page was "made at the request of Pedro Sanchez in 1860."[29]

The first settlers of the San Luis Valley were a group of Conejos grantees led by "Tata" Atanacio Trujillo of El Rito, a beaver trapper, sheepman, and trader to the Utes, who for some years past had been coming to the Valley. The settlers brought with them an image of San Rafael and within a few years built a chapel dedicated to this saint. Their first communities were Rincones, San Rafael, Mesitas, and Mogote,[30] all of these being communities located southwest of present-day Conejos. The morada of San Rafael still stands and is in use, for these were Penitente communities.

Other early Valley communities also had many Penitente

residents before 1870, but the New Mexican parish priests who first rode a circuit to minister to them from Taos did not report this. Bishop Lamy came to administer confirmation on the Conejos Grant in 1860, but appears not to have noticed the activities of the Brotherhood. He reported on the *jacal* (pole and 'dobe) church which had served the people for some years, and on the new parish church of Guadalupe, which was under construction.[31]

PENITENTES POLITICS AND LAND LOSS

As Salpointe moved to suppress the Brotherhood, the Brothers made efforts to consolidate their forces behind political candidates sympathetic to them or at least not hostile. The increasing secrecy which persecution forced upon the Brotherhood actually became an asset in delivering a bloc vote to candidates who could not have accepted public endorsement from Penitentes. Nobody except the Brothers themselves knew exactly which candidates had won with their support, but rumor more than made up for lack of certainty.[32]

One man whose successful career in Indian administration and politics was attributed to Penitente support was Lafayette Head, who came from Missouri in 1846, a soldier of General Kearny's forces. He married into an Hispano family and settled at Servilleta, near Ojo Caliente. In the summer of 1852, on occasional trips into Santa Fe, Head made a series of reports favorable to the Utes to Acting Indian Superintendent John Greiner. The Utes still raided in those days, but the prospect of their expulsion from New Mexico so distressed trade-minded Hispanos that Head and Rio Arriba Prefect José A. Manzanares limited their reports to friendly acts and statements by the Utes.[33]

In the early summer of 1853, Lafayette Head was named special agent for the Tabewache Utes and Jicarilla Apaches, and for the next fifteen years he continued in charge of the Utes. In the fall of 1854 he joined the settlement of the Plaza de Guadalupe near Conejos, under the leadership of José María Jaques.[34] In the Conejos Parish records, Lafayette Head's name appears as "Rafael Cabeza." He became the town's most affluent citizen; according to rumor, much of his wealth came from ransom offered by the kinsmen of Indian captives, whose names Head listed for the commissioner of Indian affairs in 1865. These captives were servants in the homes of settlers of Conejos and Costilla. According to Frank Reeve, Head was exposed for "fraud and dishonesty as agent at the Conejos."[35]

Despite rumors and exposures, Lafayette Head continued to prosper in Conejos, where the first territorial governor of Colorado, William Gilpin, visited him in 1861. Gilpin found Head a useful man because he lived in Conejos, spoke fluent Spanish, and was liked by the Mexicans.[36]

In 1876 Lafayette Head was elected the first lieutenant governor of the state of Colorado. According to Reverend Darley, Head was initiated into the Penitente Brotherhood so as to secure the winning vote. This seems hardly likely in view of the fact that Head enjoyed high prestige in a time and place where the Penitentes were being virtually excluded from the Church.[37] At the same time, the Brothers did not evangelize, but preferred to recruit as novices the teenage sons of their own members, thereby furthering social continuity. Then as now, however, the Brothers welcomed assistance from nonmember neighbors. Head may well have maintained cordial relations with the local chapters.

Settlement of the San Luis Valley and the northern periphery of the New Mexico grants proceeded rapidly in the 1850's. According to one account, the grantees feared an invasion of prospectors when news of mineral wealth in the area began to circulate. The Conejos Grant was settled by several waves of grantees, but the Sangre de Cristo Grant was settled by people under contract to Canadian-born Carlos Beaubien, who had acquired the grant through the death of his son, Narciso. Some of the Sangre de Cristo settlers, recruited from the Taos area, joined Conejos settlers in a westward move to found the communities of La Loma, Piedra Pintada, Las Garritas, and others in the Del Norte area. The names of Alarid, Silva, and Leblanc (a Canadian Mountain Man who married in the Valley) are associated with the founding of these communities.[38]

By 1872, Conejos Parish extended northward to Saguache and had a membership of approximately three thousand.[39] At

that time the population was composed largely of settlers descended from the colonial families of the Lower Chama, with a
small addition from Taos and other counties.[40] A few years
later a sudden influx of Anglo-American population followed
completion of the Denver and Rio Grande Railroad to Alamosa
in 1876. The San Luis Valley suddenly became a land speculator's paradise.

In the early 1870's, representatives of land and livestock
enterprises based on international capital and spearheaded by
the British speculator William Blackmore, in alliance with the
"Santa Fe Ring" of lawyers and bankers, began to make rapid
headway in acquiring New Mexico grant lands. By paying nomi-
nal sums to key members of certain grantee families, by representing clients in land confirmation cases with payment in land,
and by considerable trickery, speculators took whole grants
from their rightful owners.

In the San Luis Valley, the Travelers' Insurance Company
acquired thousands of acres of land and put it under irrigation
in a vast agricultural enterprise. They took up so much of the
Rio Grande flow near its headwaters that, between 1880 and
1896, 65,000 acres of the 125,000 acres farmed in the Middle
Rio Grande Valley had to be abandoned for want of water.[41]
Hand in hand with the vast expropriation of lands went a wave
of violence and terrorism which caused many Hispanos to leave
the San Luis Valley. Family histories in the San Juan Basin
relate incidents of covert shootings and public lynchings over
land and political control.

THE TIERRA AMARILLA GRANT

The Tierra Amarilla Grant came under the control of Thomas
Catron in those same years, but with so little overt violence that
the heirs remained largely unaware of their loss until 1912,
when the rangelands at the northeastern end of the grant were
sold to large cattlemen and fenced. From the time of the
awarding of Tierra Amarilla in 1832, Abiquiu sheepmen had
apparently been grazing their herds on the grant during the
summer, but establishment of communities and permanent settler allotment had been delayed by Indian hostilities. Witnesses

for Francisco Martinez in 1856 described settlement of the grant as "off and on" to the 1850's. In recommending confirmation of the grant, however, the surveyor general stated that Francisco Martinez had been in continuous possession since 1832. Martinez alone was granted the prerogative of assuming the task which the grant documents had reserved to the town corporation of Abiquiu, to put the settlers in possession of their allotments. The Martinez conveyances do not include some people who appear to have been living on the grant since before 1860. In some instances, the conveyances make separate allotments to a man and his wife or grant a second allotment to the same person. In all, some 138 conveyances of this sort were recorded between 1861 and the early 1870's.[42]

The earliest dated allotments were made in named locations, indicating that stable communities were already in existence. The town now known as Tierra Amarilla was then called *Nutritas* (little beavers), as its location had been known to Fathers Dominguez and Escalante in 1776. Before 1861, the hamlets of La Puente, Los Ojos (later renamed Parkview), Ensenada, Cañones, and Barranco were the sites of allotments. In 1864 the "Upper Town" of Tierra Amarilla was settled by some fifteen families, according to the conveyances made by Francisco Martinez. This location still had some population when the United States census was made in 1870, but it was labeled a "deserted town" in the Sawyer and McBroom map of the grant, dated 1876. "Upper Town" was located slightly southeast of the confluence of Cañones Creek with the Chama.

Traditional lore of the Tierra Amarilla area holds that small sheep ranches, set up possibly before the grant was made, were nestled in the hills near the later locations of Cañones and Barranco. Next to be settled were La Puente and Los Ojos de San José, with the other settlements somewhat later. After 1870, the settlement of Placita Blanca, south of present-day Rutheron, was made on the west bank of the Chama River with only a tree trunk as a footbridge for people going to Parkview. The town of Chama suddenly sprang into existence when a railroad line was built to that point in 1881. Most of the town names on the Tierra Amarilla Grant were borrowed from prior settlements in the Lower Chama Valley, from which the Tierra

Amarilla population had come. The town near San Juan Pueblo, formerly called Chama, became known as Chamita.

An important factor in the economic development of the Tierra Amarilla communities was the establishment of Fort Lowell, first known as Camp Plummer when a garrison was placed there in 1866 on request of Thomas Burns "to keep peace among unruly Indians."[43] Burns set up his first store near the fort.

Commerce in the area continued to grow after withdrawal of the troops in 1869. In 1872 the fort became the official center for distribution of rations to the Abiquiu Utes (mainly Capotes) and the Jicarilla Apaches.[44] During the period from the mid-1860's to 1881, a brisk wagontrain traffic wended its way northward on a tollroad from Abiquiu across the Tierra Amarilla Grant to Pagosa Springs, Colorado. The road then turned westward to "Baker City," a location at the northeast end of present-day Durango which was an assembly point for prospecting parties into the San Juan Mountains.

The tollroad board of directors in 1861 included agents for the Utes, no doubt to cope with bitter Ute opposition to invasion of their mountain valleys by prospectors. Both the agent of the Utes of Los Pinos near Cochetopa Pass and Lafayette Head of the Tabewache Agency at Conejos were board members. Another member was Canadian-born Henri Mercure, who in 1864 bought Julian Martinez' "share" of the Tierra Amarilla Grant from Frederick Muller. None of the board members were people whose names identify them as original grant settlers, and it is not clear how permission to have the tollroad built across the grant was secured. On the other hand, the many stores established along the road leave no room for doubt that it brought employment and profit to the settlers.[45]

In 1876 a wagon road was built from Abiquiu up the Cañon Largo, leading directly to the "celebrated San Juan mines and farming country on the Rio Las Animas, Pinos, Florida, Plata, and Mancos, all of which are unsurpassed for pasture and agriculture."[46] Businessmen of Abiquiu had for some time been advertising the availability of boarding accommodations, provisions, and saddle and pack animals for people who wanted to make an early spring start to the mining country.[47]

Freighting traffic picked up as soon as it became known that the terms of the Brunot Agreement, by which the Utes ceded most of their territory in western Colorado, would open the mining territory of the San Juan Mountains to prospecting. The increased traffic probably led directly to the founding of the first settlements along the San Juan River. Many of the first settlers were freighters who must have passed through the area on occasion and knew its promise for farming and raising livestock.

Shortly before ratification of the Brunot Agreement in 1874, Francisco Martinez died. Thomas Burns, who was then a resident of Parkview, soon intensified his efforts to buy up Tierra Amarilla titles. Burns had married the daughter of wealthy J. Pablo Gallegos, a director of the Abiquiu-Baker City tollroad, and Burns may very well have been the first systematic collector of Martinez family titles:

> About a year after locating in this place, Mr. Burns wrote to Santa Fe for a copy of the Spanish land grant which had been made to Francisco Martinez and companions. He began to purchase of the companions, but found that the title would be perfected only in the name of Martinez. He afterward bought directly from the heirs, purchasing 42,000 acres in one month. In his ranches, he now has 15,000 acres in the Chama Grant, 3,000 acres on the Tierra Amarilla Grant and 2,000 acres in Colorado on which is the famous Trimble Springs.[48]

During the last years of his lifetime, Francisco Martinez became involved in private speculative deals on the grant, some reputedly concluded while under the influence of alcohol. With Francisco Manzanares and others, various transactions took place, some of which were later reversed. It is noteworthy that in the census of 1870 the names of only 60 household heads among the 119 enumerated can be identified as grantees with recorded allotments. Apparently, while titles were being sold at random, including some to wealthy people in Santa Fe, some bona fide settlers received no grant papers.

In the 1870 census, households one through nine, at the south end of the grant, are largely listed as the homes of farm laborer families, although it must be pointed out that some people described as farm laborers had titles to Tierra Amarilla allotments. Households ten through forty-four were located at "Nutritas-Tierra Amarilla," while households forty-five through one-hundred-and-nineteen were listed as "Tierra Amarilla" and include allottees of the 1860's at La Puente, Los Ojos (Parkview), Brazos, "Upper Town," Barranco, and Cañones. Numerous households are listed with women heads, possibly because the census was taken in the summertime, when the men were away herding sheep and freighting. Since the women were listed by their maiden surnames, it is possible that numerous allottee families were missed in the comparison of records.[49]

Some early grantees failed to become bona fide settlers. Julian Espinosa, for instance, received an allotment from Francisco Martinez dated 1862, but departed immediately thereafter for service in the Union Army. His allotment was recorded in his name as a sale in 1888, but his descendants say that after the Civil War he settled immediately in the San Luis Valley and never went to Tierra Amarilla.[50]

THOMAS CATRON AND TIERRA AMARILLA

Thomas Catron entered officially into recorded maneuvers to acquire the grant in 1876, when he purchased from Thomas Lucero and his wife, a niece of Francisco Martinez, "right and title" to a one-eighth share of the grant. Mrs. Lucero's uncle, Father Antonio José Martinez, strenuously objected to the transaction as contrary to his niece's interests, but in any case these people had never been residents of the grant and had fulfilled no requirements to establish their rights.[51]

The people who had been trafficking in Tierra Amarilla titles may have been Catron's undercover agents in acquiring the grant. Frederick Muller, Thomas Burns, Elias Brevoort, and Wilmot Broad transferred to Catron by sale all titles they had acquired in 1881, and Catron proceeded to institute a quiet title suit on the strength of the shady transactions of himself and others, which were usual for the times. Vioalle Hefferan notes: "Only a portion of T. B.'s (Catron's) immense landholdings were acquired by direct purchase. Much of it came into his possession because he followed the then prevalent practice of taking claims for the original Spanish and Mexican land grants to court to have them confirmed. The claimants seldom had the means to stand the court expense incident to establishing their rights. The lawyers made arrangements that their fees should be a certain percentage of the land. Other properties came in lieu of fees for various legal services as well as by direct purchase."[52]

The "legal service" that gave Catron his hold over the Martinez heirs, according to Tierra Amarilla tradition, was behind-the-scenes action to hold off the arrest of Francisco Martinez' son Paz (who had killed an Apache) until he could escape to California. A José Paz Martinez did sign over his right and title to Thomas Burns in 1879 and joined the widow and other children of Francisco Martinez in signing over their right and title to Thomas Catron in 1881.[53] According to tradition, Paz Martinez escaped prosecution altogether.

Some of Catron's methods in acquiring land titles involved the manufacture of evidence. For instance, W. H. Keleher states that Catron, a silent partner of the Murphy, Dolan, and Company faction in the Lincoln County violence of the 1870's, found it convenient to be on a stagecoach bound between Cimarron and Las Vegas on the night of April 3, 1878. He was therefore immune to embarrassing questions about simultaneous events in Lincoln County. At the same time, Catron widely advertised a claim that a trunk containing land grant documents had disappeared from the stagecoach. In subsequent years, courts received in evidence Catron's unsubstantiated descriptions of the contents of these alleged missing documents.[54]

According to local tradition, Catron used several kinds of fraud to acquire the Tierra Amarilla Grant. Illiterate people were induced to place their x-marks on documents. They were told by Catron's henchmen that these were receipts for gifts of saddle horses, but they were actually relinquishing their rights on the grant. Among the papers transferring right and title from Martinez heirs to Catron are some with x-mark signatures, although the descendants of these people have documentary evidence that they were fully literate. It is important to recall that when these spurious documents were introduced as evidence in the district court in Santa Fe, Tierra Amarilla residents did not even know that a quiet title suit had been filed.

Theft of land grant documents is also claimed in Tierra
Amarilla. Thomas Burns, the story goes, persuaded some of the
original settlers, not of the Martinez family, to turn over their
title papers to him for safekeeping in the early 1870's. When
these people needed the documents to prove their rights on the
grant, Burns explained that the papers had been accidentally
destroyed by fire. Speculation naturally turns to the theory that
Burns sold to Catron the papers that would have proved that
this was a community grant.

A number of typewritten copies of Tierra Amarilla settler
deeds, supposedly stolen from the office of the surveyor general, were recently acquired by the New Mexico State Records
Center from the papers of a deceased former associate of
Thomas Catron. In these deeds, Francisco Martinez spelled out
to each grantee the rights and obligations that went with his
allotment: to remain on the grant for three years, to build a
house, clear land, open a ditch, raise crops. The use rights to the
ejido (community lands) were specified: "range, water, firewood, watering places, and free and open roads without preju-
dice to third parties, as in all established settlements."[55] These
are apparently translations of the very documents which had
disappeared when the settlers needed them most.

By the 1880's, Catron was known as one of the largest
landowners in the United States.[56] His acquisition of the Tierra
Amarilla Grant, nearly 600,000 acres, was his greatest coup. He
won his quiet title suit in 1883.[57] Captain Smith H. Simpson,
whose Valdez wife was apparently a member of a Tierra Amarilla family, filed an adverse claim based on titles he had acquired
from the Valdezes and some Medinas and Romeros, but this suit
was decided in Catron's favor. In 1901 Catron received patent
on the entire grant with small exceptions of the lands allotted
to settlers.[58]

PLUNDERING THE TIERRA AMARILLA GRANT

Catron began using the grant to his profit long before he
received the patent. In December 1881 he conveyed right-of-
way to the Denver and Rio Grande Railroad Company across
the northern portion of the grant, with space for a depot at

Chama. Then he proceeded to sell fourteen house lots in Chama to the employees who were to work in the depot and round house. The stationmaster was Catron's associate, Wilmot Broad. In 1885 Catron "corrected" the description of the right-of-way. All of these conveyances were recorded some years after they had been in effect.[59]

In 1882 Catron secured mortgage bonds against the grant in the amount of $200,000 at seven percent interest for ten years from the Mercantile Trust Company of New York. Satisfaction of this mortgage, undated but apparently in 1902, is recorded at the end of the Tierra Amarilla Abstract of Title.[60]

In 1882 Catron conveyed to the Denver and Rio Grande Railway Company a right-of-way for the "Chama Lumber Branch" to run between Chama and Tierra Amarilla. On some unspecified date he formed the Southwestern Lumber and Railway Company and in 1894 he wrote the following to J. M. Freeman of Denver:

> I am desirous of obtaining a loan of two hundred thousand dollars, for say five years. I will pay seven per cent per annum on it payable semi-annually. I will also pay five per cent commission on the same to obtain it. I will secure the same by 560,000 acres of the Tierra Amarilla grant, situated partly in Colorado and partly in New Mexico. This grant has been confirmed by Congress and patented by the Government of the United States. Its situs is Rio Arriba County, New Mexico and Archuleta County, Colorado. The Property is well timbered with merchantable timber, that is, timber out of which merchantable lumber can be made. It has been estimated by competent parties that there is on the property enough timber alone to produce $3,000,000 at a stumpage of $2 per M. board measure. The Denver and Rio Grande Railroad passes through the same from east to west. There are coal deposits on the same, some very near the Railroad, all of which will aggregate according to reliable estimates 100,000 acres. The Chama river, a bold, strong stream, and several of its tributaries, run through the property in various directions. It is without doubt the best watered property in the Rocky Mountain country. The original grant contains 594,515.55 acres. I own the whole except for some small holdings which were conveyed by the patentee during his life time to settlers and except for some small pieces to which title may have been obtained by prescription and some lots in Chama and

the railroad right of way and depot grounds, which I have conveyed, all of which will be more than covered by the 14,515.55 acres which I reserve for that purpose.... The property is nearly all grassed and good grazing. About one fourth is mountainous and is well timbered and grassed. At least one hundred and fifty thousand acres can be placed under water by a series of ditches which will not be very expensive, from the fact that the streams have a rapid fall; they will not have to be lengthy and no reservoirs will be required, although they could be made with little cost....

My selling price for the same is three dollars per acre, and with the passage of the Statehood bill for New Mexico it will be advanced to not less than $5 per acre.[61]

In 1897 the Southwestern Lumber and Railway Company signed a deed-of-trust with the Farmer's Loan and Trust Company as trustee to secure a loan of $200,000 as a first mortgage to run five years under an issue of five percent gold bonds. This mortgage was satisfied and recorded December 29, 1902.[62]

Within a few years, the area between Chama and Tierra Amarilla "was so clean cut that today it has the appearance of a grassland rather than of the Ponderosa pine area it once was."[63] Rows and clusters of stumps still stand as mute testimony of the uncompensated total deforestation of the upper reaches of the Chama Valley, with its inevitable consequences of gully cutting and silting downstream.

DISRUPTION OF HISPANIC COMMUNITIES

There is no evidence that the Hispano settlers, rightful owners of the Tierra Amarilla Grant, ever tried to prevent Catron from bestowing railroad rights-of-way, selling the Chama town lots at the 1881 railroad terminal, or disposing of the valuable timber on their grant. They may have been content with the wage jobs these transactions provided them. In any event, there was no immediate challenge to their way of life. The picture changed, however, when Catron sold a large part of the north end of the grant in 1912 to the Arlington Land Company for subdivision and sale to cattle owners. The first fences were then erected on the grant, and the settlers were suddenly deprived of their open range.

Even before the fencing of the range, however, Catron's domination of the grant began to disrupt normal Hispano community life. As the railroad was built across the grant, a series of wild, end-of-the-line tent cities sprang into existence. Chama in 1881 was a wide open gambling center with little control over those who fancied gunplay. A saloonkeeper from Conejos called James Catron, no known kin to Thomas Catron but a fellow-Missourian by birth, was the ringleader of the rowdies.[64]

Hispanos may have been participants in some of the disorders that broke out in Chama and, shortly thereafter, in Amargo and Monero. But none of the reports mentions rowdies of other than English surnames. Perhaps the only real contribution to disorder by Hispanos in the Tierra Amarilla area and elsewhere in northern New Mexico was their disregard for the prohibition on liquor sales to Indians. A member of the Board of Indian Commissioners in 1874 reported the "deplorable conditions" in which Utes and Jicarilla Apaches were living:

> They are now living in the open territory where anybody else may live, and the Mexicans and Spanish-Americans are living among them; many of these are making their fortunes by selling liquor, as we find; and our agent reports that it is very difficult to secure from the Government a proper regulation as to these matters. We have one of the very best of men there (Russell) and he finds his position very embarrassing.[65]

THE VIGILANTES

Vigilantism in northern New Mexico first arose far west of Tierra Amarilla, in the Farmington area where there was a substantial Anglo-American population. Until 1889 Tierra Amarilla was the county seat covering Farmington and all of present-day San Juan County. Problems of legal process arose which reflected the anti-Hispano bias of the Farmington area, imposing on the people of Rio Arriba discriminatory procedures in the selection of juries.

The instigators of trouble at Farmington were remnants of Alexander McSween's "Regulators" of prior Lincoln County violence. In 1878 the brothers George, Frank, and Jasper Coe rented two ranches at the site of present Aztec. A year later they were joined by "Ike" Stockton. These people, with other neighbors, formed the Stockmen's Protective Association, ostensibly to prevent theft of their cattle for sale to the government butcher at Fort Lewis. The association members, however, were as involved in cattle rustling as anybody else and association policy was largely guided by private grudges. A number of settlers of the Bloomfield-Farmington area appealed to Max Frost, the adjutant general, for an issue of arms and ammunition, so that they could form a local militia unit and defend themselves against the association.

The Bloomfield unit, according to the muster roll, consisted of seventy-three men led by Captain William B. Haines. Haines was a partner in the Bloomfield general store which held the contract with the territorial government for provisioning the militia unit. Two lieutenants, five sergeants, four corporals, and sixty-one privates composed the group. Of these, one sergeant, one corporal, and fifteen privates were local Hispanos. Their first efforts to round up cattle thieves and arrest men accused of crimes got off to a poor start when Corporal J. N. Jaques, trying to arrest an accused murderer in the Cañon Largo, was himself arrested and thrown in jail.

Trying to bring a case to trial was difficult. In the first place, the cattle-rustler-vigilante group made its headquarters in Durango, Colorado, rather than in New Mexico, where it operated. Furthermore, there were no justices of the peace functioning in Rio Arriba County, since the 1880 election ballot boxes had not been received by the Board of County Commissioners until a full month after the election. Adjutant General Frost petulantly ordered that justices of the peace be forthwith appointed by the commissioners, but Commissioner Juan Andrés Quintana objected to the illegal procedure and was upheld by Judge L. Bradford Prince. Ordering that special elections be held, Frost appointed Captain Haines as jury commissioner.

The new commissioner found the impaneling of juries tiresome. But most of all, he objected to the fact that Hispano jurors tended to see legal matters differently from Anglos. After trying unsuccessfully to get a man named Sandoval indicted, Haines wrote angrily to Frost: "Now all the lines are laid well for a new county. Rio Arriba don't want us. We know too much. Thornton and Burns promise to help us. Now County seat question. . . ." Haines naturally favored Bloomfield (where he had his store) as the seat of the projected new San Juan County. He pictured the rise in land values, which was eagerly anticipated in the Bloomfield area. The land was being fenced, and prosperous settlers were in a position to rent. From the Haines letter we learn that Max Frost also owned a ranch in the Bloomfield area, adjoining a ranch that had just sold for the currently high price of $900.

Haines was sanguine about the prospects for Bloomfield, so long as there was no danger that a Hispano majority might make decisions on public matters. "It is a decided fact that no more prisoners will go to Tierra Amarilla to be tried by Mexican Penitentes (dont know if spelt right) and get off."[66]

Haines' statement is illuminated by the assertion of numerous informants that from the 1880's to the 1930's, it was customary in northern New Mexico to exclude a Hispano venireman from district court juries if a Hispano was to be tried on criminal charges, on the mere allegation that both were Penitentes. This hardly made for equal and impartial justice.

OPEN TERROR

Added to the covert maneuvers to deprive Hispanos of their land and the rigging of the jury system to deprive them of trial by their peers, terroristic methods were used to ruin their economy. During the period when the Southern Ute Reservation was being established in southern Colorado, Hispano sheepmen from the Tierra Amarilla area enjoyed use of the Ute stock range by permission from the Indians. At the same time, the Utes were engaged in a shooting war with the cowboys of the Kansas and New Mexico Land and Cattle Company, a British-owned concern.[67] The Anglo-American stockmen decided to destroy the Hispano influence.

Among the richest and most influential of the Hispano stockmen were the Archuleta brothers, Donaciano, Marcelino, and Preciliano. In 1876, Donaciano Archuleta became Colorado state senator from that portion of Conejos County which was later designated Archuleta County. Marcelino Archuleta, who

owned a store in Alamosa, was the first judge in Archuleta
County. Their stock range was the Archuleta Mesa, which
straddles the Colorado-New Mexico border northeast of the
confluence of the Navajo River with the San Juan. The Archuleta brothers freighted rations to the Southern Ute Agency in its
first years, and Senator Archuleta served as interpreter for Ute
spokesmen in early parleys.

Just as Archuleta County was being established in the early
1880's, a group of Anglo settlers in the Pagosa Springs area
claimed that they were being unreasonably taxed, while the
Archuleta brothers and their associates were not listing all of
their livestock for tax purposes. The Archuletas, who were an
Abiquiu family, probably wintered their thousands of sheep in
New Mexico and only brought them to Colorado for summer
grazing. The sheep may well have been registered in Tierra
Amarilla where Donaciano owned a settler's allotment. Their
accusers, however, resorted to direct action without checking
the facts. A participant in this action, who was the schoolteacher in Pagosa Springs during this period, reminisced as
follows in his old age:

> In the southern part of the county was a voting precinct
> known as the Archuleta precinct, here over a hundred Mexi-
> cans from N. M. were voted to hold their gang in power. All
> this enraged the settlers who were engaged in the cattle
> business. Chas. Loucks, E. T. Walker, Judd Hallet, Wm. Dyke,
> John Dowell, Jake Dowell, Robert Chambers, Charles Cham-
> bers, Maurice, Willet and Siegel Brown, Frank Cooley, James
> and Dock Gilland, John and James O'Neal, Mr. Whitaker,
> Judge Price and his two sons and some 50 others including
> the writer organized a People's Party of which I was elected
> chairman and we began a bitter four years' fight to gain
> possession of the government of the county. The State Ad-
> ministration and the Courts were against us. [Note: the
> period of the struggle referred to was apparently
> 1882-1886.]

> Three precincts in the County we carried [included] Pagosa
> and Edith precincts with large majorities to gain which I and
> the above named men worked night and day, but 300 illegal
> votes polled under the supervision of the Archuleta brothers
> and Martinez defeated us. They worked to have me removed
> from the school every one of their wives and children were

with me. This gang even paid a Mexican to kill me, he met me on the bridge one night, knife in hand. I carried a walking stick with which I struck him on the head, he fell and rolled into the river, he swam and came out at the old bath house. I walked into the old court house, those commissioners were in session and I invited the man who planned the deed to come out and settle the matter in any manner he wished but he did not function although afterward he killed two men and a woman. Charley Johnson, Durango's criminal lawyer, cleared him although each was a cold-blooded murder.

The next May we had a school election and won out over the Mexican gang 15 to 1, and I taught the following year and had much pleasure in the work and was offered good pay to teach at Durango, Lake City, Silverton and Telluride but preferred to stay where I was and fight greasers. When the next election came E. T. Walker and I were sent to Conejos. We helped to defeat the Archuleta candidate for the legislature and I put in nominations Billy Adams for his first office and he was elected. The fight in Archuleta County was fierce and hot. Maurice Brown and I on that election went to Archuleta precinct and challenged 334 votes that lived over the line in N.M. Marcelone (Marcelino) Archuleta accepted them all as legal. Sheriff Dyke had deputized me to bring the box to Pagosa. To reach there we had to ford the San Juan. My horse lost his footing and in this way the ballot box was lost. It never reached Pagosa and we elected all officers except that of County Clerk, E. M. Taulk, good fellow and an unbeatable politician.

This was the election of 1886, Robert Chambers elected County Commissioner; John Loflene Treas.; Charles Loucks, Assesor; Barazilla Price, County Judge; Judd Hallet, Sheriff; E. M. Taylor, Clerk and Recorder.

Previous to this, when the Commissioners were in session, 100 of us led by E. T. Walker, who carried a band box with a rope in it, forced the commissioners to resign. The Governor reappointed them. At their next meeting, Benedino Martinez led a hundred armed Mexicans to the old soldiers barracks about the same number of us were in the courthouse armed, it looked as though blood would be shed but the bravery of sheriff Dyke led to a settlement of our differences and Pagosa has ever since been an orderly town.

Just what the author meant by "orderly" is hazy, for he next commences a racy account of how beef was constantly stolen by his friends from the Ute herd and from the "Englishman" who had a thousand head of cattle on the Pine River range. "Many a morning, I would find hanging before my door a fine butchered yearling, settlers in those days kept mum."[68]

The electoral battles mentioned above took place along the disputed boundary between Colorado and New Mexico. Settlers in some localities were uncertain about which state they were residing in. About thirty families of Hispano settlers, however, had been forced in the spring of 1883 to vacate settlements near the confluence of the Piedra and San Juan Rivers, on the grounds that they were trespassing on the Ute Reservation. Upstream along the San Juan, part of the old Coraque settlement, as well as Juanita and Trujillo which may have been settled by the early 1880's, were and are within the borders of Colorado. Rosa, on the other hand, was always recognized as a New Mexico community.

In the lawless atmosphere that flourished during those years, Hispanos were increasingly intimidated when Anglo hoodlums approached. Charlie Allison, former deputy sheriff of Conejos County and former ally of the Stockton-Eskridge gang of Farmington, rallied a group of outlaws who stole horses and held up stagecoaches in Chama, Amargo, and Pagosa Springs. Others from the former gang ranged through southern Colorado and northern New Mexico.[69]

A close-up view of Hispano-Anglo social relations in the San Juan Basin in the 1880's is provided by the following:

> Apparently unrelated to the Farmington troubles, although a number of the active participants in them were involved, was a tragedy which occurred on the night of October 24, 1882. J. Blanchard, brother of Moses, engaged in a row with Justice of the Peace Guadalupe Archuleta at Bloomington (Bloomfield) during which he was shot and killed. Moses Blanchard said bluntly that the killer must die, and the town split into an American and a Mexican party. The women and children fled and the militia was called out. Governor Sheldon ordered Frost to the scene to take command and insure law and order, but before he arrived Archuleta was lynched. Evidently the Mexicans were convinced of his guilt for they dispersed without further trouble".[70]

The living descendants of Guadalupe Archuleta give a different interpretation of this story. Archuleta, they relate, escaped being gunned down by J. Blanchard while engaged in the performance of his duty only to be lynched in a display of terror which effectively silenced all Hispano challenge to Anglo strong-arm tactics along the San Juan. Several other accounts of lynchings lacking the documentation of the Archuleta case have been handed down in family traditions and are cited as reasons why Hispanos sought remote areas for settlement. The Ute country provided respite from unequal clashes with Anglos as well as a release from pressure on Penitentes.

5

Hispanic Settlements
of the San Juan Basin

FACTORS AFFECTING SETTLEMENT

The timing and circumstances of Hispanic settlement in the San Juan Basin were keyed to specific historic events. Chronologically, they are as follows:

1. The Brunot Agreement to open the San Juan mining area in what had been the very heart of the Ute Reservation. The agreement was proposed in 1872, signed by the Utes in 1873 and ratified by Congress in 1874. This agreement brought a great increase in mining operations in the San Juan country with the foundation of a string of communities in the Upper Animas Valley. By 1877 the raw mining community of Animas City (later Durango) adjoined the freighting camp of Baker City, and within a few years a smelter and iron works provided employment for a growing population.

2. The opening of the Cañon Largo wagon road in 1876. This brought freight across the San Juan River near present-day Blanco to equip the prospectors who gathered at Baker City before going into the San Juan Mountains. Some of the men who moved the freight in mule trains were the first to settle the area. From Bloomfield and Blanco northeastward past the confluence of the Piedra River with the San Juan, the population that entered was almost solidly Hispano.

97

3. Establishment of the Southern Ute Agency in 1877 at a location on the Rio de los Pinos, later called Ignacio, after the famous Wiminuche Ute leader. With the establishment of the agency some Hispanos came to the area by invitation of their Ute friends to live nearby, work at the agency, and use the tribal range. Other Hispanos came in hopes of bettering their lot by activities around the reservation, including contraband trade in liquor.

4. The campaign, 1880-1896, to force either removal of the Utes from the area or division of their lands by allotment in severalty. Those Utes who refused to accept allotment eventually were relegated to a separate reservation at Ute Mountain, southwest of Durango. Throughout the period of debate and uncertainty, the Hispanos solidly opposed the projected removal and allotment, because these measures would strengthen the position of the Anglo population at the expense of both Hispanos and Utes. The majority of the Anglo-Americans vehemently supported removal or (as a compromise measure) allotment. When the latter measure was won, the Anglo population rapidly increased.

5. Construction of the Denver, Rio Grande, and Western narrow gauge railroad line from Chama to Durango in 1881. This provided new jobs in railroad building and maintenance, opened travel to hitherto inaccessible areas, and facilitated the marketing of sheep and cattle, leading to continued movement into the area. Some Hispano sheepmen became wealthy.

6. A program to furnish the Utes with houses and farms. Initiated in 1886, this program offered job opportunities to Hispanos. They cleared the lands, dug irrigation ditches, built small houses for thirty-two prominent Utes, and then, because few Utes agreed to live in houses, actually lived in these houses themselves and raised crops on the shares system. The Utes enjoyed having the crops and found the Hispanos useful and entertaining neighbors.

7. Allotment of land in severalty to the Southern Utes in 1895-1896. This was followed by the opening of surplus reservation lands for the benefit of homesteaders. As the communities of Tiffany, Allison, La Posta, Bondad, Riverside, and Sunnyside were founded, the first settlers in many cases were

Hispanos. Lands on the Piedra River were also opened to settlement, and after 1910 other allotments of deceased Utes were made available to purchasers, some of whom were Hispanos.

FIRST HISPANIC SETTLEMENTS

The communities founded south of the Southern Ute Reservation acquired and retained the characteristics of Hispanic communities, while communities north of the reservation, no matter how large their Hispanic component, were Anglo-dominated in both physical layout and social controls, either initially or after a period of contention, such as occurred at Pagosa Springs. In the communities north of the reservation, Anglo and Hispano population elements remained sharply distinct, with a variety of mechanisms operating to maintain social exclusiveness. But in the communities south of the reservation, the few Anglos who did settle tended to marry Hispanos and to become assimilated into the Hispanic culture.

By 1880, the communities west of Bloomfield were decidedly Anglo, dominated by Lincoln County "regulators" and Mormon cattlemen. East of Bloomfield, settlements were founded by Hispanos and the question of founding dates may never be solved. The earliest date claimed so far is for a widow, Juanita Valdez de Lobato. Her descendants say she settled a homestead under the Timber Act of 1864. Her location was at present-day Turley, and when she moved to Aztec before 1880, she also moved the adobe church of Santa Rosa which had been built on her property.

The family of Epifanio Valdez, along with Valdez, Manzanares, and Archuleta relatives, had moved from the Abiquiu-El Rito area to Huérfano County, Colorado, where they were included in the census of 1870. According to their family tradition borne out by the dates of related events, they moved to the location of present-day Bloomfield on the north bank of the San Juan River in 1872. The Wiminuche Utes prepared to drive them out, on the grounds that all lands north of the San Juan River were on their reservation. A Ute-speaking settler, Cruz Antonio Archuleta, persuaded the Wiminuches to accompany him to Tierra Amarilla to find out what the boundaries were to be under the Brunot Agreement.[1] As a result, peace was established between the Utes and these settlers. The latter eventually became the first interpreters, herders, horse tamers, land-clearers, and home-builders employed at the agency. Their descendants, under contract with the Utes, still continue these activities. Tradition has it that the labor employed at the agency until well into the twentieth century was largely recruited from the Hispano communities of the Bloomfield-Blanco-Cañon Largo area.[2]

The first settlers of that portion of the San Juan riverside which became known as Rosa, as well as settlers of the Río Piedra and of Coraque on the San Juan (upstream from its confluence with the Piedra) came from a variety of areas. What is extraordinary is that many people of diverse origins already were linked by kinship or common experience before coming to the San Juan Basin. These included people from California, Mexico, Germany, and various communities of New Mexico. The census of 1880 listed eight struggling Hispano hamlets in the San Juan precincts from Bloomfield northeastward with a total of eighty-seven households and ninety-two household heads, since some were extended households. These communities were Bloomfield, Blanco-Cañon Largo, and several hamlets along the San Juan, Los Pinos, and Piedra Rivers.

At what was later to become the south end of Rosa on the east bank of the San Juan River lived California-born José Perez with his half-Irish, New Mexico-born wife Rita Barry, her brother Antonio José, and several families of different origins who were his associates or employees.[3] By the spring of 1878 José Perez was grazing three hundred sheep along the San Juan River south of the recently established Southern Ute Reservation.

Perez was a great storyteller, and in his later years he used to tell his grandchildren that he had been a member of the renowned Joaquin Murieta band of outlaws in California and an intimate of "José Tres Dedos" (Three-Fingered Jack). Perez' age, however, would have been insufficient for participation in the semi-legendary exploits of Murieta in 1854. A more credible portion of his autobiography related to railroad construction eastward from California.[4]

Zaguán and outer door of General José María Chavez house at Abiquiu, New Mexico. Chapman photo from Museum of New Mexico Photoarchives.

A weaver at work in Chimayó, New Mexico. T. Harmon Parkhurst photo from Museum of New Mexico Photoarchives.

The late Candelaria Mestas with the children of one of her many foster sons. Born in 1858, Mrs. Mestas in the 1890's carried the mail on horseback from Arboles to Rosa. F. Swadesh, 1960.

The Candelaria log fort with its hand-hewn notched logs. In its latter days it served as a repair garage. F. Swadesh, 1961.

On the northwest bank of the Río San Juan, where the river has two deep bends slightly west of the mouth of the Río de los Pinos, was a little settlement called Los Pinos, settled by some Lucero and Salazar families. Just southwest of them, at a place later called Los Martinez lived Andrés Martinez, his mother, and his married brother, Gerónimo. This place was soon to become the site of the first morada of the San Juan Basin.[5]

In the winter of 1877 another group reached the San Juan Basin, just as the first Ute annuity shipment arrived at Tierra Amarilla from Alamosa. The group brought many oxcarts on their trip. As most of the men had a history of working as freighters, they may have been in charge of the annuity shipment. Their leader was Román Candelaria, and among the people included in the 1880 census was his relative, Bidal Candelaria, destined later to become the richest man in Rosa.[6]

Román Candelaria settled at what later became the north end of Rosa, where an adobe church was built in the early 1890's by the Rosa settlers on land he had donated. The Bidal Candelaria grouping dwelt further up the San Juan River at a spot called Hinsdale in the 1880 census.[7] Other people who had accompanied the Candelaria migration settled a community called La Piedra a few miles north of that river's confluence with the San Juan.[8]

A lone person of ill repute, who said he had been born in Spain and had no local kin, was José Lopez. He was listed in the 1880 census as the owner of a saloon on the east bank of the Río San Juan northeast of Rosa. His neighbors circulated rumors that he sometimes drugged and robbed his customers and was even responsible for the deaths of some. In 1881, while the Southern Ute agent was directing attention to Lopez as the possible source of liquor smuggled to the Utes, and while the government was trying to oust him as a trespasser on Ute lands, an outraged customer shot and killed Lopez.[9]

ATTEMPTS TO DISLODGE SETTLERS

The growth of Hispano population south of the Southern Ute Reservation alarmed the employees of the Bureau of Indian Affairs. The Hispanos neither provided the Anglo-American model of cultural orientation which the government was trying to impose upon the Utes, nor did they enforce Indian Prohibition. When the new railroad depot of Arboles was built in 1881 near the San Juan-Piedra confluence, gamblers and dancehall hussies crowded the tent community where the railroad builders lodged. In June 1881, troops were called to remove these wayward people from the Ute Reservation, and shortly thereafter the government took steps to remove the Hispano settlers of La Piedra and Hinsdale. A total of thirty settler households were evicted in the spring of 1883.[10] The evicted settlers deserted their homesteads and moved to Coraque (near the south bank of the San Juan upstream from Arboles), to Rosa, and to other established communities.

Another community listed in the 1880 census was that of Navajó, possibly at the same location as the present railroad depot of that name on the Navajo River west of Dulce. The settlers were extended families of the affluent Archuleta and Gomez lineages. A few years later the Gomezes successfully upheld their homestead claim against a government order to vacate the newly established Jicarilla Apache Reservation. They later settled the Lumberton area. The Archuleta families settled at Juanita and Trujillo near the Navajo-San Juan confluence. The former name does not appear in records until 1890 and the latter name in 1900.[11]

GERMANS IN THE HISPANIC SETTLEMENTS

By 1880 several German immigrants had settled in the San Juan Basin and soon became integrated into the Hispano community. One was Louis Wilmer, who settled on the east bank of the Río de los Pinos, His family included his son-in-law, George Vassmer, who became an occasional agency employee. There were scattered ranches along the Río de los Pinos northward to La Boca, where in 1881 a railroad bridge was built across the river. North of La Boca, the riverine lands were allotted to Ute families by 1896.[12]

The most famous of the German immigrants was Christian Stollsteimer. In 1870 he had a store in Conejos and was married to the French-Hispano daughter of the famous Mountain Man, Antoine Robidoux. By 1880 Stollsteimer had moved with considerable livestock to build his ranch near the mouth of a tributary of the Piedra, now called officially Stollsteimer Creek, but still known to local Hispanos as the Francés (not to be confused with the creek of the same name which joins the San Juan slightly east of the dam).[13]

ANGLO REACTIONS AGAINST GERMAN-HISPANO-UTE ALLIANCE

During the period when Stollsteimer was agent at Southern Ute (1885-1887), he initiated the system of employing Hispanos to clear land and build and operate Ute farms on shares. Stollsteimer was an ally of the Archuleta group in the fight for political control of Archuleta and Conejos Counties. For this he sustained vituperative attacks by the anti-Ute, anti-Hispano, and anti-Archuleta faction which was active in Pagosa Springs. He was accused of coddling Hispanos and conniving to permit a Ute uprising.[14]

Anglo settlers who were trespassing on lands identified as part of the reservation were particularly insistent that Stollsteimer evict alleged Hispano trespassers. Since Stollsteimer owed his access to the Ute range to his close links with the Hispanos, he disregarded these demands. Instead, he took action against Anglo stockmen who used firearms to hold the range they claimed.

The Bureau of Indian Affairs, however, was more interested than Stollsteimer in keeping the local Anglos pacified. One Anglo, E. A. Taylor, settled in one of the homesteads on the Piedra from which Hispanos had been evicted in 1883. He dared Stollsteimer to make him leave, demanding "official orders from the official officer in charge," along with proof that the house he was occupying actually was on the reservation. When Stollsteimer referred the matter to Washington, he was tersely instructed to check the reservation limits and *if* Taylor was trespassing, to remove him with the aid of the Indian police. Considering that thirty Hispano families had been evicted from those premises barely two years earlier, such solicitude in protecting the potential rights of a lone Anglo squatter is impressive.[15]

By contrast, the Archuleta county clerk and recorder, E. M.

Taylor, in the year following the 1886 electoral victory of the
anti-Archuleta forces, demanded that Stollsteimer forthwith
remove Hispano settlers from "Junto on the Reservation." The
location appears to have been either Pagosa Junction or Juanita,
near the confluence of the San Juan and the Navajo Rivers
within Archuleta County. One can only surmise that Taylor
wished to guarantee electoral victories in the future by eliminating pockets of independent Hispano population, a surer method
than dumping ballot boxes in the river. In a burst of unexpected
concern for legality, he added: "We are instructed that none are
allowed to reside on said Reservation and that it is contrary to
law and the wishes of the Indian Department and we earnestly
hope that you will take such steps in the matter as will right a
great wrong already committed."[16]

HISPANIC SETTLEMENT IN THE 1880's AND 1890's

In the 1880's several clusters of population formed on the
west bank of the San Juan River. Just across from Rosa, Serafín
and Nicolás Aragón built a homestead for which they failed to
file. They were displaced when Francisco Espinosa and his sons,
José Adán and Antonio José, moved down from Saguache,
Colorado, and filed on the same lands. Mexican-born Luis Rivas
moved nearby.

Juan José Abeyta, who had worked on construction of the
railroad across the reservation in 1881, came to settle Rosa
shortly thereafter. In the early 1890's, he moved to a location
at the foot of Miller Mesa (then known as Altos de Barry),
downstream from the Espinosas.

A few miles from Abeyta's location, about two miles in from
the riverbank, was a settlement known as El Arroyo de las
Sembritas (arroyo of the plantings, marked as Sambrito Creek
on the maps of the U.S. Geological Survey). Agapito Quintana,
an active Penitente, settled there in the early 1890's and soon
built a morada on his land.[17] The saints' images of the arroyo
were moved to the Rosa morada, when it was built on land
belonging to Vidal Quintana early in the twentieth century.
From that time until 1925, the Rosa morada was chapter
headquarters for most Brothers living east of the Rio de los

Pinos and was an important center for pilgrimages during Lent and Holy Week.

Several canyons that run into the San Juan from the southeast were settled some years after 1880 and continued to have a population at least until the 1930's. The Gobernador, Francés, and La Jara Canyons had several ranches each, and there was even a small center called La Fragua (The Forge), near the junction of La Jara and La Fragua Creeks. This center had its own church. In the early 1900's a number of people moved to these communities from Coyote and Canjilon, possibly due to loss of the San Joaquin Grant and appropriation of its range by the forest service.

One of the Bloomfield settlers of 1880 was a Navajo, Juan Mateo Casías, who was married to a Tierra Amarilla heiress, Guadalupe Trujillo. Casías had been raised as a captive by Miguel Casías of Conejos and had become a teamster. According to local tradition, he had stolen his master's California gold cache from its hiding place beneath a fence post when he left Conejos. Casías and his wife were popular among both Indians and Hispanos and maintained close friendships with the hispanicized Utes of the Animas Valley. Several of their children married half-Hispano heirs to Ute allotments.

ABIQUIU DESCENDANTS AND OUTSIDERS

Of the eighty-seven households enumerated in the 1880 census between Bloomfield and Hinsdale, fifty-seven were headed by people whose ancestry traced back to Abiquiu, while only thirty household heads had roots outside the Lower Chama Valley. In subsequent generations the people of "outsider" lineage who left the riverine hamlets for town residence were more numerous than Abiquiu descendants. Consequently, by 1960 outsider lineage among those remaining in the hamlets was largely traceable through females. People whose ancestors came from areas less frontier-oriented than Abiquiu have been more adaptable to the idea of living in towns and cities than the Abiquiu descendants, but the factor of relations with Utes has probably been even more important. No outsider name has ever been linked with work on Ute farms, employment at the

agency, or with rare exceptions, baptismal godparenthood to
Utes. The names of certain outsiders, however, figure prominently in records of disputes with Utes and the sale of alcohol
to them.

LIQUOR AND THE UTES

In the early days of the San Juan settlements, whenever the
Utes received annuity payments or distribution of livestock,
people arrived to ply them with liquor, gamble with them, and
relieve them of whatever they had received. The gambling away
of annuities was first reported in 1877 by the first Indian agent
at Ignacio, but he noticed no liquor consumption. He described
Navajos as the instigators of the gambling. Two years later,
however, agency leaders were worrying about the "whiskey
shops of the San Juan" as possible sources of supply for the
Utes. Utes did not enter saloons but obtained alcohol through
intermediaries.[18]

An investigator was hired to track down the source of supply.
He reported that he found eight empty whiskey bottles in a
dugout about sixteen miles from the railroad and that moccasin
tracks were visible. He surmised that Mexicans were engaged in
silent trade with the Utes, leaving bottles in remote spots where
the Utes would find them. The flaw in his guesswork was that
Hispanos wore moccasins more often than shoes, and many
enjoyed a bottle just as much as the Utes. The detective also
mentioned that "10 miles east of Arboles station another Mexican settlement with dram shops" was a likely center for the
whiskey traffic. The settlement was probably Coraque, and the
saloon no doubt belonged to Pablo Velasquez, assisted by his
son Maximiano.

The detective further surmised, on the basis of current rumor, that the liquor was not brought in by railroad but was
transported from Durango. He thought it might also come from
Pagosa Springs across the reservation "in small packages say in 5
or 10 gallon kegs." He also surmised that wagons or burro trains
made nighttime deliveries, concentrating their efforts at annuity
time. Then "these unscrupulous rascals who are at the bottom
of these transactions will make preparations to lay in a considerable stock of liquors for the purpose of making these Indians

intoxicated so that by gambling or other iniquitous devices they may cheat and rob them of their money."[19]

Descendants of those Hispanos who drank and gambled with the Utes at annuity time corroborate the detective's interpretation of their motives. Bidal Candelaria and his brothers and cronies are identified as the ringleaders in setting up the drinks and organizing the gambling that immediately followed the distribution of goods, livestock, or money to the Utes in the 1880's.

The favorite stake was sheep, and by the turn of the century Bidal Candelaria owned some eleven thousand. Information on how he won them is supported by an 1883 hearsay report in the *Durango Herald* that the Utes were turning over to Hispanos, at 50-75¢ per head, five thousand sheep purchased by the government for them at a cost of $2.70 per head.[20]

At this time, Bidal Candelaria operated a store and saloon in Rosa. His brother Anastasio set up another store and saloon on the heights across the river from Rosa, near the so-called "Darlington Spur" of the Denver, Rio Grande, and Western Railroad. The latter enterprise was not profitable, and Anastasio in later years moved back to the Piedra to homestead a location near that of the first Piedra settlement. Bidal's business, however, flourished. After his marriage in 1898 he took his brother-in-law, Jose Vidal Quintana, into partnership with him. Quintana had recently lost a battle for grazing lands on the Tierra Amarilla Grant. Bidal Candelaria was now recognized as the rico of Rosa, and Vidal Quintana was the second richest man.[21]

The partnership between "the two Vidals" was of short duration (1903-1908), ending soon after Candelaria took Maximiano Velasquez as a partner to run the saloon. Quintana, a very law-abiding man, refused to be involved in bootleg transactions with the Utes. He set up his own store in partnership with his three oldest sons and built a saloon operated by his brother Pablo.

Maximiano Velasquez was the son of Pablo Velasquez, the saloonkeeper of Coraque whose bootleg operations had long been the subject of complaints from the Ute Agency. In the early 1900's the agent succeeded in having the saloon closed.[22] According to contemporary scandal and retrospective opinion, the saloon jointly owned by Candelaria and Velasquez was the source of a great deal of bootleg alcohol consumed by the Utes. People hostile to the Utes and Hispanos, however, tended to exaggerate the problem. The sheriff of Allison, for instance, once reported truculently to the Ute Agency: "There are about 20 or 30 Indians down at Rosa drinking and they threaten to come here and clean out Allison. So you had better get here as soon as horse will carrie you if you care to have their lives spared."[23]

As a matter of fact, the Utes were in Rosa celebrating the Feast of Santiago, as they did each July 25. The Utes always camped above Rosa at that time and participated in the horse-races and footraces. They also gambled and drank, but the liquor transactions were so indirect that even a scrupulous dealer might unwittingly sell bottles that would later fall into Ute hands.[24]

TRAPPING THE LIQUOR DEALERS

Over the years government agents baited traps and paid Indian decoys to catch the people they believed were providing the Utes with alcohol. The easiest people to catch were the operators from Durango who came to Ignacio by train each annuity day, bringing playing cards and liquor for an evening of fun. In the course of the evening, they would relieve the Utes of most of their assets. Apparently the Utes felt that the fun was worth its cost, for the operations were not betrayed until Bidal Candelaria was indicted on a bootleg charge in 1917. A Ute who held a grudge against him agreed to act as a decoy, and within view of a revenue officer disguised as a tramp, he persuaded Bidal's relief bartender to smuggle a bottle to him. The bartender served a prison sentence, but Bidal used his waning influence in Santa Fé to escape prosecution.

THE CAREER OF FABIAN MARTINEZ

No liquor dealer was hunted down more relentlessly than Fabian Martinez, born in Antonito, Colorado. He was already a thorn in the side of the Ute Agency by 1903, when the town of

Ignacio was in its infancy. Martinez had established himself on the heights west of the railroad depot and had built a racetrack patronized by Utes as well as Hispanos every Sunday. Rumor held that in various remote canyons he was operating hidden stills; if so, these would have been the first of many stills which later operated on or near the Southern Ute Reservation. In 1903 Martinez applied for a license to trade with the Utes. The commissioner of Indian affairs denied the application, questioning whether Fabian was "a proper person to be allowed to reside on an Indian reservation," since his influence might be "detrimental to the interests of the Indians."[25]

After years of effort, revenue officers caught Fabian Martinez and his wife selling liquor without a license in 1907. Fabian gallantly offered to plead guilty if the case against his wife were dismissed. But Special Agent Flanders lost his case by trying to add evidence of violation of Indian Prohibition to the charges. A year later the superintendent of the Southern Ute Agency was told: "I hope you will stick Fabian this time. Mr. Flanders lost out because he gave the witnesses money and they proved a conspiracy." Fabian had meantime applied for appointment as the first postmaster of Ignacio. He did not win the post, but later ran for the office of town mayor and nearly won.[26] People recollect that a good deal of effort and money was expended to bar his victory.

In 1910, Chief Special Officer William E. Johnson assured the agency superintendent that he would try to carry out his request "regarding that old Fabian joint. . . . I see absolutely nothing I can do so far as the Federal courts are concerned except to run in a Navajo Indian on Fabian and get him that way." Officer Johnson expressed surprise that the county sheriff, over the years, had been unable to break up "Fabian's joint," and hinted that less than a wholehearted effort had been made. Somewhat later Fabian's first wife Librada died of complications following a gunshot wound from a bullet intended for her husband.[27]

Following the enactment of Prohibition in Colorado in 1916, Fabian Martinez moved to Rosa and opened a saloon there. For a time, barely across the Colorado-New Mexico state line, seven saloons did a booming business. In the flurry of activity to stop the stream of trade, revenue officers succeeded in closing down three of the seven. They baited the previously-mentioned trap for Bidal Candelaria, but Fabian Martinez escaped the net.

In 1925, years after national Prohibition was in effect, Fabian Martinez and his second wife were finally and firmly caught on a liquor charge. The wife escaped prosecution because she had a small child, but Fabian was sentenced to eighteen months at Leavenworth.[28] This was the end of Fabian's colorful career. After completing his sentence, he moved to Lonetree where he operated a sawmill until his death in 1932.

In the opinion of his surviving relatives and many friends, Fabian Martinez bore little resemblance to the villain depicted in the Ute Agency records. His reputation, while conceded to have been a little racy, was nonetheless that of a talented entrepreneur with legitimate political ambitions. It is said that more dirty work was done to defeat him in his bid for the mayoralty than anything he may have perpetrated in the course of his life. Since his day, no Hispano has emerged in Ignacio as an independent leader.

While Agency Superintendent E. E. McKean (1917-1925) left a copious record of written statements slurring Fabian Martinez, people who knew them both state that McKean depended upon Martinez to provide a sufficient number of low-paid Hispano laborers to complete the program of building Ute homes, and that McKean had a gentlemen's agreement with Fabian to leave his liquor operations undisturbed as long as they were conducted discreetly. Some people claim that McKean received a payoff for his favors.

AGENCY DISCRIMINATION AGAINST HISPANOS

The career of Fabian Martinez can be assessed only in light of the strong anti-Hispano bias that prevailed in the town of Ignacio and in the Southern Ute Agency during the first two decades of the twentieth century. Few Hispano employees of the agency ever got a civil service rating, and those who did were sometimes dismissed on thin and trumped-up charges.

This trend became particularly marked following the dismissal of Superintendent Charles Werner in 1912. He was charged with using his official railway pass for a private business trip. The investigation which immediately followed concerned every aspect of Werner's administration and the activities of each employee.

At this time it was discovered that Assistant Farmer José Velasquez, employed since 1906, had entered into shares agreements with five Utes for the care of livestock. No one questioned that the terms on which Velasquez had contracted were unusually liberal within the established Hispano pattern of livestock management. The inspector who made the discovery judged that such contracts did more good than harm, but they happened to be in violation of a recent Indian office regulation.

Once apprised of this fact, Velasquez terminated his agreements and made an identical contract with a local Anglo farmer for the care of his animals. At the time he reported this action Velasquez also revealed that during the investigation, he had been intimidated and threatened into signing an exaggerated statement concerning the drinking habits of a young half-Indian agency clerk.

In early 1913 a new superintendent with a West Point commission arrived at the Southern Ute Agency. Captain Stephen Abbot promptly initiated morning parade drills of agency farmers, herders, laundresses, and other personnel, whom he found distressingly short on "discipline." He lost no time in communicating to Velasquez his intense bias against Hispanos and his fervent desire that Velasquez resign. Velasquez took the hint, but then lodged a protest with the Indian Office.

Abbot justified his action to the commissioner of Indian affairs in the following words: "Because I am convinced that ninety percent of white farmers will do more than twice as much work as any Mexican I have ever seen, I told Velasquez I would accept his resignation. . . . I do not believe a Mexican is capable of teaching the Indian. The average Mexican is too much like the Indian." Abbot conceded that everyone agreed that "Joe was a fine fellow, that he got along well with the Indians," but apparently did not consider a capacity for empathy to be a desirable characteristic. When further pressed by the commissioner, Abbot took refuge in allegations that following his dismissal, Velasquez had entered into partnership with a "Mexican saloonkeeper alleged to be a bootlegger, and who introduced liquor on the reservation."

Velasquez denied all charges in a statement supported by sworn affidavits of several witnesses. He explained that about 1910, he had loaned $1,000 to the late Librada Martinez to build a combined poolhall and dancehall. He had soon sold the mortgage and invested the proceeds in construction of the Commercial Hotel in Ignacio. This, Velasquez held, could not be construed as constituting a partnership with Fabian Martinez, Librada's husband. Furthermore, Velasquez continued, after his forced resignation he had moved his family to Durango where he made a loan to some saloonkeepers. None of these people had been identified as bootleggers or purveyors of liquor to Indians, nor were they in any sense Velasquez' "partners."

Subsequent actions of the Indian Office in this case are forecast in Commissioner Cato Sells' response to an inquiry made on Velasquez' behalf by Representative H. B. Fergusson of the U.S. Congress. Admitting that the Velasquez affidavit had effectively shaken the factual base of the charges, Sells added: "Since the receipt of the affidavit direct testimony has been filed tending to prove the charges." As a matter of fact, this testimony was little more than an inflated rehash of Abbot's first allegations.

Abbot had sent an inspector into Durango to prove that Velasquez was a liquor dealer and the inspector reported he saw Velasquez selling drinks at a bar. Velasquez did not dispute this, but he pointed out that it had occurred while he was unemployed and while his father-in-law, Antonio Salazar, was confined with a broken leg. Therefore, Velasquez had simply been serving as a relief bartender. The candor and clarity of José Velasquez' written statements lend them added credibility.[29] Nonetheless, he was never again employed by the agency.

The Velasquez case is the outstanding instance of anti-Hispano discrimination on record at the Southern Ute Agency. The argument that Hispanos were poor workers and infected the Utes with "backward" work habits was used in various forms to justify an employee's dismissal. Anglo employees, generally on civil service, could only be dismissed for extreme

misconduct or excessively hostile relations with the superintendent. Some Anglo employees who were otherwise honest
and diligent were so inflexibly ethnocentric that the Utes could
not accept them, but this was never grounds for dismissal. Yet
during the painful forced transition of the Utes from the life of
hunters and gatherers to settled and regimented life on the
reservation, the modest, consistent influence of the best Hispano employees was so underrated that dismissals occurred on
the thinnest of grounds.

José Benito Ulibarri worked faithfully and with good results
for years as agency stockman at Ute Mountain. In 1925 Superintendent McKean proposed to replace him with a more Anglo-
Saxon-Protestant type of employee, one who would have "such
principles of discipline as is absolutely necessary for successful
work among these Indians." It was insufficient to McKean that
Ulibarri had helped the Utes develop a good herd, had helped
develop an adequate water supply on the reservation, and had
set a good example in his personal and family life. Ulibarri
spoke little English and had little formal schooling; McKean
wanted to hire a stockman who could teach stockraising from a
textbook.[30]

Hispanos had been employed by the agency from the beginning, but the bulk of their work was conducted at a distance
from the agency, on the Ute farms along the Rio de los Pinos or
on the stock range. Most Hispanos lived some miles from the
agency before 1900, except for some seasonal workers who put
up tents. The majority of the Hispano population of Ignacio
moved in after 1910, when the town was platted and town lots
were put up for sale. Ignacio became an incorporated town in
1913.

HISPANIC EVANGELISTS TO THE UTES

The first Hispano to take up residence close to the agency
was the Presbyterian missionary, Reverend Antonio José Rodriguez, who came in 1895 at the invitation of his Ute convert
Julian Buck. He lived in a jacal owned by a Ute family but not
occupied by them. It was within a mile northeast of the agency.
Reverend Rodriguez founded a school which continued opera-

tions into the 1920's. Although founded for Utes, it also provided educational opportunities for Hispano children. A certain number of Hispano converts to Presbyterianism were won by the missionary, but some of these became backsliders. Reverend Rodriguez was admired and loved by many people, even those who were not attracted to his doctrinal beliefs.

The Catholic Church had no building in Ignacio until 1900, when a small chapel was built for baptisms. The Utes had begun to bring their children for baptism in the late 1890's. By 1903 a young priest exiled from Guatemala came to found Sacred Heart Parish, which began to administer the Ignacio area from headquarters in Durango. Mass was celebrated monthly, and a concerted effort was made for the baptism of whole families of Utes. Hispanos mainly served as godparents, as did the small group of Utes who had been raised in the Catholic faith. A few Anglo Catholics also served as godparents.[31]

WAGE WORKERS AND A PENITENTE LEADER

By the end of the first decade of the twentieth century a number of Hispanos had come from the Conejos area to reside near Ignacio. Most were relatives of Fabian Martinez, who had recruited them for available wage jobs. There were Garcias, Gonzaleses, Salazars, Herreras, and others in this group. Almost all shared the same ancestry from the Abiquiu area which pervaded the Southern Ute Reservation. Some were employed hauling lumber from a sawmill near Bayfield to the Ignacio railroad depot. Their first dwellings were unoccupied Ute jacals near the depot, as the Utes still preferred to dwell in tents or, in summertime, in brush shelters.

The most notable personage of the new grouping was José Roquez Casías, brother-in-law of Fabian Martinez. He soon became the hermano mayor of the Rosa morada. Although he never took up residence in Rosa, he spent every Lent and Holy Week there until 1924, when he returned for good to the San Luis Valley where he died in 1925. Casías is remembered by all who knew him, Penitente and non-Penitente alike, as one who commanded respect and affection.[32]

In the years when José Roquez Casías was hermano mayor of

Rosa, this morada became the principal Penitente center of the San Juan Basin. The morada at Los Martinez closed down altogether in 1920 because the Penitentes decided to relocate at the Cañada Bonita, where they felt they would have less interference.

The people of the Arroyo and other neighboring communities came to Rosa, but after the death of Casías the saints' images from the arroyo were taken from the Rosa morada and eventually transferred to a morada near the Francés (Stollsteimer Creek). A morada in Coraque, which had been in existence possibly for many years, became an important Penitente center only after the death of Casías.

RISE AND FALL OF ROSA BUSINESSES

The Lenten pilgrimage to an important morada by Brothers from surrounding communities was a custom which brought business to Rosa. After Easter, the feeding and lodging of the many pilgrims was followed by sales of clothing and supplies for the season and the outfitting of sheep camps. The two general stores of Rosa carried a remarkable variety of merchandise, from canned goods and toiletries to farm implements and furniture. Since too much of the business was done on easy credit terms, the boom was shaky and vanished completely in the 1921 panic.[33]

Bidal Candelaria had propped his careless business dealings and his second wife's extravagant tastes by taking out loans. By 1910, he had incurred an indebtedness of $9,253.33 to Frank Bond, the big sheepman, banker, and storeowner of Española.[34] In 1912 Frank Bond, Ed Sargent, A. H. Long, and Bidal Candelaria formed a partnership called the Rosa Mercantile Company. Each of the four held four thousand shares, representing a capitalization of $16,000 in Bidal's store, which was greatly enlarged. Al Long became the manager of the store at a salary of $100 per month. Bidal, who was indebted beyond his share, organized his neighbors in *partido* (livestock shares) agreements with Bond and Sargent, in which the partidarios lost steadily due to overextended credit at the store. In short order Bond and Sargent owned all of Bidal Candelaria's sheep and a good percentage of all the sheep of the Rosa residents. They rented out the sheep on three to five year partido contracts, with a wool rental averaging two pounds of wool per sheep. By the end of 1916, the sheep account had grown to $6,767.65, representing 2,935 head of ewes, all of them leased out. Unlike the traditional Spanish-Mexican system of partido agreements with shared risks, the Bond and Sargent contracts laid the entire risk on the renters. They opened the way to call in debtors for accounting at will. By 1920 Bond and Sargent had more than recovered what Candelaria owed them. After the panic of 1921 and subsequent drop in the price of wool they simply liquidated their sheep and wool operation in Rosa and sold the store to A. H. Long.[35]

Bond and Sargent left Bidal Candelaria utterly ruined. It is a consummate irony that in relating the history of his rapid rise to economic dominance in northern New Mexico, Frank Bond paid tribute to the Hispano sheepmen's willingness to accept notes for sheep delivered to him in the panic of 1907, when he faced ruin if cash was demanded. "I never forgot how those Mexicans stood by me," commented Bond.[36]

6

The Flowering
and Decline of
San Juan Basin Communities

THE INSTITUTIONS OF ROSA

Of all the autonomous Hispano communities which arose along the San Juan River and its tributaries, Rosa was the largest, richest, most influential, and most organizationally complex. None of the communities ever became incorporated, but Rosa by 1889 had a justice of the peace court with a local justice and constabulary personnel. Authority of this court for civil cases and for preliminary investigations in criminal cases extended as far as Coraque and into San Juan County, across the river from Rosa.

From the records of this court, it is evident that every effort was made to resolve cases within the community-controlled court rather than let cases go to the district court. This court was under Anglo control and operated under a system of law unfamiliar to most Hispanos. The justice of the peace courts, created under the laws of the New Mexico Territory, had enough flexibility so that traditional customs and procedures could be followed within the law.[1]

By village effort, the adobe church of Santa Rosa de Lima was built about 1890 on land belonging to Roman Candelaria. The name of the church stressed the ancestral roots of the Abiquiu descendants who bestowed it and also provided the

117

name by which the entire community was then known. Priests came irregularly from Parkview or Durango to minister to the church. In 1896 the young Alsatian priest, Albert Daeger, later the archbishop of Santa Fe, became a circuit priest in the San Juan Basin. In 1914 he was priest of the church at Blanco, from which he rode to Rosa each month to say mass.[2] In later years, after a new church was built on land belonging to Vidal Quintana, the priests who came to Rosa were Mallorcan missionaries of the Theatine order.

Before the turn of the century the people of Rosa had organized and were supporting their own school through the contributions of parents. During the six-month school term, the teacher was boarded free and taught classes at the home of one student after another, receiving only a token salary. Despite its limitations, caused by the general low income level, the requirement that students and teacher alike work for their subsistence during the growing season, and the fact that a state-supported school system did not reach into this remote area of Rio Arriba County until the 1920's, the students of this generation became literate, at least in Spanish. The effort involved in creating and maintaining a school is a measure of the importance Rosa parents gave to the principles of education.

The mercantile establishments of Rosa were the largest and earliest on the San Juan River upstream from Farmington, their growth being stimulated by the nearby railroad and the sheep industry of the area. Rosa was the leader and model for nearby Hispano communities with regard to the organizational means and social code by which it operated, well recorded in the court and store documents. While many of the means were not available to smaller communities, the code was well known and functional for all.

UTES AND HISPANOS OF LA POSTA

During the early twentieth century, the pioneers of Rosa gradually slipped under the control of the Bond-Sargent interests, and Ignacio's growing population came under Anglo institutional control. But two other communities emerged which for some years maintained an independent economy and traditional

Hispanic autonomy and social relations with Utes. These were La Posta on the Animas River and the Cañada Bonita, between Middle Mesa and the east bank of the Rio de los Pinos.

Neither of these villages ever reached a prosperity comparable with Rosa. They lacked stores, saloons, and large herds of sheep. Their residents were small farmers who were partly dependent on wage labor. The Cañada people supplemented the subsistence they gained through dryland farming; they worked as laborers and herders for a variety of employers, mainly Anglos. The settlers of La Posta worked the irrigated Ute allotments on shares, and they also managed their own tiny farms.

La Posta started as a stagecoach stop on the road between Aztec and Durango. The route up the Animas Valley had long been heavily traveled by prospectors going to the San Juan mines. In the mid-1890's several Ute allotments were located in the Animas Valley. All the Ute allottees were hispanicized and some had Hispano or part-Hispano spouses.

The leading household was that of María Antonia Head. She received her allotment and allotments for Celestino and Crisanta Tucson, the children of her first marriage, through the efforts of her second Hispano husband, Juan José Vasquez. Vasquez also secured an allotment for Luis Head Vasquez, the son of his own marriage to María Antonia.

"Filomena," the wife of a man listed on the agency rolls as "Corup Charley Chavez" and on the parish rolls as "Juan Manuel García," may have been a sister or cousin of María Antonia Head. She was raised with her in the home of Lafayette Head, where both were enumerated in the 1870 Conejos census. People who knew both women thought they were closely related.

The Head-Vasquez household, along with the García, Williams (or Weaselskin), Rabbit (or Espinosa), and Russell families, had more irrigable land than they cared to cultivate by themselves. Juan José Vasquez, therefore, brought Hispano families from the Río de los Pinos and Blanco area to work the irrigated lands on shares and raise livestock for the Utes.

The arrangement was highly successful. In 1901 about thirty Hispano families lived in the Animas Valley and near the allotted Utes of the La Plata Valley. As the daughter of a bilingual schoolteacher of La Posta who arrived in that year recalls: "These people seemed to have plenty to eat. They raised a lot of their own food stuff, and with their herds of goats seemed to be well fed and happy. Anyone seeing La Posta of today can not realize what a busy and bustling little place it was."[3]

La Posta had its own church by 1903 and later became an important Penitente center. By 1920 some people from both Los Martinez and Ignacio visited La Posta during Lent and Holy Week. Although the Animas Valley Utes were fairly observant Catholics, they stayed away from the morada. María Antonia Head, however, followed the Hispanic woman's penance for Holy Thursday: she put peas in her shoes, as women of Santa Fe used to put wheat grains in theirs.[4]

Guadalupe Trujillo, wife of the Navajo, Juan Mateo Casías, was an honored person among the Brothers of La Posta. During Holy Week, she wore the badge of a religious confraternity and spent a great deal of time in the morada when no other women were present. She may have served as *rezadora* (prayer leader) for the Brothers, a function which was not restricted to initiates of the Brotherhood and which actually was carried out (in one other instance) by a woman in the San Juan Basin.[5]

CAÑADA BONITA, A PENITENTE SETTLEMENT

The other settlement, the *Cañada Bonita* (Beautiful Dale), became a Penitente center in the 1920's. First settlement of the Cañada was made under the leadership of Taos-born José Ignacio Suazo. He came to cut railroad ties above Cuba in the early 1890's and began to spend a part of each year in the San Juan Basin. First mention of the Cañada community in official records dates from 1906, but the community had existed before then, populated by small dryland farmers who cultivated friendly relations with their Ute neighbors.

Suazo welcomed Ute visitors and used yard goods for trading purposes. The women of the community baked bread and cake in their outdoor ovens and made yellow soap for the Ute trade. Some gambling and drinking with Ute friends also entered the relationship, but on a modest scale, since the Cañada had no saloons and the gambling stakes were low.

Until the morada of Los Martinez closed in 1920, the Brothers of the Cañada went there, maintaining only a small prayer chapel dedicated to San Antonio in their own community. After the closing of the Los Martinez morada, José Ignacio Suazo built the morada of the Cañada Bonita with the help of his half-Indian friend, Patricio Salazar. Suazo's son-in-law, Donaciano Trujillo, has been mentioned by some as the first hermano mayor of the Cañada. But since he died in 1918, it seems more likely that he was the last hermano mayor of Los Martinez and that it was his death which caused the abandonment of that morada. José Ignacio Suazo, in any case, was soon the hermano mayor of the Cañada chapter.

The Cañada Brotherhood included all adult male residents of the community and many from east of the Río de los Pinos. Some Brothers from Rosa moved to the Tiffany area and the slopes of Middle Mesa, so as to be close to the Cañada. As the Brotherhood disbanded in neighboring communities, the Cañada chapter became increasingly ingrown and socially isolated.

PIEDRA VALLEY SETTLERS

In 1898 some of the Ute lands on the Piedra River were put up for sale by the agency. At this time, residents of the Piedra Valley were Anastasio Candelaria and Rubio Gallegos, a young shares herder with a flock from Tierra Amarilla. Gallegos built a hand-hewn log cabin chinked with clay above the confluence of Stollsteimer Creek with the Piedra and settled down for good. In his first years he was completely isolated, since he had no neighbors and even the Utes rarely came to his part of the valley. He lived a completely self-sufficient life, even making his own moccasins.

In the early years of the twentieth century, two related Martinez families who had been involved in freighting and railroad building moved from the Sebastian Martín Grant. They came to homesteads in the Piedra Valley, below Stollsteimer Mesa. Antonio María Abeyta of the Rosa family settled on

Yellowjacket Creek, a small tributary of the Piedra. Another Rosa family, that of Juan Román Gurule, also moved to the Piedra, as did several Anglo families—the Pargins, Ayers, and Thompsons.

The main irrigated acreage, which had ditches constructed by Navajo labor, was sold to Anglo purchasers. Hispano purchasers, with more limited means, had only sufficient acreage for their kitchen gardens and some fodder crops. Their main activity was running livestock.

The town of Arboles began to re-form as inherited Ute lands above the railway depot were put up for sale. Both Candelaria and Quintana built warehouses near the depot, and the residents of Arboles were mainly occupied with railroad maintenance, the hauling of mail and freight to Rosa, the operation of small stores and the sheep dip. Sheep being moved between New Mexico and Colorado in boxcars had to be dipped and were unloaded at Arboles for this purpose.

The Hispano ranchers of the Piedra Valley formed autonomous clusters based on residence, kinship, and marriage. By 1907 Arboles had a church, but the people of the Francés (the Stollsteimer-Piedra confluence) built their own church. The priest from Durango traveled by train to Arboles and by buggy up the valley to celebrate a monthly mass there. A school was organized for the Francés children, with participation of Anglo as well as Hispano parents.

Relations with Ute families along the Piedra and also in the direction of Pagosa Junction were generally cordial, with seasonal labor exchange and mutual help. A number of Ute babies, whose parents were at least partly hispanicized, had Hispano baptismal godparents with whom they shared enduring relationships. The famous Ute leader, "George Washington," generally considered a cantankerous bully by Anglos, maintained a cordial relationship with Hispanos. He charged Anglos five dollars to move their sheep across "Washington Flats" on his allotment on their way to the upper range, and at times he threatened force to collect his fee. When Hispanos moved their sheep across the same flats, the transaction was accomplished as an exchange of courtesies. One Rosa elder recalled his experience as a child sheepherder when he received an invitation to have lunch at the

Bidal A. Candelaria with his young bride Ana Maria Quintana of Tierra Amarilla. They were married in the latter 1890's. From collection of Mrs. A. C. Marquez.

José Velasquez, the Southern Ute Agency Farmer who protested his dismissal in 1913, pictured with his wife, María Perfecta Salazar. From Tri-Ethnic Project collection.

José Vidal Quintana, in his declining years, with some of his grandchildren.

Young cowhands Benancio and Adolfo Garcia in Rosa, mid-1920's. From collection of Mrs. A. Maez.

Officers of the dance in the flourishing bootleg-era dance hall
of Pedro Marquez. Front row: musicians Onofre Gallegos and
Carlos Velasquez. Back row: Cornelio Velasquez, Pedro Marquez, Carlos Ulibarri, and Abrán Quintana. From collection of
Mrs. A. Maez.

Toasting the New Year in bootleg-era Rosa: Celestino Ortega (seated on
washtub) and José Délfido Maez, January 1, 1930. From collection of
Mrs. A. Maez.

Washington camp. Before leaving, he presented a lamb to his hosts, as previously instructed by the sheepowner (Bidal Candelaria). When George Washington died, his widow sought out Hispano friends to take care of the burial.

After being widowed of her first husband, Porfiria Martinez (of the Francés family) married the hispanicized Ute variously known as "James Allen" (tribal rolls), "Felipe Velasquez" (parish rolls), and "Cuatagá" (his Ute name). He was born in 1865 and was baptized—along with a twenty-two year old Ute, Miguel Velasquez—by Jesús Maria Velasquez of Conejos, who raised him. It is worth speculating that both Ute fosterlings were the sons of Moache Chief Chico Velasquez. He parleyed with the Canadian trader, Auguste Lacome, near the Culebra in 1850. It appears that Chico Velasquez was the Moache chief, Ankatash, father of James Allen. On the agency rolls Ankatash was listed as "John Allen."[6]

THE BOOTLEG ERA

At the time of their founding, the Hispano communities had prospered from cordial relations with the Utes. These relations continued to exist between individuals, but as far as community prosperity was concerned, the relationship diminished. The business enterprises of the Hispanos were too dependent upon credit and the fluctuations of the sheep market to have a sound base. Furthermore, agency policy constantly favored Anglo business concerns and investors, regardless of Ute opinion. The penetration of the Bond-Sargent financial interests into the economy of Rosa and neighboring communities brought about the ruin of Bidal Candelaria and many other sheepmen in 1917. Candelaria, now in his sixties, had to go to work as a herder to support his family. He died some years later, while employed on a railroad crew. The panic of 1921 finished off sheepraising for many years in the San Juan Basin. Vidal Quintana, a more cautious businessman than Candelaria, barely managed to keep his store open until the 1929 crash. Through the 1920's, only one commodity—sugar—had a high rate of turnover in the general stores, because of the production of bootleg.

Bootleg whiskey had been made in stills hidden in canyons

along the San Juan watershed since at least the early 1900's, if
not before. Some say Santiago Candelaria built the first still;
others say it was Fabian Martinez. When Prohibition was enacted in Colorado in 1916, seven saloons operated in Rosa, New
Mexico—some built within a few yards of the state line. Thirsty
people came from many miles around to drink at Rosa. When
nationwide passage of the Volstead Amendment caused saloons
and legal distilleries to close down in 1920, the bootleg business
reached its peak. For Rosa, economically wrecked by Bond and
Sargent, this was a reprieve from eclipse. Tradition holds that
bourbon whiskey from the stills of Rosa eased most of the
thirst of Durango and may have traveled as far as the Colorado
mining center of Silverton.

A. H. Long, whose wife was a devout prohibitionist, abided
by the law. But he turned his head the other way when his
assistant at the Rosa Merc sold thousands of sacks of sugar from
the back door. He departed from Rosa in 1924, leaving the
store leased to a family of active bootleggers.

Whatever prosperity bootlegging brought to Rosa was illusory
and associated with social disjunctions which many remember
with sorrow. The town was becoming depopulated as outsider
families moved away and as some Rosa businessmen opened
businesses in Ignacio, trying vainly to cover their losses. During
the 1920's, a period of nationwide crisis for the family farmer,
young men from the San Juan Basin hamlets spent brief periods
in the mining towns, earning wages adequate for a night's fling
but inadequate for the support of the families they left behind.
This was a form of "sowing wild oats," frequently practiced in
the first years of marriage while the bride remained at her
parents' home. A few Rosa families continued to farm, raise
sheep, and live at a bare subsistence level, but most supplemented subsistence by bootlegging. As a result, some of today's
most respected elders spent several years in a federal peniten-
tiary following a pre-repeal crackdown. One novice bootlegger
"took the rap" for the local bootleg king on a promise of
subsequent reward which was never fulfilled.

Teenage boys of Rosa served as purveyors of hidden bottles
to customers at Rosa's three dance halls of that period. Many of
the boys tasted the merchandise and seriously overindulged.

Traditional parental controls began to crumble. Bootlegging was the mainstay of many communities of the San Juan Basin, with considerable competition between Mormon and Hispano moonshiners. Rosa, however, was the acknowledged leader, exercising the entrepreneurial elan which had always been its chief characteristic.

THE DEPRESSION AND WORLD WAR II

The bubble of the twenties broke with the Wall Street Crash, the Depression, and the repeal of Prohibition. The people of Rosa and neighboring communities entered a period of grinding poverty. This was only eased when jobs became available under the Works Progress Administration and the state highway construction program.

Regionwide, jobs vanished and unemployed miners and other wage workers returned to the home community to survive as best they could. Seasonal agricultural jobs in Colorado were closed to people from New Mexico, and patrols were posted at the state border to keep would-be workers from crossing. During these difficult years, small ranchers, Anglo as well as Hispano, learned to eke out a livelihood by combining farm and livestock production with whatever seasonal wage labor and welfare assistance they could obtain. Rural Hispanos, however, constantly had difficulty conforming with welfare regulations. The Hispanos traditionally shared economic resources among larger groups of kin than the law permitted. Welfare regulations, therefore, created either "chiselers" or broken kin groups.

Certain federal programs initiated during the depression years were directed toward restoring the foundations of village life. In some areas villagers were assisted in recovering at least a part of their range and in obtaining livestock. Improved seed and farming methods were introduced, and health services began to reach some villages. Some of the reforms, like the Taylor Grazing Act of the 1930's, which was supposed to increase the grazing lands available to villagers, actually had the reverse effect of strengthening the hold of corporate livestock interests on the range.[7]

All favorable developments of the thirties were canceled, when a high percentage of young Hispano village men were

called into military service at the beginning of World War II.
The largely Hispano New Mexico National Guard bore the brunt
of the Bataan Death March and prolonged internment in Jap-
anese prisoner-of-war camps. Due to increased government meat
purchasing, the New Mexico range was appropriated by concerns delivering to the major packers. When surviving veterans
returned from the war and completed courses in modern sheep
husbandry under the G.I. Bill, they found that there was little
range left open to lease and build a herd. Many young men who
returned to their villages to raise a family found that they had
to leave again to seek wage work.

Throughout northern New Mexico wage jobs were scarce and
people began moving from the villages. Families from the San
Juan Basin moved to the railroad and mining towns of Utah, to
Pueblo and Denver, Colorado, as well as to California. Among
the people of each village were some with fair to excellent skills
in raising crops and livestock, homebuilding and maintenance,
cooking and food preservation, and the repair of worn-out or
broken down items—from electric appliances to automobiles.
However, these subprofessional skills did not conform to the
demands of the labor market, and like village Hispanos from all
over New Mexico, many people from the San Juan Basin had to
depend on welfare assistance to survive in an urban environment.

Many of the families who left the San Juan Basin returned to
the home community as often as possible and frequently expressed the desire to return permanently. In fact, those who
were able to lay aside savings did return to make new starts as
ranchers. Thus, Rosa and other Hispano villages, during the late
1940's and early 1950's, had fluctuations in their population
depending on economic conditions. The efforts to restore a
viable economy to the riverine communities of the San Juan
Basin received their death-blow in the mid-1950's when impend-
ing construction of the Navajo Dam was announced. Rosa,
Arboles, Río de los Pinos, and ranches south of Allison would
be covered by the waters impounded by the dam. Los Martinez
was at the site of construction.

In 1956 Congress appropriated funds to construct the Navajo
Dam and Reservoir, on the strength of the claim that this would

be of great economic benefit to Navajos. No consideration was given to the problems of nearly two hundred families, mainly Hispanos, who would be displaced by the reservoir. To date, not a single Navajo has benefited from the impounding of these waters. The only visible benefits seem to go to the owners of power boats who come from several states to enjoy the lake, and to the operators of the marina and campgrounds. The merchants of communities surrounding the reservoir had anticipated a profitable growth of their trade with visitors to the reservoir, but have found that the owners of the luxurious and well-stocked campers, trailers, and boats that come to the lake provide less trade than the marginal ranchers displaced by the reservoir.

THE FINAL EXODUS

The final exodus took years, beginning at Los Martinez and the ranches on the Río de los Pinos, continuing upriver until Rosa and Arboles were finally emptied of their population in 1962. By 1960, only one-third of the population of Rosa on both sides of the river remained in residence. Most who remained were aged people and a few families that sought to fight the low rate of compensation for their condemned homes and lands.

People attempting to replace the irrigated lands, for which the government was compensating at the rate of $125 per acre (drylands were $85 per acre), found that comparable lands in the area had gone up to $600 per acre. The situation was most desperate for elderly people living on the New Mexico side of the reservoir area, since they were not eligible for the reasonably adequate pension received by retired people in Colorado. Their compensation and the pitifully small New Mexico Old Age Assistance payments for which they were eligible could not provide them with substitutes for the pleasant ranch homes they had owned. They were forced to move to towns, to live in poor housing, and, in some cases, to become burdens upon their impoverished children.

The dominant impression gathered from interviewing in the condemned communities in the early 1960's was one suffused with the melancholy of untimely death. In many interviews, people expressed their fear that a way of life was about to be lost, that the autonomous Hispanic community was doomed. Some community leaders tried to rally their neighbors around a demand for compensation in land from the national forest in order to reconstitute the entire community, but one of the appraisers hired to negotiate with the villagers managed to sow so much distrust among them that understanding and unity came too late. He told a number of ranchers privately that he would grant them a generous appraisal if they would keep it a secret from their neighbors. At the same time, he called an elderly man who challenged his appraisal a "smart Mexican" and threatened to cut the price per acre to the minimal $85 if he continued arguing.

The aged people forced to move to towns died at an accelerated rate, leaving the impression that they could not adjust to the dislocation of their lifeways. The rate of alcoholism and of mental and physical illness apparently rose during the period of community dissolution, the least affected families being those who managed to replace their ranches. The stresses of displacement and transition experienced by the San Juan Basin Hispanos were nearly equal to those experienced by the Utes during the early reservation days.

HERITAGE OF THE FRONTIER

In retrospect, the autonomy and vitality possessed by the Hispano communities of the San Juan Basin in their best years were qualities nurtured in such a frontier outpost as Abiquiu. The riverine communities of the San Juan Basin saw a late flowering of the symbiotic relations between Hispanos and Utes which had originated in Abiquiu. Both the Hispanos and the Utes with whom they maintained contact over a long period of time became more culturally adaptive because of the contact and found areas of mutual interest that stabilized their relations. These relations continue to be practiced among those Hispanos and Utes of the Ignacio area who have found harmony of interest. No comparable relation exists between Utes and Anglo-Americans of the same area.

Even during their good years in the San Juan Basin, Hispanos were aware of the impoverishment and social downgrading which had been the lot of their kinsmen in the Chama and San Luis valleys in the years since 1846. Now displaced by the Navajo Reservoir, many have been exposed to a similar fate. Land loss has once again marked the end of residential and economic closeness of expanded kin groups, thereby initiating a process of harsh transitions. The San Juan Basin people, as well as others before them, have been left with a feeling that life has lost its meaning because they must now live in communities where their lifeways have been submerged. The people of Rosa and neighboring communities kept a relatively intact way of life longer than many other communities of northern New Mexico, and the shock of the dissolution of their villages was correspondingly acute.

THE ALIANZA

The disasters which befell New Mexico's land grant heirs and which eventually destroyed the riverine communities of the upper San Juan Basin were man-made and not inevitable. What *was* inevitable was that resistance to those social forces that destroy the rural Hispanic way of life should mount and explode. While Rosa, Arboles, and the other San Juan Basin settlements were losing their last residents in the early 1960's, an organizational nucleus concerned with the problems of dispossessed and impoverished Spanish-speaking people began to stir new hope throughout the Southwest. Known first as the *Alianza Federal de Mercedes* (Federated Alliance of Land Grants) and later as the *Alianza Federal de Pueblos Libres* (Federated Alliance of Free Communities), this organizational nucleus funneled efforts to induce a reconsideration of the disposition of the land grants. Besides the question of acres lost and their cash value, the Alianza members sought to spotlight the workings of Yankee internal colonialism. The Alianza claimed that this colonialism had denied them access to the resources of their ancestral lands, depopulated and destroyed their communities, and blighted their lives with intractable poverty.

The story of the Alianza has been told elsewhere and will only be briefly recapitulated here.[8] The Alianza movement was founded and led by Reies Lopez Tijerina, son of impoverished Texas farm laborers and descendant of dispossessed Texas land grantees. With little formal schooling but extraordinary innate talents, Tijerina became a minister of the Assembly of God sect and preached his faith as he and his family followed the migrant labor stream from Texas as far north as Michigan. His evangelical work also took him into Mexico, where he learned in detail about the Mexican Revolution and its subsequent land reforms. In the 1950's, with nineteen farmworker families, Tijerina founded a cooperative village on cheap desert lands in Arizona. This village was burned down in 1957 after business interests had come to consider it desirable real estate. The Tijerinas then moved to northern New Mexico and became acquainted with land grant heirs and their various groups, each engaged in the futile process of trying to assert their rights. They attempted to recover their livelihood in the face of government indifference and to alleviate their oppressive dependence upon welfare. It was then that the idea of the Alianza, as the agency to unite all land grant heirs, was born.

Through disciplined self-denial shared by his family and friends, Tijerina managed to spend three winters in Mexico, studying land grant law and history in the national archives and consulting with scholars in the field. When he felt that he had sufficient facts at his command, he moved once more to northern New Mexico and began to meet with heirs to the many land grants. He laid out the advantages of uniting into a single organization, and the Alianza was formally launched in 1963. It commenced its program with a concerted demand for a congressional investigation into the circumstances under which the grants had been handled since 1846.

The claims of the Alianza were greeted with ridicule and with allegations about Tijerina's motives. Stung by the contempt they met and inspired by the tactics of the Black movement, Alianza members began to adopt tactics of public demonstration and direct action. They won prompt attention, some of it violent. In a walking pilgrimage to Santa Fé to ask New Mexi-

The Chama canyon near the 1808 plaza of San Joaquin. El Grito del Norte.

The Cañon de Chama Grant. El Grito del Norte.

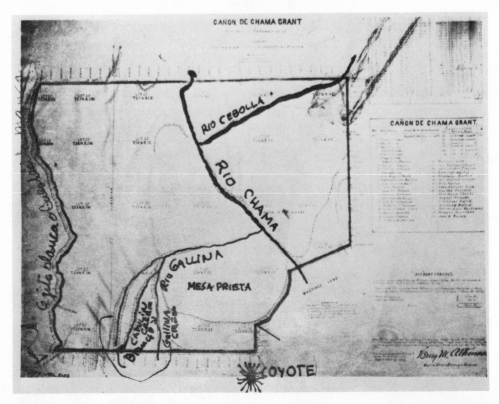

Acquitted! Reies Tijerina with his wife Patsy after the first Tierra Amarilla trial in December, 1968. El Grito del Norte.

Tierra Amarilla, scene of a major land-grant steal and of historic protest actions. El Grito del Norte.

co's governor to aid their cause, Alianza participants had to dodge stray bullets from passing cars. On one occasion a large group of Alianza members occupied a national forest campground to publicize that it was within the San Joaquin del Rio Chama Grant. They also wanted to provoke the government into prosecuting them for occupying land they owned, a case they might win. National forest employees first provoked a scene and then charged Tijerina and other Alianza leaders with assault, a criminal charge. Tijerina, while not accused of so much as laying a hand on any forest ranger, was held responsible for the actions of some of his followers. The followers themselves were not prosecuted while Tijerina was sentenced to a federal prison.

Facing increasingly repressive measures, the Alianza members decided to give supremely dramatic expression to their protest. They tried to make a citizen's arrest of a district attorney who had resorted to trumped-up charges and arrests without a warrant in order to prevent a public gathering in the Rio Arriba country. Citizen's arrests are thoroughly legal and traditional in New Mexico, as was eventually admitted in a district court. The arrest effort, however, exploded into shooting; and injuries resulted when a state policeman drew his gun. The citizen's arrest attempt made newspaper headlines all over the world as a "shootout" and as the "Tierra Amarilla Courthouse Raid." The news media played up sensational aspects of the incident but fortunately kept good pictorial records of events following the "raid." State police and National Guard armored troops assaulted the communities and homes of the people of northern New Mexico, ostensibly looking for Tijerina.

Despite the brutality of the manhunt for Reies Tijerina, the aftermath of the Tierra Amarilla episode was largely positive. The Human Rights Commission and the New Mexico Civil Liberties Union made inquiries into the massive violation of civil liberties that had taken place in Rio Arriba County, and they began to learn that such violations were not out of the ordinary. The appalling poverty of Spanish-speaking New Mexicans came to light: 41 percent of all families live on an income below $3,000 per year. Poverty is most heavily concentrated in the northern counties of New Mexico, where the majority of the population is Spanish-speaking. There were congressional hearings and the promise of massive federal programs.

Amid all the unaccustomed attention, the people of northern New Mexico experienced a fresh surge of pride in their identity and new hope for the future. Even people who claimed to be opposed to Tijerina and the Alianza program expressed their awareness that it took the "raid" at Tierra Amarilla to focus attention on the problems of southwestern Hispanos. In the years following the incident, large numbers of Hispanos, including some of the former residents of the San Juan Basin communities, have come to challenge the ways used by the dominant Anglo society to subordinate Hispanos in economic, social, and cultural life. The increasing use of Spanish as a language of instruction in schools—perhaps a small advance—can be credited to early efforts of Tijerina and the Alianza members.

A new chapter in social relations is barely opening, but it requires no particular prescience to realize that irreversible changes are taking place. The vitality of the descendants of Hispano frontiersmen will find many new forms of expression which will offer viable alternatives to incorporation into the dominant culture. The following chapters will provide analytical review of some of the characteristics of the frontier society which developed in the Chama Valley and San Juan Basin during the eighteenth and nineteenth centuries and which still display adaptive potential for future social frontiers.

7

Hispanic Community Structure

SETTLEMENT PATTERNS

The pattern of Hispanic community development in northern New Mexico has been one of multiplying, not enlarging, single units. Even in valleys sufficiently broad and with sufficient water resources to support a fairly dense population, new plazas (settlements ranging in size from a hamlet to a village) were founded as the population grew; therefore, no single community became an urban center. Even Santa Fé, the administrative center of colonial New Mexico and its most concentrated nucleus of population, remained a slightly overgrown village of 4,194 vecinos and fewer than 500 Indians at the close of the eighteenth century. In fact, cornfields surrounded homes along the river within a stone's throw of the governor's palace.[1]

The colonial settlement pattern of the Chama Valley was even more dispersed. For years, Abiquiu and Ojo Caliente were described as *parajes* (encampments) and *puestos* (outposts) because they consisted of a few small, scattered ranches and lacked a local administrative machinery except for a *teniente* (deputy to the alcalde of Santa Cruz). Each family grouping was dependent upon its own efforts for subsistence and defense.

Settlement in small, discontinuous clusters was partly the result of the terrain and the available technical means. The

133

settlers possessed the simplest of agricultural implements, most of them homemade and unequal to the task of clearing the river benchlands of their piñon and sage cover.[2] Therefore, only the narrow, discontinuous bottomlands of the Chama Valley were cultivated. Agriculture was practiced almost entirely at the subsistence level because once the lands were cleared and planted, women, children, and old people raised the crops. The able-bodied men and older boys spent much of the year herding, buffalo-hunting, trading, and performing militia service.

The dispersed settlement pattern ran absolutely counter to colonial regulations.[3] Over the years, governors and alcaldes made repeated efforts to force settlers to group in the required walled communities of grid-plan design. In 1772 Governor Pedro Fermin de Mendinueta penned the following report to the viceroy of New Spain:

> In this considerable district, the inhabitants of this kingdom live, both Spaniards and reasonable peoples, such as the Christian Indians, but with this difference, that the Indian pueblos are all formed in union, and for that reason are more defensible, but the towns of the Spaniards are not united so that to the dispersion of their houses the names of ranches or camp-houses fit with more propriety, and for this reason they are incapable of any defense, a thing which has been the motive for the depopulation of some weak frontier settlements without my having been able to prevent them permanently with the squad of soldiers destined for their defense.

At this time there was a total regular military force of eighty men in all New Mexico. For all practical purposes, they could provide only sporadic protection to the frontier outposts. The settlers had to defend themselves; and Mendinueta related how, with low numbers, few mounts, and rudimentary weapons, they had to face Apache attacks from the south and west, Comanche raids from every direction, and harassment on occasion from Utes and Navajos to the north and west. Effective defense, said Mendinueta, was impossible without uniting the settlers in walled towns:

> One of the opportune means that may be taken is to compel the neighbors of each settlement who, as I have said, live in such a scattered manner, to get together and form plazas and

streets in such a way that a few men could defend them, from which it would follow that they would the more quickly join in their own defense, or be ready to give help to some other place. Towns arranged according to this plan would be respected by the enemy.

The attainment of this end is impracticable to a governor because of the rustic temper of these neighbors who are accustomed to live separated the ones from the others, for not even parents and sons unite, and if I attempted to oblige them to congregate, it would amount to making them my enemies, and the road to this court would be filled with complainants who, with apparent lamentations (as is their custom), would try, by all means, to frustrate the object of the governor.[4]

There were several reasons why the settlers persisted in violating the regulations, even under conditions which most endangered a scattered population. In the first place, building homes close to the croplands was vital during periods when the able-bodied men were absent from the community. Lookouts were posted to watch the trails leading to the settlement. When they warned that a raiding party approached, the women, children, and elderly people would race home and bar the doors and few windows against attack. Many settlements had a defensive *torreón* (a windowless stone and adobe tower in which the settlers could barricade themselves). Food, water, and weapons were stored in the torreón and tradition holds that women and young boys would occasionally climb to the slit parapet on the roof to fire arrows at the raiders.[5]

Pitched battles with the Indians were generally avoided. Retaliation for a surprise raid was usually a surprise counterraid inflicted by a tracking party. It was not too hard to assemble a party of the local militia for this kind of warfare, because members could regain their stolen goods.

CAUSES OF DISPERSED SETTLEMENT

The raiding pattern influenced the settlers' organization of their activities. Owners of sheep found that they lost fewer animals to Indian raiders if they kept their herds scattered. For this reason, the range of the Piedra Lumbre, Polvadera, and

Upper Chama Valleys was apparently used for grazing long before grants were located there. And herders, often accompanied by their families, might spend the better part of the year far from the home plaza. Only when raiding was most intense, especially when more than one tribe was exerting pressure on the same community, was summer herding conducted close to the home community. The settlers found no relief from stock depredations when they took refuge in the walled enclosure of closed plazas, such as the plaza of Abiquiu. The raiders could breach the defenses and drive off all the livestock of the settlement.

The dispersed settlement pattern made it difficult for the authorities to maintain close supervision over all settlers. Consequently, this reinforced the internal patterns of community authority among the residents of each plaza, who were largely related by blood and marriage. These patterns were built around gradations of deference toward senior members, especially those of the senior lineage, by whose surname the plaza was often known. The senior active males of each lineage were the *tatas* (literally, grandfathers, a term used to denote community leaders; *patrón* is a term not encountered in the archives relating to the colonial settlements of the Lower Chama).

COMMUNITY AUTONOMY

As the formal machinery of *alcaldía* administration built up in the frontier settlements and later became organized into a municipal structure, the externally-ordered agencies of authority tended to be reworked into the existing kin-controlled pattern, so that the leaders of kin groups became the local civil and military leaders. A parallel pattern of leadership prevailed in the Penitente Brotherhood, the hermano mayor being selected from the seniors of a leading family.

Control over their own institutions and independence from outside interference were vital to people whose chief path to affluence was contraband trade with Indians. The goods traded off—purloined *belduques* (hunting knives), *punche* (home grown tobacco on which the required tax was not paid), and horses—were handled as illegally as the child captives for whom they were often traded. The desire of the settlers to keep their activities private earned mention in the 1793-1794 mission census report, which stated that people who needed more lands to work could always find them close to a mission, "without hiding out of sight." Other purposes were seen as uppermost, "more pernicious because hidden," when people put in petitions for new lands to replace the good ones they already owned close to existing settlements. Custos José de la Prada, who wrote the report, no doubt had in mind numerous instances of such hidden purposes in the Abiquiu area where he had long resided.[6]

THE GRID-PLAN PLAZA AND VARIANTS

Governor Thomas Veles Cachupín laid out Abiquiu in a rudimentary grid-plan, when he settled the Genízaros there in 1754. One side of the plaza was reserved for the church of Santo Tomás, built a few years later. The original plaza was an enclosed square surrounded by contiguous buildings. At each corner of the square, high gates barred access when they were closed. The rest of the settlement, however, followed no geometric pattern but wound up the ridges of the hillside and into a grassy dell south of the plaza. A census enumerator who recorded the Abiquiu population in the late 1820's commented that neither the main plaza nor its dependencies had laid-out streets "nor does the constitution of these plazas provide for them."[7]

The term *plaza* was used for communities lacking dense settlement in the grid-plan pattern prescribed by law. This term (*plaza*) inspired sarcastic comment by Antonio Barreiro in the early 1830's.[8] A central plaza area was always a part of the original community plan, but as population grew, families would find themselves short of arable land and would establish a new nucleus of homes close to fresh cropland. Thus, the lands reserved in the original plans for additional house lots were never occupied, and the central plaza itself often developed as an open space, not as a four-sided square with buildings on each side.[9]

The decentralized placita became even more the rule in the

nineteenth century, as the population moved northward into higher valleys. La Loma near Del Norte, Colorado, acquired the nickname of "Seven-Mile Plaza." The name *Rosa* applied to a community whose residences were built on both sides of the San Juan River for stretches of several miles. Coraque, Arboles, Los Pinos, and Los Martinez were similarly dispersed.

Some communities of the Chama watershed which today are compact were formerly more scattered, as was Abiquiu. Their present population concentration is the result of land loss. For example, the encroachment of the Carson National Forest has left Vallecitos de Lobato no room for expansion. The population has increased with the establishment of a Protestant church and denominational school and a sawmill owned by an out-of-state concern. This has almost created a grid-plan settlement pattern at the center.

Rosa once had a population center between the old church at the north end and the stores, post office, school, saloons, and new church at the south end. A boardwalk stretched for about a mile joining all these structures, and house lots facing it were bought and sold as town property. Yet the overall settlement pattern of the community was that of scattered ranches adjacent to irrigated lands. Once the business establishments of Rosa had been closed down, its original appearance of a hamlet returned. Its last residents expressed pronounced aversion to living in row houses where people could look through one another's windows. Ranchers along the Piedra said that the best distance from the next house was just out of sight of it.

HOUSE TYPES

The house styles of colonial New Mexico are not fully documented for early times but the following are mentioned: *jacals* were made with upright pole frames chinked with adobe and often covered over with such a thick plastering of adobe that the poles were completely hidden. Houses were built of molded and sun-dried adobe bricks, of *terrones* (adobe blocks cut directly out of the ground with their grass cover intact), of stone set into adobe, and of various combinations of materials.

The jacal structure was as native to Indian New Mexico as to the ancient Mediterranean world, and it is possible that the same holds for adobe brick. Prehispanic pueblos, however, were characteristically built of dry-masonry, often beautifully fitted, and adobe was usually used in coursed layers. The early Spanish settlers may have used some Indian techniques for building two-story houses, of which there is early record, but colonial homes were usually built as a single story. The settlers adopted the Pueblo-style *latia* ceilings of rows of small poles laid between the *vigas* (roof beams) which spanned the width of rooms thirteen to fifteen feet across. Over the latías went a layer of chamisa boughs covered with a six to twelve-inch packing of earth. Roofs tended to leak in heavy rains.[10]

Houses with adobe brick walls were built in one of two forms. The form most frequently seen along the Lower Chama today is the one that may have prevailed from the start, the sectional adobe or "boxcar" house. The original nucleus consisted of two or three rooms built along a single axis with a single door to the outside and a window to each room, all facing in the same direction. Inside, open doorways screened by curtains connected the rooms.

Additional sections were built along the same axis or at right angles, sometimes joined to the original section but at other times simply built adjacent. Each section was the width of a single room and housed a family consisting of husband and wife, their children, and, possibly, an aged or dependent relative. The grouping of sections created a compound around a patio shared by the several related families. In these family compounds a great deal of work was shared. Much of the cooking was done outdoors over a hearth protected by a *ramada* (brush shelter) and in adobe baking ovens, producing meals for the entire population of the compound. In wintertime, more cooking was done by separate households, using the corner fireplaces inside the homes, which also provided heat for the rooms.

The second form of house was a structurally unified version of the sectional type, built around a patio and generally entered through a massive front gate and entry corridor called a *zaguán*. This form of house is called a *plazuela* in Abiquiu, and it actually is a minimum model of the enclosed, fortified plaza advocated by the colonial authorities. Two plazuela structures survive on the hilly ridges of Abiquiu. One is the former home of a wealthy Gonzales family, and the other is a house of unknown antiquity, purchased in the late nineteenth century by General José María Chavez. Its location is very likely the same as that of the Miguel Montoya house of the 1740's, and it may incorporate some portions of that house. A room in one of its oldest sections is called "the Ute room." It has its own cooking hearth and apparently is the place where visiting Utes were lodged. According to a dimly remembered tradition, Utes who remained overnight in a settlement were securely locked into a room. General Chavez enlarged the house he bought, but left intact its crumbling torreón and its small windows, which opened toward the enclosed patio. The outer walls were all blank, providing some protection from surprise attack. It was built on a high, jutting bluff, virtually impregnable from three sides.

The Montoya residence must have been a large house, since it accommodated Montoya, his wife and minor children, his two married sons with their families, and the servants. This was the house that lodged thirteen Genízaros in 1750, the original nucleus of the Genízaro Grant.[11]

The best-described plazuela residence of the Chama Valley in the eighteenth century was the ten-room house mentioned in the will of Antonio de Beytia in 1765. The house stood on the west bank of the Rio del Ojo Caliente, some miles north of its confluence with the Chama. The rooms were built around a square courtyard fronted by a high zaguán. The doors and shutters had iron locks. Below the irrigated land on Beytia's property was a gristmill. Beytia had only one son of his marriage, but had reared an unspecified number of foster children, including at least one niece. To each of these children he left direct grants of one hundred *varas* (strips of agricultural land less than a hundred yards wide). Since the will mentions no guardian to administer the bequest on behalf of minors, these were probably adults, perhaps already married and still living at the Beytia plazuela.[12]

A more modest sample of plazuela construction is the ground plan of *La Casita* (the Little House) ruins on the Rito Colorado. Termed a "community house," it is an enclosed compound with a high wall sheltering small, joined units. Dr. Herbert Dick, who excavated the ruins in 1958, found features suggestive of Pueblo construction. Since some old documents refer to the place as *La Caseta* (Sentry House), its original use may have been military, when built some time in the eighteenth century.[13]

A later structure of plazuela type was the closed Plaza de Guadalupe on the Conejos Grant, built in 1854 by the families led by José María Jaquez. In this instance, the several associated families built a single enclosed structure, divided into apartments. While of jacal construction, the ranch of José Perez in Rosa followed the same principles of defensive construction. It is a matter of record, however, that enclosed plazas and plazuela houses were not proof against raids. Both the Beytia and Montoya homes were stormed in the mid-eighteenth century and their residents were forced to flee the area. The plaza of Santo Tomás, Abiquiu, was repeatedly breached.

Apparently, experience taught the Chama Valley settlers that enclosed plazas and plazuela houses provoked Indian raids and provided no real defense against them. To protect lives, the torreón was favored, and the settlers learned that it was better to lose some livestock to raiders than to keep their entire herds in the plaza as a focus for attack. Besides, those settlers who made friends with the Utes learned early that the more dispersed their living arrangements, the better the Utes could distinguish between friend and foe.

Multiroomed adobe houses were divided between the heirs of a family, a particularly large room even being divided among several heirs by a certain number of ceiling beams. An heir might keep a room in a house of which he had inherited a part, renting it or saving it for his own lodging during occasional trips to the community where the house stood.

The will of Severino Martinez, dated June 8, 1827, lists the following as his: one house in the Plaza de la Capilla of Abiquiu, presently in the possession of a nephew; three rooms in another house of the same plaza, the rest having been traded off for a house in Taos; 110 varas of land in El Rito, plus one room in a house of the Upper Plaza of El Rito. Severino Martinez had moved from Abiquiu to Taos in 1824 and owned several dwelling units in nearby settlements, including "one medium sized room in the house of my niece Trinidad Salazar" in Arroyo Hondo.[14]

There is scattered mention of wooden houses, jacals, and stone houses in early documents of the Chama Valley. Jacals are generally mentioned in a context of sheepherding.[15] A jacal, however, can be spacious, provided there is timber of sufficient size and abundance to make an ample frame. A majority of the first settler homes in the San Juan Basin were jacals, and some had stood in good condition for more than half a century. When a spacious jacal has been thickly mudded over, it is indistinguishable at first glance from a well-plastered adobe brick house.

The term *casa de madera* (wooden house) appears in a document referring to houses on the Polvadera Tract built by José de Riaño and used by the Montoya brothers in the 1740's. As both families were among the most affluent of their time and as several nuclear families of Montoyas actually lived in the houses, it can be assumed that they were not hovels. They were probably built of adzed logs from the tall pine stands in the mountains.[16]

There is no other mention of wooden houses in archives relating to the lower Chama Valley. It is likely, however, that herders used timber where it was available to build both jacals with upright poles and log houses. By the time the San Juan Basin was settled, many log houses were built in heavily timbered areas, implying abundant previous experience.[17]

The torreón was a specialized structure, diverse in form and in building materials. It might be a freestanding structure, like the torreón of José Baca on the Río del Ojo Caliente, or it might be built into the corner of a residence, like the torreón of the General Chavez house in Abiquiu. It might be built of stone, stone and adobe, or adobe bricks. Bunting describes a late eighteenth century torreón of the Taos area, which had a circular ground floor of adobe bricks and an upper story of logs built as six-sided ramparts. Some torreóns were square.[18]

INNOVATIONS IN HOUSE STYLE

An innovation in house style developed in Rosa, evolving from a type introduced in Las Vegas and Tierra Amarilla in the

The brand-new Rosa home of Bidal A. Candelaria in the early 1900's. From collection of Mrs. A. C. Marquez.

The Baltazar Quintana house in its last days. Photo by Patricia Dailey, Rosa, 1960, in Tri-Ethnic Project collection.

The Rosa Merc in 1960, shortly before it was destroyed by fire. Photo by Patricia Dailey, in Tri-Ethnic Project collection.

A large two-story house in El Rito, New Mexico. F. Swadesh, 1970.

1870's. Irish-born Thomas Burns had spent part of his boyhood in Wisconsin and built a two-story adobe-brick house in Parkview. Incorporating structural features that came from eastern areas, he put in a steep-gabled roof and dormer windows. Neighbors in the Tierra Amarilla area soon began to build second stories, pitch roofs on their adobe homes, and add balconies and outdoor staircases above their *portals.* As milled lumber became available, these new structures began to acquire a gingerbread appearance and the modified adobe homes looked more and more top-heavy.

Originally, the roofs were covered with cedar shakes, but this led to so many fires that sheet metal was used instead as soon as it became available. Two-story houses were not readily adopted in the Lower Chama and Rio Grande Valleys because their pitched roofs offered no great advantage in areas of moderate to slight precipitation and they needed too much firewood to heat them in the winter.

In Rosa, on the other hand, the snowfall was often heavy and firewood and coal were plentiful. Furthermore, the Rosa businessmen wanted to have headquarters and homes which reflected their prestige. At the turn of the century and in the first two decades of the twentieth century, a number of two-story houses were built in Rosa, less elaborate than their Tierra Amarilla prototypes but boasting splendid construction and a classic refinement of proportions. They were tall houses with walls two feet thick and excellent roofs sporting dormer windows.

It is said that an Anglo carpenter from the Ute Agency assisted in the building of the first such house, belonging to Bidal Candelaria. The nails used in the window frames may well have been appropriated from agency supplies, since such items were not then readily available along the San Juan River.

The houses of Rosa, with their spare, harmonious lines and their gracious, well-insulated interiors, were the flowering of a new synthesis. Using the first major architectural innovations to be introduced into New Mexico in two centuries, they suited both the physical and the social setting of the region. These houses continued in use until the 1960's, and in 1962 the adobe bricks of a house completed in 1905 were disassembled, one by one, and used in new construction.

RESIDENTIAL GROUPS

Extended families lived in these houses. Young married women sometimes remained under the parental roof for some years, raising their first children, while the young husband worked in a mine or at another job far from home. The modern version of joint-family dwelling has brought the house trailer into use in the San Juan Basin and other areas of northern New Mexico. Young couples park their trailers close to a parental dwelling and the young husband often works in partnership with his father or father-in-law next door, if there are land and livestock to be managed. In these extended-family groups, meals are generally prepared and served jointly for the whole group, with two sittings at the table if there is insufficient space for all.

The different types of residences described above are indicative of lifeways. Small dwellings in isolated locations were occupied by herders and other poor workers, sometimes with families in crowded quarters. Generally, these comprised groups too small to manage better than a bare subsistence. The larger compounds of sectional dwellings and plazuelas demonstrate cooperation in work and sharing of food among related families. In times before refrigeration was available, this made for greater economy in the use of food. When a kid was slaughtered, it would be shared among all, thereby saving food, fuel, and the labor of busy women. This management of the food supply was carried into modern times, and in the San Juan Basin today, cooking is still a single operation for all people jointly engaged in cutting hay. Residential closeness is no longer required for cooperation and sharing but is widely preferred. The most important remaining custom of community food sharing is Lenten reciprocal distribution of *charolitas* (casseroles of Lenten delicacies such as the baked sprouted-wheat dish called *panocha*).

PLAZA SIZE

Historically, the kin-based plazas of the Chama Valley had a difficult time maintaining sufficient numbers to survive and defend themselves in the eighteenth century. This was the result of desertions and the recurrent tendency of settlers to ask for new grants of land and to found new plazas. A population of about one hundred, including at least twenty able-bodied men, was needed for a plaza to survive. Such a population cluster might be scattered in several groups along a mile or more of river benchland. It included households headed by widows with young children who dwelt beside or in the household of an adult male who was a blood or affinal relative. Elderly people often shared their house with the adult son or daughter who would inherit it.

At times when Indian raids were frequent or severe, the settlers might abandon the plaza for a year or more. Some plazas never were resettled, but the larger the plaza, the greater the likelihood of resettlement, usually with reinforcements of new settlers. As the population grew until all arable land was in use, a portion of the settlers, generally young families, would petition for new lands beyond the periphery of settlement.

Whether settlement focused on a town plaza, a plazuela residence, or a compound of sectional adobe homes, its range in size and composition was not great in the eighteenth century Chama Valley communities. The smallest placitas of record included some twenty heads of household, grouped into six to ten joint households. The largest plazas included some fifty heads of household, and the grouping of households did not exceed twenty extended units. Most residents of a plaza were linked by descent or marriage or both.

KIN COMMUNITIES

The composition of eighteenth century plazas of the Abiquiu area and of their offspring communities of the nineteenth and twentieth centuries was virtually identical. In 1789, shortly before the last crippling Comanche raids in the Chama Valley, the population demarcation of Abiquiu totaled 1,152 persons in nine plazas, including Abiquiu proper.[19] The largest plaza was San Miguel, near the confluence of Polvadera Creek with Chihuahueños (or Pedernales) Creek. It combined the population of the Piedra Lumbre Grant with people of the adjacent Polvadera Grant.

The *comisionado* (civil leader) of San Miguel was Alonso Antonio Cisneros. His sister, María Manuela, was married to Pedro Martín Serrano, petitioner for the Piedra Lumbre Grant and its principal stockman. Pedro's brother, Juan Pablo Martín, had been the petitioner for the Polvadera Grant, but by 1789 he had left the Abiquiu area. Enumerated at San Miguel were forty-seven heads of family, of which ten were single women, possibly widows, and two were single men, possibly widowers. Eleven men and eight women bore the Martín(ez) surname and four men and six women bore the Cisneros (or Sisneros) surname. The military leader of the plaza was José Ygnacio Martín, who had bought the Gerónimo Martín house near Barranco in 1764. He was the grandfather of José Manuel Martinez, who petitioned for the Tierra Amarilla Grant in 1832.[20]

According to the census of 1845, Abiquiu and its dependencies had a total population of 1,565, grouped under 341 heads of household. The census taker failed to make a breakdown into plazas, but the parish records of prior years indicate that there were at least nine plazas, which suggests an average of thirty heads of household per plaza, no doubt with the same range of variation in size as in 1789.[21] The census taker did not give a count of houses or of extended households, but did list sequentially the surnames of heads of adjacent households. From the fact that 113 households are linked by shared surnames into 39 residential associations, we can estimate 67 kin-residential units.[22]

The 1870 census for Tierra Amarilla shows a similar, but even more dispersed, pattern among the eight placitas with a total of 119 heads of family. Here, too, shared surnames in adjacent households provide a strong hint that the same ratio of at least a third of adjacent households had kin links with one another, as was the case in the older communities of the Lower Chama. The same can be said for the eighty-seven households in the eight Hispano precincts of the San Juan Basin in 1880.[23]

In the studies of the modern San Juan Basin communities it has been possible to verify the kin links of adjacent households, thereby proving the existence of the residential associations. These associations can only be inferred in the majority of records of former populations. However, when the archives provide identifying data for families of the same surname in adjacent households, these are invariably the households of close relatives.

An added justification for the use of identical surnames as inferential evidence of kinship ties between contiguous households in historical records is the lack of evidence that any such households were *not* related to one another. The cumulative evidence *for* kinship links comes from data on marriage choices, residences, godparent selection, and land and heirship records. Here are some known and implied links among a series of Martín Serranos: José Ygnacio Martín married Petrona Gonzales, while José Lucrecio Martín married Andrea Gonzales, apparently a pair of brothers wed to a pair of sisters. Gerónimo Martín, from whom Ygnacio purchased a seven-room house in 1764, was married to a Salazar, as was the namesake son of Ygnacio. In 1797, this younger José Ygnacio Martín and his wife selected as godparents for their newborn daughter Antonio Severino Martinez (another Martín Serrano) and his wife, María del Carmel Santistevan; Antonio Severino's brother, Antonio José, was married to Maria del Carmel's sister, María Guadalupe Santistevan.[24]

The residential pattern resulted from the system of dividing agricultural lands into equal strips for all heirs, as long as there was sufficient land for the subsistence of all. By the third generation after a grant was settled, sibling groups would be farming in tight clusters, neighbors to their first and second cousins. The co-residence of siblings, affines, and cousins of same or different generation emphasizes the fraternal network that unified the community.

The composition of the population of Rosa, New Mexico, in the 1960's was parallel to that of the prototype communities of the Lower Chama in the eighteenth century. All residents with the exception of a single family shared links through ancestry or marriage with two cognate Candelaria lineages and three cognate Quintana lineages. The single family without links was the target of outsider treatment, despite long years of residence in the community.

POSTMARITAL RESIDENCE

Postmarital residence in New Mexico throughout the colonial and Mexican periods could be with the husband's family (virilocal), with the wife's family (uxorilocal), or at a new location (neolocal). Either of the first two choices was common in the early years of marriage. Even when neolocal residence had been established from the start, the need for assistance during and after the birth of children brought young couples back under a parental roof for extended periods during the childbearing years. Neolocal residence was often established only well after the formation of the family of procreation.

Compared with available information on other New Mexico communities, the Chama Valley records show a consistently high incidence of residence with the wife's kin. The records do not prove that men dwelt under the same roof as their wife's parents and other kin, but rather that they dwelt beside their wife's brothers and maintained cooperative economic and social relations, ranging from complete sharing of food, livestock, land, and daily activities to limited and temporary agreements.

The dynamics of the residential bias suggest that the availability of grazing land and the size of herds in the Chama Valley tended to outstrip the number of men available to manage them.[25] The factors which caused so many men to settle with the wife's family, however, were more complex than the simple ratio of labor force to size of herds.

The Chama Valley offered many roads to economic advancement, unhampered by the monopolistic practices of the ricos or by strict application of administrative controls. The vast rangelands of the Upper Chama Valley and the extra margin of opportunity offered by the (contraband) Ute trade provided doors to prosperity for impoverished young men of good family. Those whose family lands had been partitioned and whose marriage portion would be only a few sheep or other livestock were alert to find a wife who would inherit land and whose father's enterprises were short on manpower. Land-poor young men came from various parts of New Mexico and from Abiquiu itself to live on the allotment of the wife's family. Not uncommonly, they would become so integrated into this family that they would address their in-laws in the terms of blood-kinship, and their children would be known by the maternal grandfather's surname.

Affluent men of the Chama Valley were glad to put their

sons-in-law to work farming the land, serving in the militia, managing the flocks, or freighting trade goods to the fairs. Sons and sons-in-law often worked the land jointly as a single unit, at least until after the death of the man from whom they would inherit. After the death of Alejandro Martín of the Frijoles Ranch, his son-in-law, Manuel Cisneros, petitioned for separation from the land of the other heirs of the three strips of land, irrigated and stubble, that were his wife's inheritance. He and his brothers-in-law, Pedro Martín and José Antonio Torres, had been working the land jointly, but Cisneros feared that they might eventually disagree about ownership. He asked for a prompt separation of his parcels, so as "to enjoy them in peace with all the heirs and never have lawsuits or disputes with anyone."[26]

A son-in-law might move onto an unused allotment of members of his wife's family, petitioning for new lands as they were vacated by others. In 1768 Gabriel Quintana and José Ygnacio Alarid petitioned jointly for the vacant lands and house of Nicolás Martín. His widow, Gerónima Pacheco, had moved from the allotment near Ojo Caliente to her son's allotment near Abiquiu. Quintana had been living on the Ojo Caliente allotment of his father-in-law, Blas Martín, and Alarid occupied the allotment of his father-in-law, Domingo Benavides, alcalde mayor of Taos. Both men claimed that their lands were inadequate for the maintenance of their growing families. The Nicolás Martín house and lands were declared forfeit in their favor.[27]

HEIRSHIP

Heirship to a grant could be validated by descent from men who had maintained residence on their father-in-law's land. For instance, the Antonio de Beytia Grant on the Río del Ojo Caliente was deserted by Antonio's son, Miguel de Beytia, and by the unspecified number of foster children who also inherited, as a consequence of heavy Indian attack in the mid-eighteenth century. In 1809 the grant was resettled by Baltazar Cisneros and his wife, María Antonia Abeytia, apparently a daughter of Miguel de Beytia. They were accompanied by Juan Domingo Griego, Enrique Maestas, and José Hernando Torres, described as "children and heirs of the late Miguel de Beitia," probably the husbands of other daughters of Miguel de Beytia. In 1893 María Lorenza Lucero et al., as heirs of Baltazar Cisneros, claimed the entire grant on the grounds that only Baltazar and his family had remained to validate his wife's title to the grant.[28]

Under the Laws of Castilla which prevailed throughout New Mexico, equal division of property was made to heirs, both male and female. This meant that women inherited property which could only be managed with the assistance of a husband, brother, or son. Widows retained the use of one-half the total joint property of their husbands and themselves, not including property the husband may have inherited from an earlier marriage, if there were children of that marriage. After the widow's death, her share of the property was divided among the children of her marriage.

In communities where hired or captive labor was in chronically short supply, a propertied woman had to have a husband, brother, or grown son to manage her livestock, clear her land, etc. Although a strong-minded woman could retain effective control over her property and could even be her own official spokesman in property litigation, it was customary for a man of her family to act as spokesman and custodian on her behalf.

In frontier communities other than those of the Chama Valley it is not clear whether or not the pattern of uxorilocal residence and the relatively powerful position of women were equally marked. Nineteenth century traveler accounts and informant recollections for Taos and Galisteo, for instance, suggest that residential groups were more commonly composed of a couple with their married sons and that the daughters usually moved to dwell with their husband's relatives. By the early nineteenth century, both communities had a stronger nucleus of ricos than existed in the Chama Valley, resulting in a more clearly stratified society.

REGIONAL DIFFERENCES IN RESIDENCE PATTERNS

These apparent differences in rate of social change in frontier communities are seemingly due to several factors. In the first place, lax external controls along the Chama offered opportunities for affluence created by contraband trading with the Utes. This trading, as well as the recurrent chances of being reduced to poverty in a raid, kept the society of the Lower Chama Valley flexible—a feature which persisted in the San Juan Basin.

In the second place, the colonial government was particularly liberal in restoring title to deserted lands and giving title to large new tracts to the settlers of Abiquiu and Ojo Caliente, presumably in order to maintain adequate frontier defenses. Considering how frequent and sometimes prolonged were the desertions of Abiquiu and Ojo Caliente plazas between 1747 and 1790, it is remarkable that the same lineages bridged successive periods as the recognized grantees. Changes in the assignment of a grant over the years tended to increase the number of owners rather than to bar return to former owners or their descendants. New grants to a settler group were made within the borders of a grant previously made in the name of a single settler, as the history of the Juan José Lobato Grant abundantly demonstrates.[29]

A factor which particularly favored residence with the wife's family was the series of activities which took young married men away from their home communities. Livestock management accounted for relatively short absences, but trading journeys, buffalo hunting trips, and militia service could consume months. Young wives usually stayed with their families when a baby was due, to have the help of their mothers with the birth and early care of the infant. The custom of staying close to one's parents in anticipation of the birth of a baby has lingered on in the San Juan Basin, although most births now take place in hospitals.

RESIDENCE PATTERNS IN PREGNANCY

There was no professional assistance for parturient mothers in the Chama Valley of colonial times. Even midwives are not mentioned in the local archives. Contemporary informants of the San Juan Basin, especially those who have lived in inaccessible locations, are familiar with births which have been attended

by only the baby's father or some relative. Many women have
given birth entirely unattended. Between 1880 and the 1920's,
there were two women in the San Juan Basin who were skilled
in midwifery, but many women of the 1920's could not afford
the modest midwife fee of $25.00. There is a tradition going
back to colonial times that Indian women were skilled midwives. Until modern times, most of New Mexico had to do
without a professional doctor.[30]

Despite the fact that childbirth was considered a relatively
simple, "natural" function, the *dieta* period of forty days entailed restrictions which put a woman in need of aid from other
women. In emulation of the Virgin's forty-day seclusion after
the birth of Jesus and her subsequent purification rites, postpartum mothers of northern New Mexico kept largely to their
beds for this period, barred from connubial relations and fed a
rich diet of *chaqueue* (the Tewa term for blue corn atole), to
which was soon added diced, boiled lamb, or the flesh of a male
black goat. There was no rule as to where the dieta should be
spent, but under normal circumstances the parturient mother
stayed with her parents.[31]

This residence pattern during pregnancy and parturition
deepened the ties between young married women and their
parents, and could only favor continued uxorilocal residence.
The woman's parents often took care of the baptism of her
infant as godparents, and this, in turn, favored their adoption of
the baby, which was especially common with a first child. Close
relations with the parents of each spouse are still common in
the San Juan Basin today, but more frequently the closest ties
are maintained with the wife's parents. It is probably significant
that older people comment with more nostalgia if a daughter
lives far from them than if a son is far removed. Today, as in the
past, when a couple lives close to the parents of one of them,
affinal terminology is replaced by the use of blood-kin terminology. The son-in-law, for example, becomes "son" and the sister-in-law is addressed as "sister."

DOMINANCE AND SUBORDINATION

The kin-community network which united a village was organized along lines of dominance-subordination and also along

lines of cooperation with an absence of significant class distinctions. Some subordinate households were partly dependent upon employment by dominant households, but in turn, they were the employers of members of other households. Fray Atanacio Dominguez noted when he visited Abiquiu in 1776: "Some are masters; others are servants; others serve in both capacities."[32]

Less than a quarter of the Abiquiu households enumerated in colonial census reports listed Indian captives among their members. Such captives as were listed were largely children, raised from infancy in the household and trained to work at an early age at a level not much more intensive than that of the master's children. Of the many captives presumably obtained by Abiquiu settlers, most were apparently sold elsewhere, to the enrichment of their captors.[33]

The round of labor in frontier plazas was ceaseless and heavy, with none but the simplest of tools. Only joint labor and cooperation for mutual benefit could help ease the burden. From an early age, children were all expected to help with the work, and as a child grew to adulthood, the obligation grew. Before a boy was "emancipated" and "placed in the estate of matrimony," he was expected to work for his father and to help earn the land and goods with which he would be able to start supporting a family. It was customary, even in relatively well-to-do families, to hire out one's sons as farm laborers and as herders under partido agreements. The proceeds were pocketed by the father of the boy and were supposed to be returned to him upon "emancipation" as part of his inheritance.[34]

Hand in hand with the parental obligation to place sons in the estate of matrimony went the filial obligation to care for one's parents in their old age. These obligations were and still are discharged in the Chama Valley and San Juan Basin in ways which are reminiscent of certain customs in Spain and eastern Europe.[35] While the responsibility of the eldest son was a matter of formal record, it was not uncommon for the youngest child of either sex (*socoyote* or *socoyota*) to remain at home, possibly even foregoing marriage, to take care of elderly or ailing parents. The marked parental attention and indulgence shown toward the youngest child may be geared to the expecta-

tion of being emotionally—if not economically and physically—
dependent upon this child in one's declining years.[36]

Dominant status within a family carried with it the responsibility to aid the less dominant. Older brothers, in particular,
must help their younger siblings. Today, bearing responsibility
for the welfare of a widowed sister continues to be "the right
thing to do." At the same time, the means for meeting these
obligations have become increasingly elusive, and points of
contradiction in the code of family interdependence are sharp-
ened. There has always been some ambiguity concerning the
extent of mutual obligations between half-siblings and stepsiblings. Today, many people who uphold the family code
within the circle of close relatives are more selective with
distant relatives, only maintaining the ties of mutual obligation
with the individuals they like.

COMMUNITY INSTITUTIONS OF SOCIAL CONTROL

In the colonial, Mexican, territorial and modern periods,
there was no formal institution of social control—civil, military,
religious, judicial, economic, or educational—which gained dominance over or independence of the local kin groups of northern
New Mexico.

Colonial laws were made a nullity, decisions of governors
were jeered at, and the power of the Church was largely super-
seded by the lay Brotherhood, the structure of which paralleled
and rested upon the existing web of kinship. The only authority
that had final say in the plazas was the echelon of command
within the kin groups. Even today, when a stranger appears in
the San Juan Basin, he is closely questioned about his family
origins. If a link through kinship is found between him and his
questioners, he is automatically a friend. It is fortunate that
such links can usually be found, because one who is totally
unrelated through blood or marriage necessarily remains an
extranjero (outsider). The idea of maintaining neighborly relations with people who are not relatives, as institutionalized in
Anglo-American society, is foreign to the Hispanic tradition.

Because of outmigrations from the original plazas of residence to communities of Colorado, Utah, and California, *cam-*

panilismo (loyalty to one's home community at the expense of all others) is expanded to include respectful attitudes toward communities where many relatives reside.[37] People who have never been to the villages and towns of the San Luis Valley or Utah, where they know they have relatives, refrain from including these communities in the gibes and satirical ditties showered on nearby communities where they have no relatives. The rules of hospitality extend to relatives from these distant communities without including the specific code of constant reciprocal obligations prevailing in the family compound. To fail to meet the latter set of obligations is to expose oneself to the sharp weapon of gossip—more anxiety-provoking than direct criticism.

Community opinion of a person, reinforced by gossip, is transmitted to the target person by delicately worded innuendoes, *indirectas*, or *maliciadas*, often so subtle that it is hard to tell if the concealed jab is intentional. Mocking *sobrenombres* (nicknames) are used when their target is ostensibly out of earshot. In the San Juan Basin no one would admit knowing the nicknames of his relatives, let alone his own or those of people of high standing. The nicknames of many of the less respected Utes were the first offered, then those of Hispanos in low standing with their neighbors. Only some of the nicknames had possible obscene connotations, but all were mentioned with the mirth that accompanies off-color jokes. The nicknames of people higher on the scale of respect came later and were only uttered in a context of cautious confidentiality. It would probably have taken years to find out all the nicknames of the riverine communities.[38]

SOCIAL LEVELING AND CROSS-CULTURAL RELATIONS

The code of behavior which grew out of life in the frontier plazas of the Chama Valley was constantly subject to modification due to changes in the social milieu. The code that was brought into New Mexico was rooted in Hispanic institutions with colonial modifications, pervaded by *casticismo* (the values of an elite caste). In the Chama Valley, however, the social mobility of people of diverse ancestry was so great that social leveling was the dominant process. It is possible, as some claim, that Santa Fe maintained permanent distinct social strata, due to its function as the administrative center dominated by elitist appointees from Mexico and Spain. Yet even here, the Tlaxcalan barrio (Mexican Indians settled near the San Miguel Chapel) disappeared without a trace. Tlaxcalans must have constituted a distinct caste at the outset and must have experienced speedy and virtually unnoticed incorporation into the segment of society called *español*.

In the communities around Abiquiu we have documented the ways in which Genízaros, Indian captive children, and people of mixed backgrounds assimilated culturally and rose in affluence until they were incorporated into the español segment. We have also noted that people from the español segment, from early times, either were captured by Indians or escaped the authorities to take refuge with them. Many settlers thus became fully assimilated into Navajo, Comanche, Apache, and Kiowa communities. During exchange of captives, it was customary for Indianized español children to be exchanged for hispanicized Indian children, thus intensifying two-way cultural exchange.

The occupation which most affected community development, contraband trade with the Utes, was centered in different areas during different periods of the historical span. Abiquiu, Ojo Caliente, and (for the Moaches only) Taos were for a long time terminals of trade routes that stretched deep into Colorado and Utah. Abiquiu and Ojo Caliente were partly replaced as contact centers by the San Luis Valley settlements and the communities on the Tierra Amarilla Grant by the mid-nineteenth century, but the Moaches continued to come to Taos until they were forcibly removed.[39]

Because contact between the Utes and the Chama Valley settlers was based on trade in articles each desired of the other, without dominance of one group by the other, an egalitarian spirit prevailed between them. The military and civil bureaucrats who controlled New Mexico during the territorial years constantly denounced the freedom of relations between Utes and Hispanos and considered each group a negative influence upon the other. Hispano spokesmen, on the other hand, defended their relations with the Utes. Francisco Salazar, agent in 1874 for the Tierra Amarilla Utes and Apaches, stated: "These

Indians have been very good friends of the people of New Mexico for many years, and if any tribe deserves the favor of the Indian Department, it is the Utes of the Tierra Amarilla Agency."[40]

With the location of the Southern Ute Agency at Ignacio, Colorado, a new center of symbiotic and egalitarian Hispano-Ute relations began to develop. The former centers began a period of slow decline in Hispano fortunes, only a few favored families rising through their profitable alliance with the conquering Yankees. The traditional egalitarianism and openness of the communities of the Lower Chama Valley shriveled in each community as land and livelihood were lost and as family groupings were decimated by out-migration.[41]

DECLINE OF FRONTIER COMMUNITIES

While Rosa and Arboles were at their peak, the Chama Valley communities from Tierra Amarilla down to the confluence with the Rio Grande were losing access to their traditional range. This land was being fenced off by the U. S. Forest Service and by new private owners, the beneficiaries of courtroom chicanery and tax sales. The reaction of heirs to land grants, when their range was fenced off, duplicated previous reactions in San Miguel County in the 1870's and early 1880's. Groups of nightriders, known in San Miguel County as *Gorras Blancas* (white hoods) and in Rio Arriba County after 1912 as *Manos Negras* (black hands), rode through the country at night, cutting fences, slashing the bellies of livestock, and burning down barns and haystacks of the people they considered illegal intruders. The Mano Negra movement appears to have some links with the Spanish Anarchist movement of the same name, which developed at the turn of the century.[42]

From 1846 on, the societal structure of New Mexico, which had progressed from that of a colonial frontier to a nascent republican territory with rudimentary machinery for managing its own affairs, became that of an internal quasi colony. The municipal organization which linked towns together under *ayuntamientos* (municipal councils elected by manhood suffrage with representatives from each of the municipal dependencies and which, since 1837, had been under the command of a regional prefect) was first supplanted by full control by the prefect; then, after the formation of a county system, by the county commission. This was an inadequate system of government for widely scattered communities under alien rule.

Several institutions remained or were developed during the territorial period for the internal control of communities. These were: (1) the kin groups, with the dominance of some rising through several adjacent communities as other kin groups became impoverished and displaced; (2) the Penitente Brotherhood; (3) the Community Ditch Association, whose importance rose during this period because it was the only institution that unified the economy of neighboring villages; (4) the Justice of the Peace Court; and (5) the Church—an institution that was an integral part of the community though its authority came from forces alien to the community. As long as these institutions remained intact and population was sufficient to man the various activities they mediated, communities remained stable and unified.

In many communities today, only the kin-groups and the ditch associations remain as unifying and organizing forces that prescribe behavior and mediate activity. Yet the psychic reality of the traditional community lingers as a memory and as a set of values which still condition the social behavior of Hispanos in northern New Mexico.[43]

8

Frontier Hispanic
Social Relations

NEW MEXICO'S LANDED GENTRY

The settlers who established the Spanish colony of New Mexico came because they were promised the status of *hidalgo de solar conocido* (landed gentry), a goal which they apparently felt was worth the great physical hardship, danger, and isolation that they would have to face. The leaders of the first colony led by Oñate received encomienda grants and profited by the forced labor of many Indians. But the recolonization that took root in the eighteenth century was built out of the labor of the colonists themselves. Comments of both colonial and Mexican-period officials and visitors from the United States make it clear that the settlers were largely yeomen of very limited means, but also that most possessed independent means of subsistence. Unlike populations in the rest of Latin America, they had neither a well-defined class of hereditary aristocrats nor a class of destitute beggars.[1]

Many people acquired some wealth, lost it, and then later recovered their losses. A family did not lose its standing in the eyes of its peers because it had fallen upon evil days, and the mutual aid of large kin groups tended to cushion the blows when they fell. Even so, some families stood higher on the

159

social scale than others, such as the least landed, the most subject to debt and to laborer status and, in many instances, those with the most recent Indian ancestry.

There were ways, however, whereby even poor Genízaros could mend their fortunes. In 1740, for instance, a Genízaro of Ojo Caliente named Francisco Saes was accused by Felipe de Riaño of doing away with 374 of the 600 sheep he had rented from him on partido. Saes laid the losses to winter storms, wolves, and other difficulties. Upon investigation, however, 212 sheep that he had hidden, plus 14 more which he had sold, were located. The judgment against Saes ordered him to work out his debt for all of the remainder which could not be found. [2]

All the landed gentry of New Mexico, whether affluent or of marginal means, had a proud awareness of their hidalgo status. This has puzzled outside observers, since Anglo-American tradition requires visible proof of means to validate middle-class status, and they could recognize only the larger ranchers and more affluent businessmen of New Mexico as members of the bourgeoisie. Elderly people of New Mexico, however, still ask one another upon introduction: *"Dónde está su merced?"* (Where is your land grant?), in recognition of their mutual status as hidalgos.

Until 1824, the vecinos had an advantage over the Genízaros with regard to expanding economic opportunities, since they could settle a grant for four years, fulfill all requirements for receiving full title, then sell their allotments at a profit and request new grants. Genízaro grants, under the same regulations as the Pueblos, forbade sale of an assignment of land to anyone outside the pueblo. Genízaros only gained mobility and the chance of becoming affluent persons through booty or profit in trade, proceeds of which permitted them to buy land and to rise to vecino status. A vecino who had enjoyed good fortune, therefore, had a better chance of having property to bequeath to his children than did most Genízaros. The system of inheritance, however, was subject to many variables because a widowed parent often remarried and produced new offspring to complicate the picture.

PROBLEMS OF PROPERTY RELATIONS

Second marriages set up new networks of affectional ties which might crowd out the old ones. Two clear examples of this process in the Abiquiu area demonstrate the fissional effects of multiple marriages upon both emotional and property relations. The first case is that of Maria Manuela Sisneros, widow of Pedro Martín Serrano.

At the time of the estate settlement in 1806, the widow had retained her customary half of the property she had shared with her husband, while the other half was divided among their four children, only two of whom had attained majority. An equal division of land, livestock, hides, tools, furniture, roof beams, and cloth had been made, the portion for the minor children being received on their behalf by their uncle, Antonio Martín. The widow received her share only for her lifetime, with the understanding that upon her death it would be divided among the four children.

Shortly after the estate settlement, however, María Manuela married a retired soldier, Miguel Tenorio of the Santa Fé presidio. At this time, she drew up an agreement with her children that in exchange for selling to the retired Lieutenant (Juan?) Cristobal Quintana some of their inherited unenclosed land, she would sign over to them an equal amount of enclosed land on the ranch of her late father, Antonio Silberio Sisneros.

A short time later, the heirs discovered that María Manuela had given her husband permission to sell to Quintana the whole ranch of their inheritance, not just the unenclosed land, for one hundred pesos to pay a debt he owed Blas Trujillo. The heirs sued, on the ground that their mother was trying to disinherit the children of her first marriage. María Manuela coldly replied that she had every right to do as she pleased with land that belonged to her by an estate division made eight years previously. She more than hinted dissatisfaction with the attitude of her children and objected to the proposed division of ranch lands into five three hundred vara strips, one for herself and one for each of the four children. The intention of the proposal was to prevent Tenorio from either planting on the ranch or selling it. The division was actually put into effect in 1814.[3]

The second case is that of Gregorio Martín. In his last will and testament of 1826, he tried to bar his two oldest sons, both married, from any share in his house or lands. The reason given for the ban was that these sons had refused to give him work-time after he had lost fifty ewes in a blizzard. He had been managing the sheep under a five-year partidario contract. The surety on the flock was Martín's house and land, and when the terms of the contract ended in 1824, the owner claimed his indemnity.

Gregorio Martín had then taken his three sons before the alcalde, asking them to bind themselves to take monthly turns working for the creditor for a total of ten turns apiece, until the house and lands were free of debt. The oldest two demurred, saying that they could only comply if their father would take care of their wives and children while they were working away from home. The third son, still single, agreed to work as requested.

Further testimony showed that Gregorio Martín's rancor against his oldest two sons arose because they had married against his wishes. A former priest at the Abiquiu mission described how he had to argue with Gregorio for over a year to secure the "rights of the estate of matrimony" for the young men. Gregorio had called his sons "ingrates" and had vacillated between reluctance and rage. Another witness described the partidario contract drawn up between Gregorio and the witness' father shortly after the blizzard. Gregorio's eldest son had been the herder and had secured an increase from 35 to 140 ewes, plus rams born each year, and the ewes' surplus milk. From the profits of this enterprise, Gregorio Martín had been able to acquire a house and lands to replace those he was about to lose.

The aggrieved sons added their statements. Their father, they said, had married a second time and had a son by the second wife. While Gregorio was preparing his testament, this wife's uncle was present, urging that she and her child receive bequests at the expense of the offspring of the first marriage. The disinherited sons said that they had always been obedient to their father and deserved no such treatment as they were receiving. These allegations are borne out by Gregorio's emphasis on specifying bequests to the third son, while excluding the first two from their share of the real property.[4]

The record of inheritance among past and present residents of the San Juan Basin shows that the greatest difficulties arise when limited property is to be divided among many people, especially if there are heirs from two or more marriages. The sharpest disputes arise among people who have experienced recent reductions in their total property. Impoverishment has a predictable negative effect on human relations, in that it reduces capacity to fulfill traditional obligations and undermines the rules of behavior toward kin.

TRADE RELATIONS

Trading was a major source of livelihood for settlers in the Lower Chama Valley. However, if the volume of data from the archives is any measure, more of the trade in which the settlers were involved was illegal than legal. While caravan trade to Chihuahua out of Abiquiu is not even mentioned until 1800, there are repeated references to unlicensed trade with Utes in merchandise on which the required taxes went unpaid or which was altogether banned.

In 1735 Teniente Diego de Torres, deputy of the alcalde mayor of Santa Cruz, was accused of having opened trade with a group of Comanches at Ojo Caliente before arrival of the responsible authorities. Juan García de la Mora said that Torres had sent a servant to negotiate for buffalo robes in exchange for belduques. In his own defense, Torres stated that the Comanches had threatened to burn their own goods unless the trading started, because they were nervous about the Utes camped in the vicinity. Paulín de Beytia, who had arrived in the midst of the unauthorized trading, stated that Juan García de la Mora and his brother were also bartering when he arrived.[5]

Not long thereafter Abiquiu became the official center for an annual trade fair attended by Capote and Sabuagana Utes. The Capotes at that time ranged the San Juan Basin and its tributary valleys, while the Sabuaganas ranged to the north and west, from the Dolores River to the vicinity of present-day Grand

Junction, Colorado. By mid-eighteenth century, these Utes were well supplied with horses and were moving southward, dislodging Navajos from the Governador-Cañon Largo area' and committing depredations on the settlements of the Chama watershed from time to time. Albert Schroeder credits the Capotes with the stock depredations complained of in 1736 by the settlers of the Río del Oso. This led to a large tracking sortie in which no Utes were found before cold weather put an end to the venture. The next major sortie followed the August 1747 raids on Abiquiu and Ojo Caliente, for which Sabuaganas and Capotes were blamed, although the real culprits were apparently Comanches with some Moache Ute allies.[6]

By the early eighteenth century, the Moaches were remaining largely east of the Rio Grande, moving between Taos and the eastern portion of the San Luis Valley and hunting seasonally on the Plains, where they maintained a friendly relationship with the Comanches. By the 1750's they had fallen out with the Comanches, shifting their friendship to the Jicarilla Apaches. Although the range of the Moache Utes is sometimes shown as extending westward deep into the San Juan Mountains, their main contact with colonial settlements focused on Taos, where they traded and intermittently raided.[7]

The Sabuaganas encountered in late summer of 1776 by the Dominguez-Escalante party near the Gunnison River were horsemen who dwelt in skin tipis, gathered in large groups, and hunted the buffalo. The expedition was met on the trail by a party of eighty mounted warriors who conducted them to their camp of thirty tipis to buy a supply of dried buffalo meat. This was the band which the Genízaro interpreters and their uninvited companions had been seeking for purposes of trade. Disregarding the objections of the priests, they immediately proceeded to carry out their purpose according to a well-established routine.[8]

Since they had ready access to the nonequestrian bands of the Great Basin of Utah, the Sabuaganas were probably the main source of captives traded at Abiquiu. Both the Capotes and Sabuaganas camped regularly in the vicinity of Abiquiu, apparently remaining at some distance in order to be able to trade without supervision.[9]

The Capotes participated with the Sabuaganas in early raids against the Hopis and Navajos, but later developed friendship with the Navajos. Schroeder suggests that the specific interdiction on unlicensed trade with the Utes in 1778 was based on fear of strengthening the Capote-Navajo alliance.[10] An equally plausible purpose, however, would have been to reduce the number of horses going to the Capotes and Sabuaganas in exchange for their child captives. The Sabuaganas seem to have been the main partners in this kind of trade, and a number of nomadic tribes originally received their horses through Ute middlemen, the better to harass the settlements.

ATTEMPTS TO CURB CONTRABAND TRADE

Interdictions on unlicensed trade with the Indians were decreed early and often but were weakly enforced. In 1737 Governor and Captain-General Olavide y Michelena issued a decree forbidding the purchase or ransom of Indians, male or female, converted or heathen, without recording the transaction before the appropriate justice. Penalties for this infraction included a hundred peso fine or, for Indian transgressors, two hundred lashes. The punishment automatically carried with it loss of the human merchandise.[11]

Despite the severity of the announced penalty, its enforcement was exceedingly lenient in 1739, when Miguel de Salazar of Santa Cruz was found guilty of illegally purchasing a girl captive from nomadic Indians in Taos. Salazar's companion in the transaction was allowed to keep the girl in order to be able to raise his share of the fine, since he was too poor to make immediate payment.[12]

Governor Francisco Trebol Navarro's 1778 edict banning unlicensed trade with the Utes replaced an edict published three years before by Governor Mendinueta. Trebol made a stronger ban, mentioning that Mendinueta's ban had been flouted not only by vecinos, Indians, and Genízaros, but by the very alcaldes and other officials whose duty it was to enforce regulations. Trebol stated that transgression of this type "leads not only to defiance of submission and respect to the prohibitor but injury to the common good of the Republic, since a few enjoy the benefits which would accrue to all if they did not go to the Ute country, since the Utes would then come to ours as they did before these troubles started."

The governor feared that the greed and thoughtlessness of the unauthorized traders might provoke new outbreaks of hostility between settlers and Utes. He also feared that the settlers might "participate in idolatrous acts or uphold Gentile errors . . . all of which have been incurred by those who practice this illicit commerce, according to reliable information which has reached me and caused me grave concern." This would naturally lead the "infidels" to persist in their "barbaric beliefs," and would also increase the danger that the traders, to curry favor with the Utes, would reveal military secrets.

Governor Trebol further added to the penalties by promising a reward to be divided three ways among those who informed on violators of the edict, the judge who prosecuted them, and the royal treasury. Copies of the edict were sent to all Spanish settlements and Indian pueblos and were returned with a signed statement by the town authorities that they had publicly announced its provisions.[13]

Despite the lure of reward for informing on illicit traders, the first such revelation on record implicating Abiquiu traders is dated 1783. In this case, the mission father, Fray Diego Muñoz de Jurado, notified the alcalde mayor of Abiquiu, Santiago Martín, that his own son was among a group of eleven unlicensed traders who had gone to the Ute country. The alcalde and a party of ten "Spaniards" and two Indians overtook eight members of the trading party, jailed them, and confiscated their belongings. The traders were carrying small supplies of corn, wheat flour, tools such as awls and trade knives, punche tobacco, *bizcocho* (hard, sweetened biscuits), and a few spare horses and mules. The tone of the final report suggests little intention to inflict severe punishment on the wrongdoers.[14]

In the 1780's, Governor Juan Bautista de Anza continued trying to curb unlicensed trade into the Ute country, which had already depleted the horse herds in the colony and had involved men of the highest and lowest standing, both directly and indirectly, in irregularities. In response to the governor's report of July 29, 1784, Comandante General Jacobo Ugarte y Loyola[15] stated that several unlicensed traders from the Santa Cruz de la Cañada jurisdiction had protested the fines and confiscations ordered by former Governor Trebol in 1778, and that a number of punishments had been suspended. In January 1784, the mission priest of Santa Cruz admitted sending a servant on such an unlicensed trading expedition, and neither he nor the servant had been punished.

Ugarte noted that since peace had been restored with the Utes and Comanches, and since the Navajos had been induced to serve as allies and spies in the campaign against the Gila Apaches, trade could be considered as a desirable corollary of peace, but only to the extent that it was kept under official scrutiny. Uncontrolled trade could readily lead to "excesses and disorders" of a kind that could stimulate antagonisms and war. Ugarte cited the prevalence of the "floaters and criminals" who stole horses from the settlements to trade with the Indians. When a rightful owner recaptured his livestock, the Indians felt they had been robbed. Some irresponsible traders, upon concluding business with Indians, would steal the Indians' livestock as they departed. Ugarte wrote that such vicious practices could only be stopped by arranging between colonial and Indian leaders for official trade fairs at specified times and places.

The Genízaros of Abiquiu, wrote Ugarte, were demanding their promised reward (presumably for informing on unlicensed traders to the Utes). The balance of fines collected would be spent constructing a secure prison in Santa Fe and purchasing gunpowder for the colony.

In October 1786, Ugarte added instructions for excluding irresponsible elements from the proposed trade fairs. Supervision should be furnished by soldiers from the presidio or by the alcalde mayor of each community selected as the fairground. Ugarte further instructed that Indian leaders be kept informed of trade regulations and be urged to lodge complaints against violators with the appropriate authorities.[16]

During this same period, however, the prosecution of unauthorized traders was in the hands of local authorities, and the penalties were far from the maximum. In 1785 a trading party of five was brought before the Abiquiu alcalde, José Martín, at Santa Rosa de Abiquiu. They had just returned from a trip on foot to the San Miguel River of western Colorado. One of the party had gone off alone in search of Ute customers, had fallen ill, and died on the homeward trail. The survivors were fined and condemned to two months' labor in the "royal houses of this villa," Santa Cruz de la Cañada, probably working at road or bridge repair.[17]

In 1797 about two dozen small, unlicensed traders went before Manuel García de la Mora, alcalde mayor of Santa Cruz, for a hearing. Traveling alone or in pairs, mostly on foot, they had made trips to the Río de los Pinos, the La Sal Mountains, and the Uncompahgre River, all in western Colorado. They had traded corn and flour for dressed deerhides, buffalo robes, and the prized chamois of the mountain sheep. Although none denied their guilt, several justified their actions by the poverty and debt which had driven them to seek illegal means to quick profit. It is possible that some of these traders actually were poor, but one of them, Mateo García (de Noriega), was a member of a prominent and wealthy family.

All the accused in this case were given a month in jail, and those who said they had not succeeded in making any trades were fined twelve pesos. Those who admitted completing trade were fined twenty pesos and were threatened with six months in the Santa Fé jail and a fifty peso fine if they repeated their offense. The alcalde mayor denounced the authorities in the partidos and plazas from which these traders came, because not one had reported the violations. Apparently, some Genízaros had informed on the traders.[18]

EXPANSION OF ABIQUIU TRADE

The authorities continued to bear down on illicit trade, but with recognition that there was no stopping it. In 1802 Governor Fernando de Chacón reported to the comandante general in Chihuahua that he believed it was impossible to stamp out the cultivation of punche tobacco (which he also called *tabaco zimarrón*), because in both the Rio Arriba and Taos jurisdictions it was an important trade item with the Utes and Jicarilla Apaches. Chacón suggested that fully domesticated tobacco be taxed in open, legal trade, but that the cultivation of punche be banned only in areas where there was no *cambalache* (barter trade) with Indians.[19]

Trade with the Timpanagos Utes of the Utah Lake, its date of origin unknown, was already well established by 1813. In September of that year, a party of traders who had been on a trip to central Utah from March to July were called before the alcalde mayor of Santa Cruz for questioning. Mauricio Arze, Lagos García, Miguel Tenorio, Felipe Gomez, José Santiago Vigil, Gabriel Quintana, and José Velasquez were the members of the party. The first two spoke fluent Ute and may have been of at least part-Ute ancestry.

Tenorio, Gomez, Vigil, Quintana, and Velasquez all answered the questions put to them as though they had rehearsed in advance. They said the Timpanagos had greeted them very warmly and had immediately brought for their inspection children of both sexes whom they wanted to trade for horses. The traders said they had refused, explaining that the *tata* (in this instance the comandante general) had forbidden them to allow the Timpanagos to sell their own children. The Timpanagos were bitterly disappointed, saying that this trade had helped them greatly in the past. They wanted the horses badly and tried to stampede the *caballada* (the string of horses, of which the traders had apparently brought a large number).

By their own account, the traders then went further west until they found Utes willing to trade *gamuzas* (dressed hides) for the horses they had brought. This trading seems to have been accomplished near Sevier Lake. According to their account, the traders had finally been able to return with a large number of hides.[20]

If this account leaves the impression that trade in central Utah was institutionalized by 1813, it was even more so in 1820 when the Sandoval party conducted trade with the "Timpanagos, Sampuchis and Saguarichis . . . according to custom."[21] The number of captives who passed through Abiquiu as a result of this trade is hard to determine, since only those who remained in the homes of local people were baptized by the missionary of Santo Tomás. The earliest Ute baptism recorded at this mission was that of a ninety-year-old man who requested baptism in 1759 and who apparently was not a captive.[22] After 1760 most baptisms recorded were of infants or children "bought of the Utes," also listed as "heathen infant" or "Indian child of unknown parents." These listings became more frequent early in the nineteenth century but were never very numerous. The child's master was the godparent.

After trading with California began to develop over the "Old Spanish Trail," Abiquiu became an important center of trade, some of it legitimate. The 1827 census enumerated six merchants and forty-eight craftsmen as Abiquiu residents.[23] This did not necessarily mean that contraband trade declined; in fact, the market for Navajo captives rose in the 1830's and reached its peak in the 1860's. The commerce which developed in later years in Tierra Amarilla and the San Juan Basin under the impetus of settlement and the gold rush in Colorado followed a pattern of combined legal and extralegal transactions. By the late nineteenth century, however, the twilight zone between permitted and proscribed activities had vanished.

FORMAL ADMINISTRATION
AND COMMUNITY LEADERSHIP

During the colonial period the governor at the provincial level and the alcalde at the local level had to administer without such needed personnel as notaries, legal advisors, and other administrative aides. They also had to combine military leadership with important judicial, police, civil, fiscal, and other functions. Due to population growth and governmental reform measures, a more complex apparatus of government began to emerge late in the eighteenth century. The establishment of new posts to fulfill special functions was stimulated by the constitutional movement, which was heartily endorsed throughout New Spain. Even so, the shortage of trained personnel left many functions concentrated in the hands of a few in peripheral communities like Abiquiu. The local leadership continued to flow from the tatas, the lineage and community elders, who tempered their authority with greater conformity to local tradition than to colonial regulations. Thus it was that the very administrative inadequacy which permitted the growth of extralegal commerce in the settlements of the Lower Chama Valley and other peripheral areas also stimulated the growth of an internally-controlled community ethic.[24]

Whenever the colonial authorities issued regulations which conflicted with the prevailing community ethic, the settlers resisted, and it can be said that in Abiquiu such resistance was usually effective. The history of refusal to form grid-plan towns, to comply with regulations on trade with the Utes, and (on the part of the Genízaros in 1831) to bow to the alcalde's measure of their grant lands, has already been documented. In later times the tensions of clashing values have centered on the ecclesiastical demand that Penitentes forego their special ritual observances, the current Anglo-American objections to what are seen as "nepotic" political practices by Hispanos, and the grave and continuing conflicts occasioned by land loss under a dominant system which treats land purely as a chattel.

STRAINED RELATIONS OVER BOOTY

The best long-term example of tension between the values of the state and those of the community is provided by the issue of war booty.[25] In early colonial times the winner took the spoils, and the lure of booty was a sufficient inducement for settlers, Genízaros, and Pueblo warriors to serve as volunteers in the militia. In 1746 Miguel Martín Serrano, listing his meritorious acts in hand-to-hand combat with the Comanches, boasted: "During your Excellency's term, they carried off my entire herd of horses and I and my sons went forth with some of the residents and took it away from them and I took those belonging to the enemy away from them, together with their leather jackets and saddles."[26] Militia service was hazardous and the unpaid volunteers had to furnish their own mounts, arms, and supplies. With reasonable luck, however, the hazards and sacrifices were amply rewarded.

An 1818 report submitted to the captain of cavalry volunteers of the militia company of Santa Cruz de la Cañada includes the records of three officers from Abiquiu. The *teniente* (lieutenant), Francisco Salazar, rated as *noble* (meaning that his honor was so well established that he could not be imprisoned for debt), had participated in three campaigns. In the first one, five stolen horses and a captive vecina had been recovered from the enemy. In the second, a bloodless campaign of 1817, French infiltrators were induced to withdraw from the frontier. In the third, a current Navajo campaign, Salazar had killed seven enemies and had taken two prisoners, ninety-three mounts and twenty-three hundred head of sheep. In two campaigns, the *alferez* (standard-bearer), Mariano Martinez, had killed four braves, taken a boy prisoner, and captured fourteen horses. He also shared in the booty taken by Salazar, as did the third militiaman, First Sergeant Diego Sisneros.[27]

In 1821, however, new regulations on division of spoils required that they be turned over to the highest ranking officer of the unit for his decision as to their disposition. The reaction to this regulation in Abiquiu was so indignant that it became difficult to raise a levy of infantry, the least prestigious rank in the militia. The alcalde of Abiquiu reported to Interim Governor Facundo Melgares: "Dissatisfaction with your order concerning booty in war is the cause of the cooling off of opinion, since people complain bitterly that they exposed themselves and had no reward."[28]

A few weeks later, the same alcalde reported on the insubordination of the citizen, Miguel Sanchez, when called to campaign duty. Sanchez hid at his home, and when the alcalde finally came in person and "flung the king upon him" (brandished his rod of office in sign of royal authority), Sanchez replied defiantly that he would not obey the alcalde nor even the governor himself.[29]

In 1834 the people of Abiquiu petitioned the political chief to conduct campaigns "according to the custom and well-liked practice which general preference and long observance have given the status of law in this Territory." At this time the town officials announced that the militia could not go out on campaign at the moment because of the severe winter and the poor state of their horses.[30]

In 1845 the issue of booty was still alive. José María Chavez, commander of a punitive expedition against the Utes, departed for the northern frontier, and he received instructions from the prefect of the north, Juan Andrés Archuleta, to leave small amounts of booty in the hands of the individual takers. In the case of a big haul, however, Chavez was to supervise its distribution among the entire group. Chavez was eager to win this campaign, even if it meant crossing the Arkansas River and entering territory of the United States, where the Utes apparently received arms and encouragement to continue raiding in New Mexico. However, the large militia force under Chavez' command was less than enthusiastic. Although drafted for two months' service, militiamen flooded Chavez with petitions before the end of the first month. They complained about their lack of arms, supplies, shoes, and mounts and insisted on going home. Archuleta's solution to the booty problem clearly was not to their liking.[31]

THE EXTENDED-KIN MODEL OF INTERACTION

Thus, from 1821 to 1845, although the settlers were not entirely successful in imposing their will on the authorities, they were able to win leniency in enforcement of regulations. And when they were sufficiently annoyed by a new regulation, they could successfully withhold their services. The government truly lacked the power to enforce a regulation which the settlers rejected. This does not mean that the New Mexican frontier communities were without the law. In all the Chama Valley settlements, the extended-kin model of interaction produced orderly sets of relations.

This interaction model extended even to Utes and to other Indians with whom the settlers maintained close relations, reflected in the use of kin terminology and in the practice of "respectful" behavior. Such terminology and behavior prevailed between Atanacio Trujillo and his Ute friends, when he consulted them about taking a group of settlers to the Conejos area in the spring of 1849. After their parley at the Ute camp near San Antonio Mountain, the Utes took leave of Atanacio, saying: "Go, Atanacio, and don't worry. We are just like your sons and you and your sons are just like a father in our hearts." Soon after the settlement was made, the Utes came to visit, shared a meal, and exchanged gifts.[32]

No such courtesies were extended to individual Utes with whom friendship had not yet been established. In 1820, the

Sandoval trading party visited the Timpanagos and other Utes in central Utah and learned of a plot to kill them. However, one of the Utes agreed to guide the party to safety, and he went with them back to Abiquiu.

The Ute asked only one reward for his aid. His wife and daughter had been captured by Kiowas and he asked Sandoval to tell him in which settlement they had been sold. Sandoval replied evasively that he had heard of three Indians recently purchased in Taos, one by "Bautista the Frenchman" and the others by the alferez, Don Juan Cristobal García. Aside, Sandoval boasted: "I didn't try to enlighten the Ute to the fact that his daughter was in our community but rather tried to conceal it." The Ute set out for Taos with an interpreter who apparently revealed the truth, for presently, he was back in Abiquiu demanding the return of his daughter from Juan Trujillo. At Trujillo's request, the alcalde of Abiquiu confiscated a horse belonging to Sandoval as indemnity for the loss of his captive, since the governor had decreed that a Ute was worth one horse.

Sandoval appealed to Governor Facundo Melgares, who denied making any such ruling, except for payment to Utes protesting the wrongful killing of a fellow-tribesman. Melgares pointed out that the purchase of "gentile" (unconverted) Indians was forbidden, that whoever had purchased the girl was guilty of an infraction, and that no indemnity whatever could be exacted for her loss.[33]

Sandoval's conspicuous ingratitude to the Ute and the inconsiderate treatment he received at Abiquiu seem to have been because this Ute was a stranger and nobody's trading partner. Even today, San Juan Basin Hispanos make a distinction between Utes with whose families they have maintained a friendship for a generation or more and those with whom no close ties have been developed. The ties of padrinazgo and compadrazgo have been important evidence of links, although they operate in one direction only, no Utes having been recorded as godparents of a Hispano child. There is a tradition that when an Indian captive was raised in a Hispano household and remained there as an adult, he or she was to be addressed by the children of the family with appropriate kinship terminology, such as "aunt" or "uncle," always using the respectful second-person pronoun *usted.*

AGE AND GENERATION: RESPECT

The most decisive factor in shaping social relations in the Chama Valley and San Juan Basin was the hierarchy of status defined by the relative age, generation, and honor of the inter-acting parties within an expanded-kin network. The hierarchical ordering of relations was most clearly reflected in the use of the second-person pronouns *tu* (intimate) and *usted* (respectful), in which the regional usage differs markedly from usage elsewhere in the Spanish-speaking world. Elsewhere, servants of whatever age are normally addressed with the familiar *tu*, since the very word for servant (*criado*) has the connotation of a minor who has been raised by the family. The unusual stress placed by the descendants of the Chama Valley pioneers upon emphasizing the respect elements in the most intimate relationships, includ-ing those with Indian servants, tends to limit the use of *tu* largely to people of a younger age group or generation.

Today in the San Juan Basin, brothers and sisters close in age address one another as *tu* in childhood. But once grown, siblings of opposite sex address one another as *usted,* as younger siblings from early childhood address much older siblings of either sex. Even a husband and wife often address one another as *usted,* although husbands more often address wives as *tu* than the reverse. It is customary for people of an older generation to address younger people, whether related or not, as *tu*. In the San Juan Basin this usage is customary only with younger people of the same sex as the speaker. Elsewhere, *tu* is used in addressing younger people of both sexes. There are times when even parents address their own children as *usted,* as when an adult child serves as godparent for its newborn sibling, creating a compadrazgo relationship between parent and child.[34]

According to San Juan Basin informants, this marked prefer-ence for formal terminology among close-knit kin groups is an important way to express affection. Intimate forms are more readily used among people whose relationship is casual and of diminished intensity.

At times, contradictions arise between the principles of age and generation which create awkwardness for children learning which behaviors are appropriate between different categories of kin. These are uncertainties similar to those experienced when learning the forms of irregular verbs. In a large family, children may grow up with uncles and aunts some years younger than themselves. One day, in a community of the San Juan Basin, two children were observed walking down the street and dragging between them a tiny girl, screaming in protest. When asked what was the matter with their little sister, they replied that she was not their sister, she was their little aunt: "Come along, Auntie, please do," they added politely, as they continued dragging her down the street.

People of one's own generation who are much older are addressed in terminology implying a distance of a generation, but only if the relationship is close and the emphasis on respect toward one's elder is vital. This principle can be further extended, as when a child raised by her father's elder brother grew up calling him "Gram'pa."

The term "cousin" in New Mexico connotes more respect and affection than in Spain and Mexico, where it carries a connotation of "fool."[35] The term is used among near and distant cousins and among people whose relationship is unknown if they share a surname, always in a context of friendliness and egalitarianism. An elderly Hispano of the San Juan Basin uses cousin terminology in addressing a family of young people of mixed Navajo and Hispanic ancestry who share his surname. They acquired the surname from their Navajo grandfather, who was raised as a captive in the household of a wealthy relative of the old man's stepfather, from whom the old man's surname derives. This usage is considered very friendly and courteous in the San Juan Basin.

Equal divergence from other Spanish-speaking regions is apparent in the northern New Mexico use of honorifics. "Don" is never used as a term of address but only in respectful reference to people not present, frequently to people long dead. Nonrelated adults, even close friends over many years, express respect for one another by addressing one another as "señor" or "señora." Here again, terminology which would be considered coldly formalistic outside of New Mexico marks relationships of great warmth and intimacy.[36]

FRATERNAL RELATIONS

The most enduring and vital relationship in the frontier communities of New Mexico has been the fraternal bond between people of the same generation. They had to place reliance upon one another in the daily tasks of raising crops and livestock and the hazardous enterprises of trading with and raiding against nomadic Indians. In time of need they could rely upon one another. Relations of a fraternal type between equals were marked by slight but distinct dominant-subordinate differentiations based on relative seniority.

The pattern of fraternal relationships is formed in early childhood, when parents delegate authority to older children so that they may begin to assume responsibility for younger children. As the children grow, the adolescents and late preadolescents form an authority group in relation to their younger siblings, while each child bears a particular responsibility for the child next to him in age.

Fraternal relationships go beyond the nuclear family and even beyond closely related families who live close together. Within a small and close-knit hamlet, the entire community is informally age-graded, with all who form an age-group oriented toward fraternal relations with one another. Within each age group, precise degrees of deference are accorded to senior members. Work relations bring together brothers, cousins, and affinal relatives. Men, much more than women, are drawn into small, informal hierarchies of decision-making and job-assigning.

Fraternal terminology was particularly developed through the Penitente Brotherhood, which channeled fraternal activities, such as care for the sick or incapacitated or for families of recently deceased members. In the San Juan Basin hamlets today, the term of address used toward and between people of Penitente or formerly Penitente families is "mano" (short for *hermano,* brother) and "mana" (short for *hermana,* sister). Penitentes are often referred to as *manitos,* especially by migrant laborers from Mexico, who find their fraternal relations too rustic for anything but humorous reference. The *hermano mayor* (elder brother) was the chief authority figure among the group of officials of each morada, known collectively as the *hermanos de luz* (brothers of light). The hermano mayor was treated according to the rules of seniority, although he might not in fact be chronologically senior to all.

THE POSITION OF WOMEN

Hierarchic rules in Hispanic countries have universally placed women in a status subordinate to and dependent on men, with a large element of custodialism derived from both European and Near Eastern sources. The code regarding women in relation to men applied theoretically in New Mexico, but in practice it was often disregarded. This was due to frontier conditions and low population, which made it impossible to maintain the sexual division of labor that prevailed elsewhere in New Spain. Women and girls apparently never took up mining or the herding of livestock in distant pastures, but they did care for animals grazing in the *dehesas* (community irrigated pastures) or for goats grazing on the hillsides near the placita. Men, on the other hand, did their own cooking in sheep camps or on buffalo hunts and trading journeys. They were and still are willing to cook the meals and mind the children if the wife is ill. Fathers still take an active part in teaching skills and values to their children. [37]

Even in the forms of recreation most associated with masculinity, women were not excluded. Contests of horsemanship are the traditional outlet for male display. And in Rosa as in many other New Mexico villages of the past, the Feast of Santiago on July 25 was celebrated each year with horseraces and *corridas de gallos* (rooster pulls) with frequent accidents due to the recklessness of the male participants. The following day was the Feast of Santa Ana, and women would mount on horseback and hold tamer contests with a chicken destined to be cooked. There was a great deal of betting on the races and women gambled—if not more than the men, at least as much.

Women knew how to butcher and skin animals and make *carne seca* (jerky), as the Indian women did. There is no record, however, of Hispanic women who made *teguas* (moccasins).

People usually obtained their moccasins from Indian women, and sometimes the men made them.

Male settlers cleared the fields, dug ditches, and prepared the soil for planting, unless they had hired hands or captives to do the job for them. Women, old men, and children did the major work in planting, irrigating, and harvesting, with the exception of those wealthy or elderly women who were sometimes specialists in handiwork, herbal medicine and midwifery, or reading for purposes of religious observance.

Today's women of the San Juan Basin and Chama Valley are equally active in assuming tasks which in other Hispanic societies are reserved for men. They handle trucks and tractors as a matter of course, and frequently earn anything from egg money to a full-time wage. These tasks, performed in the name of the family, make it possible for them to continue living on ranches. Girls and women constantly phrase their intention to earn wages—not as the fulfillment of a personal ambition, but in order to help their menfolk keep up the ranch. Teaching, secretarial work, and nursing are the preferred vocations, especially because they can be suspended during years of intensive child-rearing and then resumed in later years. Two women had taken night and summer courses whenever possible since the 1940's to earn teacher certification, while rearing their families.[38]

PARENT-CHILD RELATIONS

Relations between parents and their children are seen as a process of guidance into becoming an adult capable of functioning within a well-understood code. The tradition-oriented parent unhesitatingly communicates the rules of right and wrong, offering little room for alternatives and few explanations, since children simply must be told and discussion is not necessary. Younger or more flexible parents do give time to discussion and explanation. Infants and small children receive a great deal of tender attention and little demand from all members of the family. But between the ages of approximately four and eight, they are subjected to fairly intense pressure for conformity, and in late preadolescence discipline reaches its peak. At this age children are often described as "lazy" or "stubborn" and overt or covert signs of rebellion cause their parents frequent anxiety. Once adolescence is well underway, severity is relaxed and teenagers are treated as young adults. At this age they are expected to assume responsibilities commensurate with adulthood, such as earning wages in part-time or summer jobs in order to purchase their school clothes and textbooks. Throughout northern New Mexico today, the scarcity of jobs for teenagers contributes heavily to the high school dropout rate.[39]

Parents counsel their teenage children, but do not necessarily expect to be obeyed. They do insist that respect and honor be upheld in the family home and the home community. If boys and young men must be drunk and disorderly, it is better that they be far from home. This is one reason why the young men of Rosa used to work for a time in mining communities, not so much to make money as to sow wild oats. In prior generations, the escape valve for men who found the village code of behavior too constricting was provided by trading journeys, buffalo hunts, and other strenuous activities.[40]

CONCEPTS OF MASCULINITY AND FEMININITY

The New Mexico code of respect and honor as the guide to behavior within the family and home community applies to men and women alike and somewhat displaces the Hispanic concept of *vergüenza* (shame). This term has been described as belonging particularly within the sphere of values of the female in Andalusía, Spain, and also as the dominant ideal for New Mexico villages.[41] Vergüenza centers on an ideal of female modesty, purity, and reserve which requires more sequestration of women than was ever possible in the Chama Valley and San Juan Basin. Even the term *sin vergüenza* (shameless) carries less sting in the San Juan Basin than in Andalusía, being used most often in good-humored reference to the behavior of small children who cannot be expected to know better. *Sin vergüenza* is a term sometimes applied in referring to those Utes who do not observe Hispanic norms of behavior; but since many Utes do actually comply with the norms considered most basic by Hispanos, they do not constitute in relation to Hispanos of the

San Juan Basin a stratified group of sin vergüenzas as do the Gypsies of Andalusia. *Sin vergüenza* as a term used in northern New Mexico carries its greatest sting when applied to Hispano businessmen who profiteer in the Anglo pattern, in violation of the code of kinship solidarity. In this context, *sin vergüenza* connotes the antithesis of respect and honor, as concepts defining the quality of relations among people, rather than expressing concern for reputation and the *quédirán* (what will people say), traditionally the focal concern of vergüenza.[42]

An example of the contrast between the values of northern New Mexico and other Hispanic societies is revealed in the treatment of women who have given birth out of wedlock. Critical population shortages in New Mexico and the overwhelming desire for children guaranteed that such a woman would have no difficulty in finding a decent man to marry her and adopt her child. The importance of being a *pater* (sociological father) even takes precedence over being a *genitor* (biological father), so that men of the San Juan Basin who have married and adopted under these circumstances assert with pride that they really *are* the father of the child they have fostered. The model for this relationship is Saint Joseph, the pater of Jesus, for whom veneration is profound in northern New Mexico. There are many images of Saint Joseph to be found throughout the area, showing him as a standing, crowned figure holding the infant Jesus on one arm. His other hand holds the flowering staff which is the symbol of his purity. Men pray to him for strength against earthly temptations and also for a "good death," meaning death preceded by the full benefits of the last rites.[43]

There are recorded instances of a man repudiating his wife on the claim that she was pregnant by another man. Commonly, community members explain these instances as expressions of "insane jealousy" on the part of the husband, even when his accusations may have been based on fact. On the other hand, when a man accepts as his a child who may have been another man's, the sly innuendoes about the presumed cuckold are tempered by the approval the community feels for his willingness to serve as pater.[44]

Cultures of Hispanic derivation have always had highly differentiated ideals of masculinity and femininity, expressed in role-differentiated behavior and separation of life domains. In part, the ideal of a man as defender of the family honor and custodian of the honor of his wife, daughters, and sisters has been influenced by the Arab occupation of Spain during nearly six centuries of the Christian era. Anglo-American perception of these behaviors and domains, however, has been affected by sensationalized interpretations of *machismo* (virility) to be found in the works of Ernest Hemingway and many social scientists.

In New Mexico the masculine ideal is best expressed in the term *hombría* (manliness), exemplified by the hardworking, responsible, loyal, and affectionate man of the family. There is a strong emphasis on fulfillment of work roles, as witnessed by the term *mujerota* (meaning a lot of woman), which is applied to women who are tireless and tender wives and mothers, superb housewives, devoted Catholics, and active in their communities. In sum, masculine and feminine ideals are linked with family functioning, and the family model is the Holy Family.

Behavior which is often seen by Anglo-American observers as machismo constitutes deviant behavior so far as the Hispano community is concerned. For instance, the young men who go to dances to start fights, a recurrent phenomenon since public dances began to be held in the San Juan Basin, are always identified by community members as marginal people, rejected by both Hispano and Anglo society and resentful of both.[45] Male assertiveness within limits that are acceptable is confined to daring and even reckless action, such as riding half-tamed horses, "going wild" in horseraces, and laying "crazy bets" on the outcome. The association of equestrian display with assertions of irresponsible maleness is widespread in New Mexico. Curiously, it is laid at the door of the very nomadic Indians who learned their horsemanship from the Spanish settlers. "It is the horses who make men wild," declared a Las Vegas buffalo hunter of the 1860's as he refused to teach his small son to ride. "With a horse under me, I myself am no better than a Comanche."[46]

9

Paths of Change

SHIFTS IN KIN-LINKED INSTITUTIONS

Preceding chapters have related the history of Hispanic settlement of the Chama Valley and San Juan Basin, documenting
the constant contact between settlers and Indians, especially
Genízaros and Utes. The social structure of these communities
was analyzed, emphasizing population factors and the weakness
of institutions of control external to the community. In this
concluding chapter, focus will be on the processes of change
and on the kinds of sociocultural change which have taken place
and continue to take place in the same communities.

Because of the central importance of kinship as an organizing
force in the communities of northern New Mexico, what might
appear to be minor shifts in kin-linked institutions are important indicators of change processes. Reference has already been
made to tendencies in colonial times for certain categories of
relatives to marry one another, and for baptismal godparents to
be drawn preferentially from the kin group (See chapter 7,
footnote 24). Through pedigree studies in the San Juan Basin, it
has been possible to show the dynamic relationship between
these two institutions and the nature of observed changes.

MARRIAGE CHOICES

The marriage choices of a single lineage group of the San Juan Basin and of the families into which they married were traced over four generations, and baptismal godparent choices for the children of these marriages were also traced. In all, 331 marriage choices and 152 baptismal godparent choices for which pedigree information was available were analyzed.[1]

From the church dispensations listed in eighteenth and nineteenth century marriage records, it was already evident that there had been for a long time a high incidence of marriages within the second or even the first degree of cousinhood. Unions within proscribed categories for which no dispensation is permitted and which cannot be solemnized by the marriage sacrament, but which have nonetheless been known to occur, include marriage between stepparent and stepchild, between stepsiblings and various polygamous arrangements. The latter has usually involved a relationship with a close relative of the official wife, particularly a younger sister.

Table 2 shows the marriage patterns which emerged from study of the 331 marriage choices in the San Juan Basin for which considerable pedigree information was assembled.

Table 2 shows the persistence of patterns in selecting marriage partners, of which there is record from colonial times, particularly the marriage of people who are blood relatives and the marriages over generations between people of two large lineages.

In his 1812 report to the Spanish Cortes, Pedro Bautista Pino stated that poor people wishing a dispensation in order to marry a relative were barred from doing so by the expense of traveling four hundred leagues to Durango, Mexico, the seat of the nearest bishop. As a consequence, "many people compelled by love, live and rear families in adultery." The compulsions of love may have determined choice of marriage partner among people who owned little property. However, marriages requiring dispensation because of kinship between the partners were regularly contracted among propertied families, who arranged marriages without extensive prior consultation with the proposed marriage partners.[2]

TABLE 2

Spouses are known blood relatives 9

Spouses share surname of at least one
grandparent, hence are by inference
related to one another 25

Spouses are known affinal relatives 35

Siblings marry spouses who are kin to
one another 32

Siblings marry spouses who share surname
of at least one grandparent, hence are by
inference related to one another 23

Siblings share a single spouse, serially 3

Siblings share a single spouse,
polygamously 8

Spouses are related through one
previous spouse 9

Siblings follow one another in marrying
Anglo spouses 18

Siblings follow one another in marrying
Indian spouses 6
                                         ———
                                         168

 Cliofes M. de Jaramillo correctly notes that arranged marriages between close relatives were common among the most elite families of New Mexico in the late nineteenth century. Her explanation that "since there were so few pure Spanish families in the small villages and so few opportunities of becoming acquainted with outsiders, there was a great deal of intermarriage between first and second cousins, in order to keep the Spanish blood from mixing" need not be taken too literally.[3]

 The extent to which "Spanish blood" did mix through the adjustment of ethnic labels has already been demonstrated, since no amount of the ideology of casticismo could prevail in a society of such critical population shortage and so little secure hereditary wealth. As a matter of fact, the best way to guarantee relatively pure Spanish lineage was to seek a spouse from the colonial aristocracy of Mexico, people who were no kin to the settlers of New Mexico. But such marriages rarely occurred, while cousin marriage and sibling exchange were commoner among the settlers of visible means and prestige than among those with the least apparent means.

MARRIAGE AND MEANS

In Andalusía, Spain, both cousin-marriage and marriages between pairs of brothers and sisters are most common among families who own small farms. The arrangement is advantageous because it delays the partition of the farm lands and increases the labor force on them, united by ties of blood and marriage. It continues to be advantageous as long as the property unit can provide adequate livelihood for the whole group.[4] The same situation seems to have been operative in colonial New Mexico, where the subdivision of irrigable lands into narrow strips occurred sooner if the heirs to a property were married to nonrelatives than if they were married to relatives.

As population increased in any community and the land base became proportionally more limited, petitioners for new grants associated in groups which crossed kin lines. In the early stages of settlement of a grant, fewer people were close relatives than after the passage of a couple of generations. In the first generation of settlement, therefore, more marriages took place between unrelated individuals than in later generations, which characteristically had more cousin marriage and sibling exchange. Starting with the eighteenth century, the record of each community shows marriage choices moving from an open to a closed system and reopening whenever old families moved away and new ones took their place.

The record of marriages in the San Juan Basin demonstrates the transition from many marriages between nonrelatives in early times to a relatively closed system among related ranch owners in more recent generations. As ranchers lost their lands, and the base for joint residence of labor-sharing kin groups was undermined, the marriage pattern again became more open. Consolidated schools, paved roads, and the freedom of young people to select their own mates have further opened the pattern, but cousin marriage and sibling exchange continue to be popular.

The age at which marriage is contracted has varied over the centuries and has also varied according to economic status. During colonial times the wealthiest people married young, while the poorer families had to delay marriage in order to amass sufficient property to emancipate the sons and place them in the "estate of matrimony." The situation in New Mexico, however, never approached the inflexibility of the lot of small freehold farmers in County Clare, Ireland, where reduced acreage and the firm rule of patrilineal inheritance limit heirship to a family farm to one son. Other sons receive a "fortune" and are sent on their way to seek a livelihood elsewhere, while the "boy" who is to inherit must remain subordinate until all his siblings have departed and his parents are ready to retire, leaving him as master.[5]

The Castilian system of inheritance which prevailed in New Mexico provided for equal inheritance of land by all children of a landowner. Increased access to land was provided by the fact that landless young men could live on the lands of the wife's family and that new grants could be obtained under the Spanish and Mexican governments. Under the United States government, title to land was available under the Homestead Law. The continued availability of land and the willingness of family groups to move as a body to vacant lands maintained a strong system of extended kin and a tendency to favor marriage between relatives which showed no signs of weakening until after World War II.

Limitations on the extended family and upon early marriage were most marked where poverty was greatest. In 1845 Abiquiu had suffered heavy military losses due to hostilities with the Navajos and Utes, and out of a total 338 households, 91 were headed by widows. Only 203 households were headed by husband and wife, 7 were headed by unmarried men, and 14 by unmarried women. One hundred and thirty-two single men over age eighteen and 14 single women in this age group lived in households in which they were nonheads. By contrast, the undated census of El Rito from the same general period listed only 44 households out of a total of 297 as headed by widows, 3 headed by single men, and 2 by single women. Throughout the colonial period the daughters of well-to-do families married as early as age fourteen and the boys soon after age eighteen.

VALUES OF THE MARRIED STATE

Some of the shifts which can be observed in New Mexico marriage records over the centuries undoubtedly are the product of cyclic population changes operating upon an institution of Hispanic derivation. Others suggest the impact of contact with Indian societies in which different systems prevailed. For instance, the belief that full adult status is only achieved through marriage and parenthood appears to have firmer roots in Indian societies of New Mexico than in the Spanish tradition, which extols religious celibacy. Prior to New Mexico's conquest by the United States, most priests native to New Mexico were married men with children. This fact gives evidence of the New Mexicans' deep commitment to marriage and parenthood; it does not evidence corruption on the part of the priests. Father Antonio José Martinez had studied and written on the issue before taking his postordination wife.[6]

In the Hispanic society of New Mexico, polygyny is an institution which remains covert. It is accepted, however, possibly because sororal polygyny was part of the Navajo and Ute traditions and because the Utes accepted cohabitation of a man with a woman and her mother or daughter. Relationships of this kind, banned by the Church, nonetheless were often stable and did not lead to rejection by the community. The incidence of sororal polygyny may also have been influenced by the preferential marriage of widowers with a younger sister of the late wife. This likelihood is strengthened by the frequent marriage of widows with a brother of the late husband and by the sparse record of women's marital infidelities, which often implicate a close relative of the husband. The occasional woman who took her husband's brother as a long-term lover conformed neither to Indian nor Hispanic norms. But because of flexible attitudes which developed toward unusual domestic arrangements, such women did not become total social outcasts.

GODPARENT CHOICES

The pattern of selection of godparents for one's children, especially the baptismal set, follows one variant of the Hispanic tradition. Furthermore, it is dependent upon the question of marriage partners, actual or potential. Compadres are spiritual relatives, and in past centuries marriage between them was forbidden.[7] Although the regulations have been revoked, Hispanos of northern New Mexico still consider marriage between compadres scandalous. In view of the fact that communities were small, that a couple might have to find baptismal godparents for ten or more children, and that widowhood and remarriage were common for both men and women, it seems reasonable that people preferred to select compadres who were already excluded as potential marriage partners.

At the same time, the compadrazgo relationship in New Mexico was atypical of the New World in general, except for upper class strata. George Foster has noted that compadrazgo in the New World won a preeminent place as an integrator between minimal groups in the same society, between classes or ethnic groups for whom contact is necessary or unavoidable, and also as a mechanism of mutual aid in crisis situations. Foster also showed that in Spain, these same functions were undertaken primarily by the cofradías, which blended religious lay brotherhood with the function of trade guilds. In Spain, therefore, compadrazgo remained secondary to the kinship system. The same has been true for New Mexico, with mutual aid functions being undertaken across kinship lines by the cofradía, the Penitente Brotherhood.

In the New World compadrazgo has become in many regions the chief cohesive and integrating force in a community, channeling reciprocal behavior and often widening ties to include sponsors from the upper strata of the community. Only among the upper classes in Latin America is there a tendency to follow the Spanish type of compadrazgo, whereby existing kin relationships are intensified, while avoiding ties of pseudo-kinship. The Spanish system limits godparents to a pair of baptismal sponsors, not necessarily man and wife, a single confirmation sponsor of same sex as the child, and a pair of wedding sponsors. The latter set is not required by canon law. Elsewhere in Spanish America there may be a proliferation of occasions requiring godparents.[8]

In part, the New World system of compadrazgo helped to stabilize relations between native Indian populations and the Spanish and mestizo groups. To this extent the institution of compadrazgo in New Mexico conforms to the general New World model, since the settlers regularly served as baptismal godparents of Indian children and adults. At Abiquiu the baptismal godparents of Indian children brought in by the Utes were usually settlers, but the Genízaros interchanged godparent roles for their children with one another, rarely selecting settlers for this role. At Genízaro weddings it was customary to do without sponsors and record the whole congregation as witness to the ceremony.

Even the fragmentary genealogies that can be reconstructed for the eighteenth century settlers of Abiquiu indicate the operation of the same system of godparent selection which has been verified in the San Juan Basin communities of modern times, the system already described for Spain. Parents select for their children in preferential order their parents, aunts and uncles, sisters and brothers, and, finally, their own oldest children as baptismal sponsors. Godparents are expected to provide the baptismal outfit, the church fees, and the refreshments for the occasion; but the primary relationship resulting from baptismal sponsorship is not between the compadres but between sponsors and godchild. The latter must address his godparents with unfailing respect and affection and must help them and do their bidding.[9]

In the San Juan Basin, as in Spain, the ideal order of selection prescribes the mother's parents as godparents of the first child, the father's parents as godparents of the second child, while succeeding children are sponsored by other relatives. Of the 152 case sample of baptisms for which pedigree information was available, 27 baptisms were of first-born children. In Table 3 we see the breakdown.[10]

This sample shows much lower incidence of mother's parents or father's parents in godparental roles during the first generation of settlement in the San Juan Basin than was the

TABLE 3

Godparent Selection in the San Juan Basin

Sponsor's Relation to Child	First Child	Other Children	Total
Mother's parents	4	4	8
Father's parents	2	10	12
Mother-Father siblings	7	15	22
Mother-Father relatives	8	56	64
Penitente Brothers	5	14	19
Nonrelative	1	24	25
Older sibling of child		2	2
	27	125	152

case in later generations, because migrating families often left the older generation behind. Furthermore, many migrating families already had baptized their first children before coming to the San Juan Basin. And since they came from so many different places, it was impossible to trace back the baptismal records.

Table 3 shows clearly that real or fictive kinsmen (since Penitentes are Brothers) have been selected for 127 out of a total of 152 baptisms to serve as sponsors. There was no justification for separating siblings and other relatives into wife's kin as distinct from husband's kin, because in a high percentage of cases the sponsors were relatives of both husband and wife. The incidence of cousin marriage and sibling exchange was high in this sample.

Penitentes routinely selected their children's godparents not on the basis of blood kinship, but on the basis of Brotherhood in the local morada, preferring chapter leaders. A small number of non-Penitente parents selected a highly esteemed Penitente couple as godparents for one child, but in every instance where more than one child in a family had Penitente godparents, the family involved was affiliated with the Brotherhood.

It was and is uncommon for parents to select their younger siblings or siblings close to them in age as baptismal godparents for their children. In recent years some priests of the Chama

drainage have made efforts to discourage parents from selecting
godparents nearly a generation older than themselves, on the
grounds that by the time the godchild is of an age for intensive
religious instruction and moral guidance the godparent will be
too aged to serve effectively. Priests feel that godparent choices
are based on the desire to provide a parent surrogate in case the
biological parents should die before the child is of age. In this
sense, the primary concern in godparent selection is focused on
the physical rather than the spiritual welfare of the child. In
view of the regularity of marriage between widows or widowers
and a sibling of the deceased spouse, near in age or younger, and
in view of the persistent belief that marriage between
compadres constitutes incest, parishioners of northern New
Mexico have paid little attention to priestly criticism.

There are few instances of godparent selection in the San
Juan Basin, however, which could be construed as an effort to
secure a wealthy surrogate parent who could adequately
support his godchild in the event of the parents' death. At the
other end of the scale, affluent parents occasionally selected a
much less affluent couple as their child's godparents. These
arrangements were considered satisfactory because few people
in the area expected gifts or special assistance from their
godparents, and all disclaimed the concept that compadres must
help one another *as* compadres. Reciprocal aid has been
channeled entirely through the kin group and the Penitente
Brotherhood.

As in Andalusía, *consuegros* (co-parents-in-law) in the San
Juan Basin are expected to address one another as compadres
and to cooperate for the benefit of their married children.[11]
This expectation, no doubt, was easy to fulfill in the days of
arranged marriages. It is still fulfilled in most cases where the
bride and groom are relatives. But as young people make their
marriage choices independent of parental opinion, the
consuegro relationship becomes a formality, with a potential for
mutual recrimination and bitterness if the marriage proves
unsuccessful. The principal stabilizing force in marriage is the
continuing popularity of cousin marriages and of
sibling-exchange marriages and their capacity to draw together
whole kin groups.

THE FRATERNAL MODEL IN RELIGION

The adaptation of religious practice in New Mexico to a fraternal (Penitente) model rather than to the paternalistic model of the Catholic Church (in which the priest is the father, who leads his flock of pious sons and daughters) appears to have been an internal adjustment to the scarcity of village priests and sacramental services rather than the effect of Indian contact. The principal religious observances in the villages were not masses. They were private prayer and prayer meetings, vigils for the dead which the Penitentes led, and dramatic reenactments of the Passion during Holy Week. Religious instruction came entirely from the home, a fact which Bishop Zubiría criticized during his visit to Abiquiu in 1833. He also noted that the cult of Saint Rose of Lima was so popular in the Abiquiu area that mass was not even celebrated on the feast day of Saint Thomas, patron saint of the Abiquiu church.[12]

Because there were so few priests in the villages, people kept holy water in their homes to baptize infants in danger of dying, and often delayed formal baptism for months. People of today who live on isolated ranches still keep holy water. In Arroyo Hondo the Brothers assisted the dying in reciting the act of contrition and led responsive prayer for the salvation of the soul about to leave the body. As a person was about to expire, the Brothers called upon the name of Jesus three times, to try to save the soul in transition from the perils of perdition. This is a vivid example of fraternal efforts to meet the crisis of death in the absence of sacramental reassurance.[13]

Funeral wakes provided emotional release for the bereaved and allowed the community to participate in formal mourning, a joint religious effort with interludes of sociability. The wake lasted until dawn, when an *alabado* (praise song) of farewell in the name of the deceased signaled the time to conduct the body, wrapped in a shroud and laid on a board or ladder, to the grave. Prayers were said for the repose of the soul, and further ceremony had to await the arrival of a priest.[14]

It will be recalled that Bishop Salpointe tried to ban Penitente-led funeral wakes in the 1880's, but village isolation made the ban impossible to enforce in such areas as the San

Juan Basin. It was not until the Brotherhood's membership
began to dwindle in the 1920's that new funeral practices began
to develop. In Rosa, the *Unión Protectiva* (Protective Union)
was formed as a lay organization of Hispano Catholics for the
specific purpose of creating a burial fund for its members.
Members paid dues and the organization ran benefit dances.[15]
The fund provided for simple burials of all members, and for
the first time, coffins came into wide use. Villagers of the San
Juan Basin, however, still prefer funerals without elaborate
display and are particularly opposed to such practices as
embalming. They feel that a body should be restored to its
Maker as intact as possible; even surgery is felt to be something
of a desecration.

The Unión Protectiva was a minimal substitute for the Brotherhood in organizing funerals and assuming the task of burying
the dead. Much of the stark simplicity of funeral observance, as
well as the realistic attitude toward death that runs through
Hispanic culture, was thus preserved in a new organizational
setting. Change of this kind created little disruption within the
community and was readily adopted. Like the Brotherhood, the
Unión Protectiva has been a community-wide unifying force.

The Hispanic attitude toward death has neither influenced
nor been influenced by Indian concepts about death. The Utes,
especially, have a tradition of fear and avoidance of the dead
and burial grounds, though Utes who are Catholics are buried
with Catholic rites. Hispano neighbors help bereaved families,
making funeral arrangements and attending the ceremonies. The
Utes traditionally buried their dead in rock shelters and never
visited the gravesites.

EFFECTS OF INTERCULTURAL CONTACT

Initial contact relations between settlers and Indians were
marked by intense efforts on the part of the colonial
government and its military, administrative, and evangelistic
forces to achieve total domination over the Indians of New
Mexico, as had already been achieved in various parts of Latin
America. The firm resistance of each Pueblo community to
interference with its theocratic way of life was relatively

successful due to the weakness and small numbers of the colonial settlement. Surrounded by nomadic tribes and isolated from centers of colonial power, the settlers had to make compromises. They also had to adapt their own way of life to the physical and social realities of the New Mexican environment. This adaptability of a nominally dominant group was the chief cornerstone of the structure of contact relations between Hispanos and Indians from the early eighteenth century to modern times, long after the Anglo-American rule had imposed its own structure of dominance over both Indians and Hispanos.

In the eighteenth century the Pueblos won back their right to the privacy of native religious practice and freed themselves from illegal demands upon their labor time. Once the settlers abated their violations of Pueblo rights, relations between the Pueblos and the settlers became more cordial, on the basis of compadrazgo and trading relationships and on joint experience in raiding nomadic Indians. A certain amount of intermarriage continued to occur, resulting in shared ties of ancestry and cultural tradition, even though sharp dichotomy existed between the two cultural types.

Present-day customs and attitudes reflect prolonged intercultural experience. The Catholicism of the Pueblo Indians more closely resembles the folk Catholicism of their Hispano neighbors than that of the mission fathers who evangelized them. Both groups have deeply religious feelings about their natural surroundings, expressed in the commonly overheard Hispanic view that "the land is our mother" and in the elaborate ritual of the Pueblos celebrating their relatedness to their immediate community and to the hills, mesas, and mountain peaks surrounding it and the sacred myth of their locus of origin.[16] Hispanos have a less formalized ritual relating to land, but on the day of San Isidro the priest blessed their lands, ditches, and ditch gates. *Tatas* formally led their grandsons into the fields to recite to them the boundaries of the family allotment and the landmarks of the community boundary. Spanish law permits buying and selling of land as a chattel. But, once settlers had been on a grant for a long time, a deep attachment to their land developed, perhaps stimulated by the attitudes of Indian neighbors and relatives.

The high status and relative freedom of women which developed in the frontier settlements of New Mexico were partly a response to conditions of existence, but may have also been the result of early intermarriage with Pueblo women by some of the most prominent settlers. In the settlements, division of labor by sex was somewhat less stringently defined than in the pueblos.[17]

In the Genízaro pueblo of Abiquiu, Pueblo dances and songs, on a recreational rather than a ritual level, have been remembered and performed in recent years on the feast day of Santo Tomás. In many villages of northern New Mexico, descendants of the early settlers attend certain Pueblo festivals and even join the Indians in the *Matachine,* a dance-drama of Spanish origin.[18]

Contact between the settlers and the nomadic tribes caused the Indians to become mounted warriors and the settlers to abandon positional warfare in favor of the surprise raid. Settlers also abandoned the defensive, enclosed plaza in favor of the scattered placita and herds, which maximized individual friendships with Indians and minimized losses of livestock. Men in the settlements apparently adopted many elements of Plains Indian attire, while Indian women, of both Pueblo and Plains, adopted the Spanish shawl. The settlers learned from New Mexico Indians how to make jerky from deer and buffalo meat and how to make the blue corn atole, called *chaqueue* by the Tewas. From previous experience in Mexico, most settlers were already familiar with techniques of raising corn, grinding its kernels on the metate, and making tortillas and atole.

The settlers brought to New Mexico mules, horses, donkeys, cattle, goats, sheep, swine, and chickens: all animals previously unknown in the New World. Settlers introduced the cultivation of wheat, cantaloupes, watermelons, apples, peaches, apricots, pears, tomatoes, and chile, the last two cultigens being native to Mexico but hitherto unknown in New Mexico. They introduced firearms and Hispanic crafts of weaving in wool, woodworking, and blacksmithing. Iron, tin, copper, bronze, and silver were the metals they worked, although the local supply was limited.

These new resources were adopted by different Indian groups with great variability in the degree and manner of adoption. Prior to the Pueblo rebellion, the Pueblos learned the skills relating to these resources through forced labor, while the nomadic tribes learned skills as captives and acquired produce and livestock by raiding.

The Río Grande Pueblos managed to adopt a number of Hispanic technological innovations and social institutions without permitting the destruction of the integrity of their own culture. The Navajos, on the other hand, sustained a profound alteration of their whole way of life by becoming pastoralists, yet wove their new resources into a new way of Navajo life far removed from the Hispanic way of life. Their handling of the weaving complex is a case in point.

The Navajos may have adopted cultivation of cotton and weaving with a belt loom from the Pueblos, prior to the coming of the first Spanish explorers. Certainly, they became familiar with Pueblo techniques during the Pueblo refugee period of the late seventeenth and early eighteenth centuries. During the seventeenth century, Navajo captives of the settlers must have learned to weave on the Spanish standing loom. By the late eighteenth century, however, the Navajos had reorganized their experiences into their own way of weaving. Among the Pueblos, the men were the weavers; among the settlers both men and women wove, but among the Navajos weaving was the domain of women, with rare exceptions. The Navajos invented their own loom, a suspended upright frame to which the warp threads were laced. Wool dyes and blanket design combined elements borrowed from both Pueblo and Hispanic sources with the Navajos' own creative efforts. Today, Hispano weavers buy vegetable-dyed yarns from the Navajos rather than prepare their own.

EFFECTS OF SOCIAL LEVELING

The factors shaping life in Abiquiu and other frontier communities maintained a constant process of social leveling in the face of Spanish casticismo and hierarchic ordering of society. The frequent opening of new lands to settlement through land grants for which any vecino could apply, the opportunity for all able-bodied men, including Genízaros, to increase their wealth through trade or the acquisition of war booty, and the recurrent possibility of losing all previously acquired wealth constantly blurred distinctions of caste and class. We have already seen that Genízaros did acquire property and vecino status and that some became recognized leaders. José Gonzales, the Genízaro leader of the 1837 Rebellion, was briefly the governor of New Mexico, with the support of the alcalde mayor of Santa Cruz and other leaders of the Río Arriba country, as well as the leaders of a number of pueblos.

The Hispanic life outlook which emerged as a result of the risks and vicissitudes of frontier existence stressed personal responsibility, business initiative, and courage. Despite beliefs molded by religion that God is the ultimate master of man's fate, the people of the Chama Valley and the San Juan Basin to this day believe that human effort has much to do with a person's life. One who has tried hard and has not been rewarded with good fortune nonetheless earns respect for his or her *fortaleza* (fortitude), while people who make little effort, regardless of their station in life, are characterized as *flojo, perezoso,* or *resolanero* (lax, lazy, or idle). Ranch families carry on a ceaseless round of hard work, and only real illness can excuse individuals from their regular tasks.

The kinds of changes which have been described thus far, the cyclic shifts in selection of marriage partners and godparents, the adaptive modifications of some concepts and practices in the direction of Indian cultures, the substitution of the Penitente funeral by the Unión Protectiva funeral, and the moderation of ideas of dominance in a colonial society: these are all examples of the capacity of New Mexico Hispanic culture to maintain its own character in a context of adaptive flexibility. Under United States rule new kinds of change processes were set in motion.

EFFECTS OF UNITED STATES CONQUEST

For New Mexico Hispanos, unlike the Navajos and Apaches or the Spanish-speaking people of Texas and California, conquest by the United States did not immediately unleash a decisive and wholesale process of violent subjugation. The Hispanos greatly outnumbered the Yankees, were widely distributed over a large territory, and were constantly needed in the campaigns to control the nomadic Indians and to drive out Confederate invaders. Consequently, between the abortive 1847 uprisings and the end of the Civil War, there was an absence of coercion, let alone genocidal tendencies, in the Yankee handling of their Hispanic subjects. By the end of the Civil War, a well-defined group of Hispano collaborators was working closely with stateside authorities, and the semicolonial mold of New Mexico life, with its superficial appearance of democracy, was firmly entrenched. Yet the continuing large Hispano majority and the continuing self-sufficiency and autonomy of the communities it occupied, as well as its fundamental compatibility with Indian neighbors, constituted such a potential challenge to Yankee control that statehood was delayed for nearly another five decades.

Change was initiated from the top, with replacement of the municipal system of community administration by the county commission and of the native clergy by a foreign clergy. The villagers adapted to these changes by placing heavier reliance on the ditch association and the Penitente Brotherhood for their civic and spiritual needs and by applying their code of action in the justice of the peace courts when these were established. Beyond this, the chief reaction of the villagers was one of withdrawal from interaction with the aggressive new rulers of their land, the better to preserve their own set of values. The process of social enclavement, which became increasingly marked in the villages from the 1880's until after World War II, advanced most rapidly in those villages where the land grants were first alienated from their rightful heirs, where grazing lands were appropriated and fenced, and where (as in Lincoln County, San Miguel County, and the San Luis Valley) there was considerable violence.[19]

Despite the trend toward physical and social enclavement, the new way of life brought in by the Anglo-Americans soon began to reach the remotest villages. Wagon traffic increased, railroads were built, the horse and buggy became a popular mode of getting about the countryside. In recent decades, the automobile has supplanted all other forms of transportation. The tin cans tossed aside by American Civil War troops permitted an unexpected flowering of the Hispanic tinsmith's art. Prior to the coming of the Americans, many village men and boys spent at least part of the year away from home, buffalo hunting and trading with Indian nomads. Now they leave their families to work in mines and in the "factories in the fields" or shear sheep in Wyoming. Sometimes the whole family leaves the village for seasonal employment.

In the Anglo-dominated towns, where cash transactions and other unfamiliar ways of conducting one's life prevailed, Hispano laborers early changed their style of dress from buckskins and moccasins to overalls and shoes, while people who managed to enter business and the professions soon wore the clothing of the Anglo middle class and assumed its mannerisms. In the villages which continued to have some autonomy, however, it was possible to adapt minimally to a cash economy and to take over some of the resources of an industrial society without seriously disrupting village life.

In the San Juan Basin, a relatively open society endured well into the twentieth century, due to the leverage which the Hispanos and Utes provided for one another. Despite the controlling hand of the Southern Ute Agency and the increasing penetration of the Bond and Sargent interests into the business life of Rosa, most community changes in the Hispano hamlets along the San Juan were chosen by the villagers. Thus, while threshing continued to be accomplished in some New Mexico villages as late as the 1930's by methods older than the Bible, the villagers of Rosa began to borrow the threshing machines and harvesters of the Southern Ute Agency before the 1920's and soon began to obtain machines of their own.

VITALITY OF THE HISPANIC CULTURE

So long as the basic demographic unit, the village, had means for survival within the framework of cooperation of extended kin groups, Hispanic culture continued to thrive. In fact, faced with years of economic ruin, the ravages of land speculation, drought, depression, and malnutrition bordering on starvation,

**Celebration of Santa Rosa Day on August 30, 1960, at Rosa, New Mexico.
Photos by James Clifton.**

The Clinica del Pueblo de Río Arriba provides health services at minimal cost to the people of the Tierra Amarilla area and is run by a citizen board. F. Swadesh, 1973.

The new maternity wing and community center currently under construction at the Clinica del Pueblo de Río Arriba. F. Swadesh, 1973.

added to recent Anglo-American intolerance of their very existence, the villages have survived with a vitality that is almost unbelievable. The moment some viable means of livelihood appears, villages are repopulated and regenerate at a rapid rate. The Pecos Valley villages during the Farm Security Administration program in the years just preceding the Second World War provide an example of this regenerative capacity.[20]

In the years since World War II, Chimayó has shown that local businesses based on traditional skills can be usefully combined with a community enterprise (apple raising and packing) and wage work. Even the small community-sponsored agricultural cooperative and clinic established near Tierra Amarilla without any government or foundation support has survived and grown because of growing voluntary support both outside and within the community.

The conditions of northern Hispano villages in New Mexico and of Indian communities in the same area continue to be bleak and threatened. But there is hope. There are factors which continue to force villagers to leave, and there are factors which bring villagers back to their home communities. The growing network of paved roads has brought the area both improvement and deterioration. On the positive side of the ledger, many more people can continue to live in the villages while commuting to their jobs than ever used to be possible. There is easier access to medical care, although throughout northern New Mexico, the distance from home to clinic or hospital still continues to be excessive. Until the *Clínica del Pueblo de Río Arriba* (People's Clinic of Río Arriba) began to offer obstetrical services in 1972 to women living in the Tierra Amarilla area, the nearest hospital was more than eighty miles distant. Until recent years, the infant mortality rate in the area was thirty per one thousand live births. Many infants were born at home, with or without the services of a licensed midwife, while many others were born in automobiles on the way to the hospital.

BREAKUP OF THE VILLAGES

Improved access to the northern villages, however, has brought other kinds of changes. The most potentially damaging is the acquisition of Pueblo and Hispano grant lands by real estate subdevelopers. Taking advantage of the prevailing low income which induces many people to sign over title to their land for even modest payments, these concerns have sold many of the lands as small parcels to gullible purchasers, sight unseen, through media advertising throughout the United States, particularly in the overcrowded cities of the East and West Coasts.

Few subdevelopers have built many homes on their tracts, since the strategy of the corporations is largely one of speculation. They do, however, bulldoze "access roads" to each parcel, creating an acute erosion problem. The potential of subdivided lands for purposes of extension and improvement of range is altogether lost, and the economy of villages is pushed into further decline. Current administration policies regarding programs for rural areas may propel many thousands of villagers into urban slum barrios, where they have little or no hope of finding a livelihood and will probably be forced to become hopelessly dependent upon welfare. Welfare regulations prohibit payment of benefits to people who own land that has even a partial potential for subsistence, so families are forced to put their lands up for sale. Usually, they leave their home villages in order to secure welfare support. Since no household headed by an able-bodied man may receive welfare funds, destitute men will desert their wives and children in order to secure aid for them. The miserably inadequate welfare support provided in the state of New Mexico has thus had a baneful effect in destroying rural communities and breaking up families.

Another by-product of improved roads in northern New Mexico has been the nearly universal closing of village grade schools and the busing of small children many miles over mountain roads to schools in larger towns. These roads become dangerous and even impassable during snowfalls or heavy cloudbursts; therefore, children often miss days at school or are bused home early when there is inclement weather.

Villagers deeply resent the closing of their schools, which have been important and unifying institutions of village life. In the less accessible communities, parents who wish their children to have a full school experience have been forced to move into a town where the problems of busing are less acute. Children who are bused to towns for schooling, as well as those who live in towns, are becoming more and more exposed to the lifeways and values of the Anglo-American society and correspondingly estranged from the values of their families and home communities. In part, the change in values is traceable to the influence of television, because most programs seen in New Mexico are a reflection of Anglo values, while few provide any reinforcement whatsoever of traditional Hispanic values. The emphasis on youth and the downgrading of old age which is so marked in the Anglo-American value system and is so antagonistic to the Hispanic value system, and the glorification of material gain, so foreign to Hispanic village subsistence values, is driving a wedge between Hispano youth and their elders. All of these new and foreign values permeate the Anglo-dominated school systems, where an equally foreign atmosphere of competition prevails.

HISPANIC COUNTERATTACK

Yet the vitality of Hispanic village culture is far from exhausted. In the wake of the innovative efforts of the Alianza movement, there is a dawning of recognition of the rights and needs of the Hispano villagers of northern New Mexico. Here and there new range is being acquired by associations of small livestockmen. The possibilities of rural cooperation are being tested in many ways, by farmers' markets in the towns, by agricultural cooperatives and community pre-schools, and by craft enterprises.

In the face of suspension of federal programs for rural communities, there is a current stream of repopulation of the Hispano villages. With growing unemployment in cities, young families are bringing their savings back to the home village to try to make a new start. There is a growing demand for rural economic programs that will provide livelihood for villagers, not bureaucrats. The forest service policy of favoring big business use of forest resources at the expense of the marginal stockmen in the villages has been so intensely challenged by the Alianza that some modifications in range management appear to be emerging.

People in political life and rural economists are beginning to challenge the long-dominant idea that village life in the United States is doomed and might as well come to an end. Social scientists are particularly interested in the viability of the interaction group provided by village populations, where people grow up knowing everybody in the community. The menace of depersonalization and alienation in the metropolis, and the absolute need of decentralizing population into smaller units in order to provide better institutions and services are winning recognition. Therefore, it is time to review the factors which may well obliterate the Hispano village in New Mexico and to ask searchingly whether these factors should be allowed to continue to operate unchecked.

WRONGS TO BE RIGHTED

The first major cause of destructive change in the Hispano community has been long-term violation of the Treaty of Guadalupe Hidalgo. This agreement pledged United States' protection of the personal and property rights of previous Mexican citizens.[21] Fraudulent and thieving disposition of land grants; the imposition of land taxes starting in 1895; creation of a vast public domain from the community lands of grants; appropriation of these lands to create national forests; the policy of national forest officials to favor exploitation of the forest resources by corporate, often out-of-state interests at the expense of the villages that surround the forest; and finally, the reckless obliteration of communities and failure to relocate them as socioeconomic units, of which the history of the Navajo Reservoir is only the most recent instance—these are the economic violations of the treaty, all of which can and should be rectified. The handling of Indian claims cases provides a precedent, although there is room for criticism of the fact that tribes have ultimately had to pay the cost of their cases.

The second major cause of destructive change is the repression of the Spanish language and of Hispanic culture, the suppression of the true history of New Mexico, and the creation of an Anglo-glorifying pseudohistory of the Southwest. Formal education is imparted in a manner clearly violating both the treaty and the New Mexico State Constitution. Even in recent years, the custom of heaping ridicule and imposing punishments on students who speak Spanish in school has surfaced again and again. Some students persist in speaking Spanish because they are unable to express themselves in English, while others are deliberately affirming their sense of cultural self-identity. For whichever cause, the right to speak Spanish or the Indian language of the home should be inalienable rights of New Mexico schoolchildren.

Ever since George Sanchez wrote his immortal *Forgotten People* in 1940, there have been voices in the wilderness preaching the need for bilingual-bicultural education and advocating an educational content enriched by the diversity of New Mexico's cultural heritage.[22] Yet for years, in the name of education, the cultural and community self-image of children has suffered assault in the schools. In recent years, the allocation of federal funds for bilingual-bicultural education has begun to move the educational establishment in the right direction, but much more remains to be done. In 1971, on the initiative of Lieutenant Governor Roberto Mondragon, educators and community leaders began to come together to chart a plan of change toward multicultural education.

Another destructive change wrought by Anglo-American dominance in New Mexico has been the loss of direct contact with and participation in the culture of Mexico which is, after all, the mother culture of Hispanic New Mexico. In the early decades following 1846 there was continuity of contact, kept alive by travel up and down the Rio Grande. Traveling performers known as *maromeros* brought theater and entertainment from Mexico to New Mexico as late as the 1920's. Known kin ties between communities of New Mexico and northern Mexico facilitated the shift of population both northward and southward. The international border remained wide open until after the Mexican Revolution of 1910.

By the early twentieth century, however, mine owners began to import groups of Mexican nationals to the Rocky Mountain states to serve as scabs against the great strikes led by the Western Federation of Miners. Miners from New Mexico who were loyal to the labor organization suddenly found it necessary to distinguish between themselves and the scabs. Speaking Spanish among themselves, they continued to refer to themselves as *mexicanos,* but when speaking English they began to use such terms as "Spanish American" or even "Spanish." Through military service starting in the Civil War they were well aware of their American citizenship and had ceased to think of themselves as mexicanos in terms of national affiliation.

STRUGGLE FOR CULTURAL IDENTITY

The identity situation became more confused then ever when some native New Mexicans working in California, Michigan, and other states, were caught up and expelled as Mexican nationals in the great deportations of the depression years. Those who had no birth identification on their persons were helpless against the dragnets that were spread in California and Michigan. In later years, large growers misused the Bracero Law and imported droves of Mexican nationals every time the farm workers of the Southwest attempted to win a higher wage. This situation created bitterness between New Mexican farm workers and Mexicans.

Today, the majority of people of northern New Mexico tend to emphasize their Spanish ancestry at the expense of New World forebears. In many cases, they resent the efforts of the Chicano movement to emphasize Mexican roots. The Chicano movement, in turn, tends to denounce the attitudes of northern New Mexicans as evidence that they are *vendidos* (sold out, collaborators), disregarding the long period of competing with Mexicans for substandard jobs and the manipulation of these attitudes by powerful elements. Only the Alianza, through its strong base of support among marginal Hispano ranchers, has been able to express the ideology of the *indo-hispano,* the Spanish-speaking person rooted in his mountain village and sharing much ancestry and historic experience with Indian neighbors. Because this is the historic experience of many people who now dwell in Denver, Los Angeles, and other urban centers, it is not surprising that the Alianza has had high prestige among many groups of Spanish-speaking southwesterners.

On that day, which hopefully will not be too distant, when economic and cultural rectifications have been made to the Hispanos of New Mexico, perhaps the displaced people of the San Juan Basin will come to feel that they did not suffer in vain. This account of their history and way of life is offered in the spirit expressed by a descendant of Los Primeros Pobladores, a grandson of the San Luis Valley pioneer, Atanacio Trujillo. He wrote:

> The main object is to remind Hispanic Americans of the glories achieved by our ancestors, heroic nourishment for the heart, in the high conviction that noble fathers of necessity have noble sons. Let us wrest from the oblivion in which they unjustly lie the great achievements made upon this soil, among the outstanding and heartwarming feats of the world.[23]

Notes

INTRODUCTION

1. *Hispano:* see glossary. This term is sometimes used synonymously with "Chicano," "Spanish-American," or "Mexican." Each of these terms, however, has different connotations.

2. *Chicano:* see glossary. This term is nowadays sometimes expanded to include Puerto Ricans as "Chicanos Boricuas" and persons of Cuban birth and ancestry as "Chicanos Cubanos."

3. For a description of grid-plan towns, see George Foster's *Culture and Conquest,* pp. 3-6 and for a description of *cofradías,* see Foster's *Cofradía and Compadrazgo in Spain and Spanish America,* p. 2. Wesley Hurt's ethnohistorical study of Manzano, a community of the Estancia Valley east of Albuquerque, documents loss of lands due to store debts in the early nineteenth century.

4. The historian Clarence Haring has compared frontier communities of both the English and the Spanish New World colonies, dividing those under both flags into two classes: the farm colony and the exploitation colony. The former predominated in the British colonies and the latter in the Spanish colonies, but each system had colonies of both types. The exploitation colony was defined by the plantation system, with great tracts of land worked by forced labor; the elite of these colonies were educated and powerful while the majority of inhabitants were impoverished and illiterate. Farm colonies prevailed in areas where the Indian population was both scattered and nonadaptive to forced labor, and where imported slaves could readily find refuge with the Indians; in such colonies, the majority of the settlers were small freehold farmers and class stratification was slow in developing (Haring, 1947: 27-30).

5. The Alianza Federal de los Pueblos Libres is an organization of heirs to the Spanish and Mexican land grants of the Southwest. Their principal membership is among small landowners of northern New Mexico. For more on the organization and its history see Swadesh, 1968 and 1969, and Blawis, 1971.

1. NEW MEXICO'S CULTURAL SEQUENCES

1. This chapter owes a great deal to the works of three principal authors who have been followed too constantly for specific references: Erik K. Reed (1964), Edward P. Dozier (1970), and Edward H. Spicer (1962). Jennings (1964) was also consulted for the section on prehistory. The author also had the benefit of discussion with the late Professor Dozier on topics relating to colonial New Mexico and the establishment of *Genizaro* (detribalized Indian) communities.

2. Hibben, 1951.

3. Haury, 1967; DiPeso, 1968.

4. Dolores Gunnerson, 1956; James Gunnerson, 1969; Hall, 1944.

5. Schroeder and Matson, 1966; Hammond and Rey, 1966; Schroeder, 1968.

6. Gibson, 1952; Marc Simmons, 1964.

7. Scholes, 1942.

8. Chavez, 1967.

9. Hackett and Shelby, 1942.

10. Espinosa, 1940.

11. In 1708, the sister-in-law of Sebastian Martin accused two women of San Juan Pueblo of using "devilish art" to afflict her with an itch so severe that it led to convulsions. After an investigation in which her evidence was flatly contradicted by members of her husband's family and a courageous San Juan Indian, the case was dismissed by the governor with a sharp reprimand to the complainant (SANM II: #137b).

Another such case concerned a witchcraft charge leading to the persecution of an Indian who committed suicide before review of the case in 1799. The investigation led to withdrawal of the friar who had launched the charge from mission service in New Mexico; suspension of the alcalde mayor of Santa Cruz and his assistant; and sentence of one of the accused, who had laid blame on the Indian, to four years in chains and on rations, in public works in New Mexico or at the presidio of Encinillas, Chihuahua (SANM II: #1462, #1495a).

12. Forbes, 1960; Haines, 1938a and 1938b; Jones, 1966.

13. Twitchell, 1911: 385; Haring, 1947: 105; Chavez, 1954a: ix-xvii; SANM I: #1340, #1342.

14. Galvez, 1951.

15. Lowie, 1963; Gunnerson and Gunnerson, 1970; Moorhead, 1958; Galvez, 1951.

16. SANM II: #409, #999.

17. Administrators and missionaries, again and again, found the frontier settlers of New Mexico uncouth and even indecent. In his study of Spanish government in New Mexico, Marc Simmons (1968) documents the attitudes of aristocratic civil and religious administrators from Spain and Mexico, who had little understanding of the adjustments being made by the settlers to the New Mexican physical and social environment. Their independence and "insolence" drew unfavorable comment, and widespread adoption of the skin clothing used by nomadic Indians was seen as nudity (p. 76). In New Mexico and other northern frontier areas, the establishment of machinery for local government was delayed on the grounds that there were not enough competent and educated people to man municipal posts (172-74, 193-98).

As late as 1833, when New Mexico was part of the Mexican Republic, Antonio Barreiro interrupted his assignment to establish a New Mexican judicial system by heaping polite ridicule on Father Antonio José Martinez' assertion that if New Mexico were granted statehood, local people could man all administrative posts: "I do not mean to say that there are no capable men in the country; truly, I do not mean this; I am grateful to all in the territory for the favors they have always conferred on me; wherever I go, I shall proclaim the kind heart and the beautiful character generally possessed by New Mexicans . . . but I do object to the statement that there are capable men to fill all positions" (Carroll and Haggard, 1942: 140).

18. Twitchell, 1963: 168-73.

19. *Rio Grande Sun*, Historical Edition 11/8/1962, Section B: 13.

20. Twitchell, 1963: 250-311.

21. Tate, 1970: 44.

22. Tate, 1970: 15, 20. See also Swadesh, 1969: 61-65.

2. EARLY CHAMA VALLEY SETTLERS

1. Chavez, 1954a: 222-26, Martín Serrano. This important and richly documented work was checked for each family surname mentioned in this book, and the author acknowledges overall indebtedness to Father Chavez' pioneering work.

2. NMLG Reel 25, SG 132: Antonio de Salazar.

3. MNLG Reel 16, SG 36: Town of Chamita; NMLG Reel 22, SG 97: Joaquín Mestas; NMLG Reel 41, PLC 68: Antonio de Beytia; NMLG Reel 48, PLC 140: Juan José Lobato; NMLG Reel 53, PLC 250: Cristobal de Torres; NMLG Reel 53, PLC 253: Juan de Ulibarrí; NMLG Reel 53, PLC 264: Bartholomé Sanchez. Also, SANM I: #110, #247, #437, #464, #520, #824, #827, #829, #833, #849, #872, #943, #944, #954. Also, NMLG Reel 53, PLC 266: Juan Tafoya. The story unfolded by these documents is that all grants listed above, except the Antonio de Beytia and Juan José Lobato Grants, were dismissed by the Court of Private Land Claims in the 1890's in favor of the Bartholomé Sanchez Grant, despite

the fact that Sanchez apparently never lived on his grant and the colonial authorities had left open the question of adverse claimants who did live on their lands. Both San Juan and Santa Clara Pueblos claimed that portions of the Bartholomé Sanchez Grant encroached upon their lands. The Antonio de Salazar Grant overlapped lands claimed by the heirs of Bartholomé Sanchez; Salazars resided for generations at their Corral de Piedra Ranch.

4. Governor Gervasio Cruzat y Góngora withdrew the following grants: NMLG Reel 53: PLC 249: Manuela García de la Riva; NMLG Reel 53, PLC 254: Juan Estevan García de Noriega; NMLG Reel 53, PLC 255: José Antonio Tórres; NMLG Reel 53, PLC 261: Antonio de Ulibarrí; NMLG Reel 53, PLC 265: Gerónimo Martín. Evidence in the archives and church records, however, is overwhelming that the García de Noriegas and heirs of Gerónimo Martín continued to occupy their grants (See SANM I; #518, #538, #561, #950, #954, #955, #976, #1000, #1004, #1022, #1225, #1242. Also, SANM II: #529, complaint of Francisco Quintana, 1754, concerning lands he was buying from Gerónimo Martín, which had been included in the Genízaro grant. The Juan Estevan García de Noriega Grant later passed into the hands of the grantee's descendant, Joaquín García, NMLG Reel 27, SG 151 and NMLG Reel 31, SG—, File 197). Bartholomé Trujillo's San José de Gracia Ranch is also mentioned in a number of documents over the years. In the 1890's the Court of Private Land Claims rejected claims to lands in the Chama Valley in favor of the claim by the descendants of Juan José Lobato, excepting only the Town of Abiquiu Grant, and the Plaza Blanca, Plaza Colorada, Black Mesa, and Antonio de Beytia grants. The historical record shows, however, that Juan José Lobato occupied his Santa Bárbara de Chama Ranch from 1744 to 1747 only, then sold it to Ventura de Mestas, whose lands abutted Lobato's east boundary. Lobato's original grant petition mentioned lands at Pueblo Colorado, and he only mentioned the larger area of both sides of the Chama between Chamita and the foot of the hill going to the Piedra Lumbre in his second petition (NMLG Reel 48, PLC 140). As alcalde mayor of Santa Cruz de la Cañada, Juan José Lobato put settlers in possession of lands which were later claimed in his name. The final note to this curious set of facts is that shortly after nearly 190,000 acres had been adjudicated by the Court of Private Land Claims to claimants in the name of Juan José Lobato and hundreds of heirs to the other grants had been dispossessed, most of this grant became a part of the Carson National Forest.

5. NMLG Reel 31, SG—, File 112; NMLG Reel 50, PLC 177: Río del Oso.

6. SANM I: #963, will of José de Riaño Tagle; #571, complaint of the Montoya brothers regarding the Polvadera Grant, 1766.

7. NMLG Reel 27, SG 148: Plaza Blanca and SG 149: Plaza Colorada. Also SANM I: #1004, protest by heirs of Cristobal Torres concerning the Plaza Colorada Grant.

8. Hackett, 1937: 399; SANM I: #20.

9. Hackett, 1937: 477.

10. SANM I: #36.

11. NMLG Reel 48, PLC 140, Frame 312 ff: letter by Juan Lorenzo Valdez.

12. SANM I: #847.

13. SANM I: #1100, proceedings in the 1750 resettlement of Abiquiu.

14. A matter kindly brought to the author's attention by E. Boyd. Further study of early Chama Valley settlements would benefit by careful scrutiny of Santa Clara and San Ildefonso Mission records, especially in the years prior to 1754.

15. SANM I: #1098. Although the Comanches briefly experimented with a settlement on the Arkansas River, neither they nor the Utes ever became sedentary.

16. NMLG Reel 26, SG 140, Frame 34 ff.: Abiquiu.

17. Father Miguel Menchero (quoted in Hackett, 1937) described the Genízaro settlements of Tomé and Belén in 1744, as follows:

> The Indians are of the various nations that have been taken captive by the Comanche Apaches, a nation so bellicose and so brave that it dominates all those of the interior country . . . they sell people of all these nations to the Spaniards of the kingdom, by whom they are held in servitude, the adults being instructed by the Fathers and the children baptized. It sometimes happens that the Indians are not treated well in this servitude, no thought being given to the hardships of their captivity and still less to the fact that they are neophytes and should be cared for and treated with kindness. For this reason many desert and become apostates. Distressed by this, the missionaries informed the governor of it, so that in a matter of such great importance he might take the proper measures. Believing the petition to be justified and carried away by the zeal of his guardianship, in deference to both Majesties, he ordered by proclamation throughout the kingdom that all the Indian men and women neophytes should report to him so that if the case were proved he might take the necessary measures. In fact a number did apply to him.

Menchero related that the governor then made Genízaro grants at Belén and, later Tomé. The latter grantees did less farming than fighting, carrying out their "obligation to go out and explore the country in pursuit of the enemy, which they are doing with great zeal in their obedience and under the direction of the said Father," the missionary of Isleta who was also directing them in construction of a church at no cost to the crown (Hackett, 1937: 401-2). Prevailing scholarly opinion agrees with Menchero in classifying the Genízaros as derived from mixed nomadic tribal ancestors, mainly from outside New Mexico. In many church records, however, Navajo, Apache and Ute ancestry is specified and Spanish admixture is known or inferred for some Genízaros (Chavez, 1954b: 115-16; Chavez, 1955: 193-94; Adams and Chavez, 1956: 42, note 71).

18. An account of repeated efforts to keep Ojo Caliente populated is

214 LOS PRIMEROS POBLADORES

given in E. Boyd, 1957. The Abiquiu Mission records, however, indicate that Ojo Caliente was populated from 1754 through 1761 and 1763 through 1765. From then on the record is more sporadic.

19. SANM I: #664, #1062.

20. Since the Genízaros were of diverse tribal origins and lived in detribalized communities, they came under the influence of Hispanic cultural patterns much more readily than the Pueblos, and were in constant demand as frontier militia. A note in the 1793-1794 census report, urging establishment of a presidio of Genízaros at the "old Pueblo of Socorrito," describes the Genízaros as warriors on a par with the Opatas of Sonora (AASF, Loose Doc. 1795, #13, note 6). Through their opportunity to collect war booty and acquire the status of *vecinos* (tithes-paying settlers who could buy or sell a house or lands) many Genízaros became fully adapted to the Hispanic cultural model (Chavez, 1955: 191-93). The Genízaros of Abiquiu, however, included many who were of Pueblo origin. Since the local Tewas called Abiquiu "Jo-so-ge" and since "Jo-so" means "Hopi" in Tewa, Twitchell speculated that the Abiquiu Genízaros were drawn from a delegation of 440 Hopis who came to Governor Codallos y Rabal in the 1740's to ask for protection and missionary friars (SANM I: #28, note by Twitchell on p. 25). Many Pueblo additions to the Abiquiu Genízaro population were from the Río Grande villages. To this day, the Santa Claras refer to people who have become too hispanicized to remain in the Pueblo as Genízaros (Edward Dozier, verbal communication).

21. AASF, Loose Doc. 1795, #13, notes 3 and 5.

22. Bolton, 1950: 142, 156, 159.

23. SANM II: #1881, #2131. The will of Don Severino Martinez of Taos in 1827 includes bequests of land to two Indian women "both now married and who were my servants" (Minge, 1963: 36).

24. Crocchiola, n.d. (1960): 13-20. This census is held by the Bancroft Library at the University of California. Portions of the New Mexico archival record are scattered in California (Bancroft and Huntington Libraries), Kansas (Truman Library), Washington, D.C. (Library of Congress), and Illinois (Newberry Library), as well as in Mexico and Spain. Some are in private collections. This dispersal represents a great loss to the documentary history of New Mexico.

25. Bancroft, 1889: footnote on p. 258, referring to a manuscript in the Pinart Collection of the Bancroft Library. Documents on this case are also listed in AASF but were not available to the author at the time the study was made. Thanks are due to Gilbert Benito Córdova for showing the author a *piedra imana* and explaining its significance.

26. Table of Missions prepared by Custos Fray Pedro Rubín de Celis, in Library of Congress, quoted by Bloom, 1913: 28-29.

27. Comparative population figures compiled from Adams, 1954:64; AGN, Californias 29: folio 199 v; Bancroft, 1889: 455; SANM I: #1191; Bloom, 1913: 28.

28. Partly documented from Chavez, 1954b: 70; plus verbal communi-

cation from New Mexico State Archivist, Dr. Myra Ellen Jenkins. The *Griegos* were of Greek ancestry; *Fresquez* came from the Flemish surname *Frishz; Archibeque* and *Gurule* are derived from French surnames *L'Archeveque* and *Grollet*. See Chavez, 1954a.

29. AASF, M-1, Box 4.

30. In 1736, after severe Ute raiding, a group of fifty settlers and seventy Indians under Teniente General Juan Paez Hurtado set out to track down the Utes; they gave up and went home when the weather turned cold (SANM II: #409). The Moache Utes sometimes raided Taos and even ventured west of the Río Grande on raiding expeditions with the Comanches. They did not often go as far west as Abiquiu, which was close to the Capote Ute range and was a favorite trading center for the Sabuagana Utes.

31. Schroeder, 1965: 73; SANM II: #548; Adams and Chavez, 1956: 252-53.

32. NMLG Reel 20, SG 73: Piedra Lumbre; NMLG Reel 25, SG 131: Polvadera; NMLG Reel 23, SG 113: Cañon de Pedernales; SANM I: #571.

33. NMLG Reel 27, SG 151: El Rito; NMLG Reel 31, SG— File 197: Joaquín García; Carroll and Haggard, 1942: Editorial Note #9.

34. NMLG Reel 20, SG 71: Cañon de Chama; NMLG Reel 45, PLC 107: Cañon de Chama.

35. NMLG Reel 31, SG—, File 183: Vallecito; NMLG Reel 48, PLC 141: Vallecito de San Antonio.

36. SANM II: #1082, #2961, #2963, #3051; Marc Simmons, 1968: 212, note 74.

37. SANM I: #613, #615, #805, #1103; SANM II: #2600; NMLG Reel 12, SG 3: Tierra Amarilla.

38. Bancroft, 1889: 300, footnote.

3. THE MEXICAN REPUBLIC AND THE UNITED STATES CONQUEST OF NEW MEXICO

1. SANM I: #387.

2. NMLG Reel 23, SG 108: José Rafael Zamora (Petaca); NMLG Reel 48, PLC 142: Vallecito de Lobato; NMLG Reel 51, PLC 204: S. Endicott Peabody; NMLG Reel 52, PLC 236: Vallecito de Lobato.

3. SANM I: #1189; Warner, 1931: 336.

4. NMLG Reel 26, SG 140: Juan José Lobato; NMLG Reel 38, PLC 52: Town of Abiquiu. Also SANM I: #709, #1066 and MANM, Roll 13, Frames 738-82.

5. Read, 1912: 371-72; Chavez, 1955: 190-94; Reno, 1965.

6. Carroll and Haggard, 1942: 188; MANM Roll 41, starting at Frame 1247 for undated census lists.

7. Hafen and Hafen, 1954: 209.

8. MANM Roll 41, starting at Frame 1257 for undated census lists.

9. The following account indicates that trips to California had become routine. In 1835 the son of the late interpreter to the Utes, Manuel Gregorio Torres of Abiquiu, offered a piece of land as security for payment on a captive Indian woman, for whom he promised payment upon his return from his next trip to California (MANM Roll 36, Frames 431-38: petition on a land dispute by María Antonia Espinosa, 2/22-5/9/1844).

10. Jaramillo, 1941: 16; Carroll and Haggard, 1942: 106-10; Bancroft, 1889: 275-76; Minge, 1965.

11. MANM Roll 35: communications in governor's letterbook (formerly numbered #7534 and #7823) concerning the 1844 massacre of Utes in Santa Fe and its aftermath. Also, calico-bound notebook of family records, handwritten by Juan Andrés Quintana, in possession of his grandson, Isaac Quintana.

12. Abert, 1962: 62.

13. Twitchell, 1963: Chapters 8-11.

4. POPULATION SHIFTS IN THE TERRITORIAL PERIOD

1. Weightman speech quoted by Read, 1912: 485-86.

2. Swadesh, 1969: 58 ff.

3. Bancroft, 1889: 646-48; Read, 1912: 596; Diaz, 1960: 1.

4. Bancroft, 1889: 703, footnote; Lange and Riley, 1969: 73-74; McCarty, 1969: 2, 8-9.

5. These grants were made by Governor Manuel Armijo, mainly in favor of Anglo-American cronies, shortly before the Kearny invasion.

6. Twitchell, 1912: 471; Westphall, 1965; McCarty, 1969.

7. Harper et al., 1943: 63; McCarty, 1969: 7-8.

8. NMLG Reel 12, SG 3: Tierra Amarilla; Abstract of Title to the Tierra Amarilla Grant, known as the "Old Hernandez Abstract," hereafter referred to as TAG: Conveyance #49.

9. TAG #54, #292, #293; McCarty, 1969: 10-14. One of the claims acquired by Catron was the "undivided 1/8 part of the tract of land known as the Tierra Amarilla Grant," which was sold in 1864 by Julian Martinez, a brother of Francisco, to Santa Fe storekeeper Frederick Muller. Julian had no valid title to the grant, since he had never lived on it, but his conveyance passed from one hand to the next (TAG #3-#14, #18).

10. Pitt, 1970: 416-19; Price, 1967: 17; Gill, 1964: 19.

11. Turley, 1935.

12. NMLG Reel 31, SG File 80: Conejos; Velasquez ms. (n.d.).

13. Carroll and Haggard, 1942: 144-45.

14. Francis, 1956: 265-89; Minge, 1963: 34.

15. Read, 1912: 523.

16. Woodward, ms., 1935: 160.

17. Chavez, 1954b: 109-20.

18. Carroll and Haggard, 1942: 88.

19. Carroll and Haggard, 1942: 53.

20. Chavez, 1954b: 110-11. Father Chavez is convinced that, in addition to having originated in Mexico or elsewhere in Latin America, the Penitente Brotherhood of New Mexico has certain features which are universal in the region and exclusive to it: kneeling on *arroz* (tiny stones collected from anthills) and the use of stone knives, yucca scourges, and cactus thorns (Chavez, 1954b: 120). Father Chavez' suggestion of an original center of the Brotherhood near Santa Cruz de la Cañada is supported by the fact that the Santuario de Chimayó, New Mexico's principal cult shrine associated with healing powers attributed to the local clay soil, parallels closely the practices of a Guatemalan shrine, studied by Stephen F. de Borhegyi (1956; see also SANM, Misc. File on Chimayó, #2, 11/16/1813). It is said that weavers from Guatemala came to settle Chimayó in the late eighteenth century, perhaps accounting for the parallels. The builder of the Santuario is described as a Penitente leader.

21. Chavez, 1954b: 99.

22. Woodward ms., 1935: 262.

23. Darley, 1893. The late Doña Candelaria Mestas, born in 1858, told me her early childhood recollection of an abortive cavalry attack on the San Pedro Church. As the soldiers charged into the plaza, the *tinieblas* commenced with such a noise of groans and cries and rattling of chains and *matracas* (wooden noisemakers) that the horses threw their riders, and the attack on the Penitentes had to be cancelled.

24. Alarid-Leblanc correspondence, 11/8/1881.

25. Read, 1912: 511.

26. Zerwekh, 1962: 215.

27. Chavez, 1954b: 100.

28. Rendón, 1963: 78.

29. Darley, 1893: 8-17. Darley quoted Pedro Sanchez to the effect that the *Hermano Mayor* (Elder Brother) led the local chapter and that the *Hermano Mayor Principal* headed all chapters. It is evident from the title page that the Rule of Brotherhood applied beyond a single local group. According to Darley (p. 35) political and religious ambitions of past years had disunited an originally united Brotherhood. The name of Bernardo Abeyta (the same name as that of the builder of the Chimayó Santuario) as Hermano Mayor Principal reinforces the suggestion that Chimayó was the original and principal Penitente center.

30. Trujillo ms., 1934.

31. *El Reino de Dios*, 6/1934: 8-9.

32. An unnamed person, apparently the hermano mayor of Abiquiu, sent a letter to a Las Vegas printer on May 29, 1900, with a proposal for reestablishing contact among the disunited Brothers of Río Arriba County, by referring to him all inquiries concerning the recently published rules of the Confraternity. The writer wished to launch a slate of Democratic candidates for county office to break the stranglehold of the Catronist Republicans. In July of that year a "Fusion" Democratic ticket was

formed. It included some candidates who were not themselves Penitentes but were considered sympathetic to the rights of the Brotherhood. The slate included two Anglo-American storekeepers, Samuel Eltodt of San Juan and Henry Grant of Abiquiu. Tobias Espinosa, who was just commencing his medical career at Chama, ran for surveyor, and José Vidal Quintana ran for assessor. A few years later, Quintana was a storekeeper of Rosa and its lone Democrat (NMSRC, Misc. Doc., Record Book of Juan de Dios Durán, 422, 445).

33. Abel, 1916: 189-243; Reeve, 1937: 135.

34. Abel, 1941: 328; Velasquez ms. (n.d.).

35. Reeve, 1937: 139.

36. Gilpin, 1962: 709. Lafayette Head raised two Ute girls in his household, sisters or cousins, one of whom retained the Head surname all her life. Both returned to live as married adults on the Southern Ute Reservation. They were devout Catholics of a distinctly Hispanic cultural orientation, as were other Utes raised in Hispanic households.

Perhaps because he was a Missourian by birth, Lafayette Head approved of the system of raising captive Indians, but his defense of Pedro Leon's 1852 practice of trading off horses and mules for Ute children was couched in Hispanic-Catholic terms. Head pointed out that heads of households having a child captive were obliged to serve as baptismal godparents and must seek a mate for the captive at the proper age (14-16 years for girls and 18-20 years for boys); once married, the captive was automatically free (Hafen and Hafen, 1954: 273-74).

37. Sanford, 1933: 176. Albert B. Sanford visited Lafayette Head in Conejos in 1876 and found him a top-ranking member of both Anglo and Hispano society. See also Darley, 1893: 35.

38. *Rio Grande School Bulletin,* 10/1962: 3.

39. *El Reino de Dios,* 6/1934: 10.

40. United States Census, Colorado, 1870: Conejos County.

41. USDA, 1936: 53.

42. TAG #92-229, #292, #294, #303, #315. The Abert Report of 1846 (see note 12, chapter 3) is perfectly consistent with the possibility that small, hidden sheep camps and ranches were located in the canyons of the Tierra Amarilla country at that time.

43. *Rio Grande Sun,* 11/8/1962, Section B: 10.

44. Reeve, 1937: 147-49.

45. TAG #4; NMSRC, Twitchell Collection #212.

46. *Rio Grande Sun,* 11/8/1962, Section C: 5.

47. *Santa Fe New Mexican,* 1/13/1874.

48. *Santa Fe New Mexican,* 12/14/1891.

49. The Abiquiu baptismal and marriage rolls were destroyed by a fire which gutted Santo Tomás Church in 1869, consuming most of the existing parish records for the nineteenth century. The church records concerning people of the Upper Chama commence in 1869, in the books of the Church of San Juan Nepomuceno, El Rito.

50. TAG #224, 10/27/1862.

51. TAG #2: María Manuela Martinez and husband Tomás Lucero, bargain and sale deed for right, title, and interest to Thomas B. Catron, 9/6/1876.

52. Hefferan ms., 1940: 26.

53. TAG #292, #293, #54.

54. Keleher, 1962: 123.

55. NMSRC, Fiske Collection: conveyance to Jesús María Córdova, 7/2/1864.

56. Larson, 1962: 164.

57. TAG #89: decree of district court, 9/28/1883.

58. TAG #85-89, and decree of probate court of Río Arriba, 2/12/1885; 23-24.

59. TAG #273, 12/10/1881; #257-270, 8/1881-4/1882; #274, 1/14/1885.

60. TAG #81, 7/22/1882: 27.

61. Quoted by Hefferan, 1940: 158-60.

62. TAG #84: 27.

63. Harper et al, 1943: 55.

64. United States Census, Colorado, 1880: Conejos County; NMT, Adjutant-General, #123, 4/3/1881.

65. Quoted by Reeve, 1937: 153.

66. NMT, 6-B, Adjutant-General, 1881: Letters #118, #120, #123, #126, #127, #133, #149, #156, #166.

67. Swadesh ms., 1962: 12-14.

68. Taylor ms., 1933-34: 15-16.

69. Rasch, 1965: 220-24.

70. *Santa Fe New Mexican*, 10/31/1882-11/1/1882, quoted by Rasch, 1965: 229.

5. HISPANIC SETTLEMENTS OF THE SAN JUAN BASIN

1. Cruz Antonio Archuleta was the father of the 1881 lynch victim, Guadalupe Archuleta. The hamlet of Archuleta, southwest of the Navajo Dam, is named after this family, whose descendants claim Indian ancestry through Francisco Manzanares, father-in-law of Epifanio Valdez. He is described as a "Chimayó," a term used with the connotation of Genízaro or detribalized Indian, as well as for a person from the town of that name. Manzanares seems to have had Ute ancestry.

2. Several other family groupings claim the distinction of being the first permanent settlers of the San Juan Basin. Descendants of José Miguel Ulibarrí say that he and his married son, Agustín, settled in a cave near the present damsite in 1870, while building their homestead in Los Pinos. In that year, however, both were enumerated in the Tierra Amarilla census tracts. In 1880 the Ulibarrís lived on the east bank of the Río de los Pinos above its confluence with the San Juan.

The descendants of Salome Jaquez claim that their ancestor accompanied the first Valdez-Manzanares-Archuleta migration from the Huérfano Valley, but give a date of December 20, 1876 for arrival in the San Juan Basin. Since Jaquez brought in a sizeable herd of sheep which would have been in jeopardy before the Utes accepted the terms of the Brunot Agreement, it seems unlikely that he was with the first settlers (see Cornelius, 1961: 155).

3. The 1880 census lists the following residents of the Perez Ranch in addition to Perez and his wife: Antonio José Barry, a widower; Santos Oliveras, born in California; Jacobo García and Guadalupe Maez, companions of Perez in the move from the San Luis Valley, but born in the Lower Chama Valley.

4. Perez first appears in the Conejos baptismal rolls in 1872, when his son, Enrique Alfredo, was baptized in Piedra Pintada near present Del Norte. The following year, his daughter Aurora was baptized in La Loma. Perez' sheep were mentioned disapprovingly in Ute agency records of 1878 (FRC 44094-005/311¬4/22/1878).

5. The Luceros were José Blas and Ramón, men from the Chama Valley, who had moved first to the San Luis Valley with their father, Felipe Enerio Lucero, and then had come to settle *Los Pinos*, at the river bend later called *La Península*. Their sister Rita was married to Teófilo Salazar, who had previously been widowed of her sister Petra. Rita would later be widowed of Teófilo and would then marry Antonio José Barry, formerly married to her late sister Madalena.

Thus we note a preexisting link between people of widely diverse backgrounds, who had probably become acquainted in the San Luis Valley. However, Teófilo Salazar's father, Francisco, may have been one of Perez' California companions. At the same time, this Francisco Salazar may have been a freighter from Abiquiu who went to California after being enumerated in the 1845 census.

Two other "Californians" are said to have been Perez' companions in his move to New Mexico. Neither of them dwelt on his ranch in 1880, but both figure in the history of the San Juan Basin. Candelario Sotelo married a granddaughter of Francisco Martinez of Tierra Amarilla fame and moved to Rosa with his brother-in-law, Pedro Quintana, who had married a Rosa girl. The other Californian was Miguel José Quintana, quite probably the son of Francisco Estévan Quintana of El Rito. Francisco had a small son named Miguel in 1841 when he moved to California and settled the San Luis Obispo Grant near Los Angeles. In 1880 Miguel J. Quintana lived at La Piedra with his daughter and son-in-law, Santiago Candelaria. His son, Agapito, was the first settler of the Arroyo de las Sembritas in the following decade (see Hafen and Hafen, 1954: 220-21).

6. The Candelarias, of a Río Abajo lineage, had been on the move as freighters for a number of years. The birthplaces of Román Candelaria's children by his wife, Mariana Griego, were varied, as follows: María Severa, 1863, "New Mexico"; Anastasio, 1866, Capulín, Conejos Parish; José,

1871, Chilili, in the Manzano Mountains; Francisco, 1874, Huérfano County, Colorado. Grown and married children of Román Candelaria were his son, Augustiniano, and a daughter Victoriana, married to Juan Román Gurule. This Candelaria kin group settled on the east bank of the San Juan River at what would later be identified as the north end of Rosa.

Roman Candelaria's party arrived in the winter of 1877, just as the Utes were being assembled on their reservation. They reached the San Juan River via Carracas Canyon and attempted to cross at the same fording place used in the previous century by the Dominguez-Escalante expedition. Their heavily laden oxcarts could not make the crossing and they therefore wintered in Coraque at the mouth of the canyon. There they assembled a two-story "fort" made of handhewn notched logs, which they had brought with them in case of Ute or Jicarilla attack. In the spring they disassembled their fort and moved on to the Rosa location.

Other Candelarias who were related to Román were enumerated in the 1880 census of the San Juan River district. The widow of Juan Antonio Candelaria, Román's first cousin, lived at Hinsdale with her bachelor sons, Anastasio and Bidal. Her elderly widowed sister lived next door. Two married sisters of Anastasio and Bidal Candelaria lived at Hinsdale; they were Catalina, married to José Lucero, and Quirina, married to Domingo José Gallegos. Other Candelaria relatives were Pablo, Santiago, and Jesús Candelaria; the latter's father-in-law was Chihuahua-born José Refugio Corrales, who lived with him at La Piedra.

The population of La Piedra in 1880 included a well-to-do sheepman from Tierra Amarilla named Felipe Madrid. He had been permitted by the Utes in 1877 to graze 1500 head of sheep on their range (FRC 44094-005/301−12/20/1877). Two other Tierra Amarilla grantees living at La Piedra were Andrés Avelino Martinez, a carpenter, and Rafael José Alire.

At Los Pinos, in addition to the Luceros and Salazars, lived Mexican-born Faustín Enriquez, who had moved from the San Luis Valley as a herder for the Gomez family of Río Navajó but by 1880 had his own homestead. The first Lucero settlers were replaced in the early 1880's by other Luceros who called them "cousin" without knowing the precise relationship; these were the offspring of José Esquípula Lucero and María Luisa Maestas of Tierra Azul. José Blas and Ramón Lucero then moved to Rosa where Blas became involved in a flaming romance with Pabla Leblanc, the estranged wife of Nicolás Aragón, a sometime musician of Tierra Amarilla. They eloped to the home of Federico Panayós (Henry Tree), a hispanicized Ute whose teenage daughter later had a child by Blas Lucero. The affair between Blas and Pabla was short-lived and Pabla later became the San Juan Basin's most respected midwife, earning a Board of Health certificate. She was a woman of strong character, the daughter of a Canadian Mountain Man who had settled and married in the San Luis Valley.

The character of José Blas Lucero is somewhat clouded in the memory of many who knew him. He was a dynamic person, often seen as boastful

and unstable, but one who was steadfast in upholding the rights of the
Utes to their reservation and to compensation for the lands they had lost
(see FRC 44015-006 Tree—4/26/1902; 44017-154/064—1925-26; 44011-
Letterbook a: 392-93—10/22/1900, also 158-59—6/2/1900, 87-8—8/8/
1900 and 392-93—10/22/1900). Living Utes who knew Blas Lucero speak
of him warmly.

7. The actual location of Hinsdale is in doubt, but may have been the
spot where the Arboles depot was later built. In 1883, at the time of the
eviction of settlers from the margins of the Ute reservation, Bidal Candelaria had an Arboles letterhead for his business stationery. In a communication written shortly after the eviction, the letterhead is crossed out
and re-addressed "San Juan River," the name then used for Rosa (FRC
44014-005/001—6/20/1883).

8. *Piedra* (rock) refers to the famous Chimney Rock for which the
entire valley and its river are named. In the early 1960's, the location of
the original La Piedra settlement was still marked by a small cemetery.

9. Lopez was shot by Anastasio Gonzales of Bloomfield. The killing
was witnessed by Serafín Aragón and his small son Pedro, but no one felt
impelled to call in the law, since the killing was considered justified.

10. FRC 44094-005/308—6/15/1881, 6/21/1881, 12/8/1882.

11. Río Navajó could have been an early name for Juanita, located at
the San Juan-Navajo confluence. Lumberton is first mentioned in church
records in 1900; Dulce had its name by 1886.

12. The other settlers of the east bank of the Río de los Pinos in 1880
were Serafín Aragón who had come from Saguache, Colorado with his
wife, small children and a Navajo servant; Cruz Antonio Archuleta; Mariano Córdova; English-born Lee Craven and his Boston-born wife; Andrés
and Gerónimo Martinez with their mother and Gerónimo's wife and
children; José Miguel and Agustín Ulibarri with their families. There were
in 1880 no settlements on the west bank of the Río de los Pinos north of
the hamlet of that name.

13. In the early 1890's Stollsteimer lost most of his sheep in a dreadful
blizzard, and had to give up his ranch. His descendants still live in the area
and are described by local Hispanos as *coyotes*. Several employees on
Stollsteimer's ranch entered the historical stream of the San Juan Basin.
German-born Herman Brachvogel and Walter von Buddenbroch served as
agency employees during Stollsteimer's term at Ignacio. Von Buddenbroch
married a daughter of the Wilmers and their thoroughly hispanicized
descendants still live in the San Juan Basin. Another employee of Stollsteimer was Francisco Marquez, who married a daughter of Román Candelaria in 1882 and was known to his grandchildren as a fervent Penitente.
At that time, Church sanctions against Penitentes were so severe that when
the second Marquez child was baptized, a note was entered in the record
that the child was illegitimate.

14. FRC 44014-005/125—11/26/1885.

15. FRC 44094-005/308—3/20/1885, 4/23/1885, 4/28/1885.

16. FRC 44094-005/308—9/14/1887.

17. Agapito Quintana was married to Cipriana Corrales, a daughter of José Refugio. Other homesteaders of the Arroyo were the Lopez siblings from El Rito: Donaciano, José Nestor, Braulio, Lucía (married to Emilio Padilla), and Luciana (married to Tomás Herrera).

Probably founded somewhat earlier than the morada at the Arroyo de las Sembritas was the morada of Los Martinez, slightly southwest of Los Pinos. A number of families who lived nearby were its first Brothers and the name of Juan Bautista Velasquez, who appeared in the early 1880's, is closely linked with the morada. Velasquez married a daughter of José Esquípula Lucero and Velasquez' son, Timoteo, married a daughter of Agapito Quintana. The location of the morada of Los Martinez, just below the Navajo Dam, was marked by a small graveyard which lay beside it.

18. FRC 44014-005/130—3/12/1878, 3/14/1878; 005/126—10/12/ 1880.

19. FRC 44014-005/125—5/1/1885.

20. FRC 44015-5/22/1883, 6/1/1883, 6/14/1883.

21. Descendants of Rosa pioneers insist that neither Candelaria nor Quintana became a patrón in the sense of gaining political control; in fact, these people reserve the term for Anglo employers who, perhaps, paid higher wages. Candelaria is recalled with more respect in the years following his bankruptcy than during his greatest affluence, because it was then that he demonstrated his *fortaleza* (strength of character). He was then in his sixties with a young second family and he hired out as a herder or for any work that would support them. When he died, he was working as a maintenance man on the railroad. Vidal Quintana was highly respected for his vigorous principles but he never succeeded in winning a single person outside of his own family to the Democratic Party. By the time the New Deal programs had won some converts in Rosa, Quintana was a poor man and was about to enter his final illness.

22. Ute Agent Joseph O. Smith was not sure if the saloon was in Colorado or New Mexico but asked that it be closed, if only on the grounds that the owner was operating without a license. His real reason for wanting Velasquez' saloon closed was that "he is selling his vile stuff to the Indians and I have a large camp of them there now working on a ditch . . . please try to pull the fellow in" (FRC 44011a-418—8/18/1900).

23. FRC 44014-005/126—7/25/1906.

24. In 1891 an investigator noted that the existing control measures to enforce Indian Prohibition would "impel persons disposed to engage in any vice with Indians to be very secret in their practices" (FRC 44019-161: A.S. Griswold, report on—4/2/1891).

25. FRC 44014-005/126—7/8/1903.

26. FRC 44014-005/126—1/2/1907, 10/22/1907, 4/14/1908, 4/25/ 1908.

27. FRC 44014-005/126—3/8/1910, 11/8/1910, 12/21/1910.

28. FRC 44014-005/126—10/5/1925.

29. FRC 44019-161: José Velasquez, 4/6/1906, 9/24/1912, 10/3/ 1912, 11/22/1912, 3/21/1913, 8/9/1913, 8/30/1913; plus the written statements of José Velasquez in 1912 and 1913, loaned by his widow, María Perfecta S. de Velasquez, for microfilming in the records of the Tri-Ethnic Project.

30. FRC 44019-161: José Ulibarrí, 7/30/1925.

31. McClellan, 1961: 112; baptismal rolls of Sacred Heart Parish, Durango, Colorado, Vol. I.

32. Like Francisco Marquez, Casías was banned from the sacraments because of his Penitente membership and his children were designated as "illegitimate" on the baptismal rolls. Casías was nonetheless highly respected by non-Penitentes as well as Penitentes. Several Utes selected him as baptismal godfather for their children.

33. The store records of J.V. Quintana and Sons, 1905-1919, show how customers paid their bills seasonally, after selling off livestock. Records were loaned by Miguel F. Quintana, for microfilming in the records of the Tri-Ethnic Project and the Western History Library of the University of Colorado.

34. Grubbs, 1960: 198.

35. Grubbs, 1962: 46-49; Harper et al, 1943: 78-79.

36. Grubbs, 1960: 194.

6. THE FLOWERING AND DECLINE OF SAN JUAN BASIN COMMUNITIES

1. The Rosa justice of the peace court records provide an example, well remembered by older residents, of how a case could get out of community control when it was referred to the district court. Donaciano Lopez, in 1891-1892, was repeatedly accused by Rosa people of stock trespass and stock theft. When called before the court, he sometimes failed to appear and sometimes jumped bond. The neighbors wanted the j.p. court to get their livestock back for them, but since this was a criminal case, it was referred to the San Juan County District Court, where delays were interminable. By 1893 community feeling ran so high that, when Lopez was ambushed and killed one night, no serious attempt was made to apprehend the assassin. Note 7, chapter 5, gives another instance of a killing which the community viewed as an act of justice (Rosa J.P. Court, Book 5: 167-68; Book 250: 181-82; plus informant data).

2. Father Albert Daeger, a diminutive man who spoke Spanish with a strong Alsatian accent, was working as a circuit priest in the San Juan Basin as early as 1896, entering baptisms in the St. Joseph, Parkview, church records. Rosa people recall that, one Sunday morning as he was riding from Blanco to Rosa to celebrate mass, his horse died beneath him. Daeger sent his assistant back to fetch a fresh mount for him while he walked on ahead, carrying his heavy stockman's saddle. By the time the assistant had caught up with him, the priest had hiked many hard miles to

Rosa and was already celebrating the mass. San Juan Basin Penitentes recall that Daeger expressed understanding of their fervor and only asked that they conduct their penitential exercises out of sight of the "Protestant heretics"; they complied so well that even the Anglos who attended the Horner School in the Arroyo de las Sembritas did not realize that each day they passed by the morada. In later years, Father Daeger became the archbishop of Santa Fe.

3. McCulloch, 1961: 195.

4. Henderson, 1937: 77. Few people with strong Indian connections of any kind were active in the Brotherhood. Patricio Salazar, son of a Navajo father and Hispano mother, was one exception. He helped build the Cañada morada and was an active Brother, having been raised in the Los Pinos community after his father deserted the family.

5. The task of the prayer leader was to "line out" prayers to which the assemblage gave the responses. The prayer leader might read from a book, usually copied by hand, or might recite from memory. The functions of a *cantor* (song leader) were similar to those of a prayer leader, but cantors always appear to have been initiates of the Brotherhood. The cantor's function was to lead in the singing of *alabados* (praise songs) during prayer vigils, wakes for the dead, and the observances of Lent and Holy Week. The unmetered verse and cantillation of alabados make them strongly reminiscent of Islamic and Jewish sacred music. The cantor served as a singularly dramatic narrator of the Passion during Holy Week exercises.

6. Conejos and Durango Parish records; informant recollection; Abel, 1915: 169.

7. Loomis and Grisham, 1943; Harper et al., 1943: 65; USDA publications; Apodaca, 1952.

8. The reader interested in learning more about the Alianza is referred to Blawis, 1971, for an excellent report, also to Swadesh, 1968 and 1969. The Alianza and the personality of Reies Lopez Tijerina have been interpreted in numerous writings, most of them sensational and distorted by ethnocentric bias.

7. HISPANIC COMMUNITY STRUCTURE

1. Twitchell, 1925: 175. Fray Angélico Chavez lists five communities in the Belén area during the eighteenth century which were called "Plaza de Chavez" or "Plaza de San Fernando de Chavez" (1954a: 160-64). The earliest center of population of Albuquerque was Alameda rather than the plaza of San Felipe de Neri. Even in the modern metropolitan district of Albuquerque, with population exceeding 300,000, the little placitas of Los Ranchos, Los Griegos, Los Duranes, Los Tomases, Martineztown, San Felipe, Barelas, San José and others are distinguishable, despite engulfment by the city. The core population of many of these placitas is still deeply rooted and attached to small plots of land on which they raise much

of their own food. Residents continue to maintain some institutions of the traditional village.

2. The wooden plow was used, its blade tipped with iron when available. The *coa* (digging stick) was extensively used in planting corn. A hoe with an iron tip was an item of sufficient importance to be mentioned prominently in wills. Metal spades were a rarity; settlers made their own wooden spades.

3. The grid-plan town, with streets laid out at right angles to one another and a central plaza serving as the religious, administrative, commercial, and social hub of the community was much more important in New World society than in Spain. As new towns were built with a formal layout, the church occupied one side of the plaza; administrative buildings, including a garrison and a jail, occupied another side; the open market and/or stores took up the third side, and the homes of leading citizens were on the fourth side (documented in George Foster's *Culture and Conquest:* 34-38). The plazas of Santa Fe, San Felipe de Neri, and Santo Tomás (the Genízaro town of Abiquiu) were examples of the prescribed central plaza in New Mexico; but the pattern of solid rows of houses enclosing the plaza and lining squared-off streets remained embryonic.

4. Translated and quoted in Read, 1912: 336-39. The term which Read translates as "neighbor" is *vecino*, meaning a tithes-paying settler-citizen. Even as early as the beginning of the eighteenth century, there were vecinos of full Indian or African ancestry, who received land grants because they were well assimilated into the colonial culture and its objectives. "Reasonable people" (*gente de razón*) refers to Christians of Hispanic, Mestizo, Indian, or African ancestry, not all of whom were vecinos.

When Governor Mendinueta wrote his complaining report to the Viceroy, he had already experienced the stubbornness of the Ojo Caliente settlers with whom he had contended in 1769. They had prevailed upon him to drop his charges of cowardice and his threats to vacate their grant title. He had settled an additional group of twenty-two Genizaros above the hot springs to aid in the defense of the community. His statement that the settlers could "frustrate the object of the governor" is well documented in the records of Ojo Caliente (SANM I: #655, #656; Boyd, 1957).

5. SANM I: #1100; informant reports of family traditions.

6. AASF, Loose Doc. 1795, #13: 4-5.

7. MANM, Misc. Doc. undated, probably 1828-1830.

8. "The word plaza is used in New Mexico to indicate a certain place where people are living" (Carroll and Haggard, 1942: 286, footnote).

9. As late as 1841, the townsite of Abiquiu apparently included not only the public square and church land, the houses and the entrances and exits, but a considerable amount of unassigned land. The translator of a statement on unassigned lands in Abiquiu, drawn up in 1841 by General José María Chavez in his capacity of peace justice, commented on the

"vague" use of the term *chorreras*, which the translator defined as "back-yards." At present, Abiquiu residents use the term to designate the access space between contiguous houses, which cannot be denied by one owner to another. In the San Juan Basin, where the settlement pattern remains dispersed, people use "chorreras" to mean the rainspouts that drain off their roofs or natural drainage channels for runoff in a community. The latter may have been the meaning used by General Chavez in his statement (see NMLG Reel 48, PLC 140: Juan José Lobato, 5/13/1841).

10. Bunting, 1964: 6-7.

11. NMLG Reel 48, PLC 140: Juan José Lobato. The General Chavez house is the residence of noted artist Georgia O'Keeffe.

12. NMLG Reel 41, PLC 68: Antonio de Beytia. The strips of land mentioned were of unspecified length, but irrigated strips usually ran from the irrigation ditch to a short distance from the riverbank.

13. Bunting, 1964: 9; Herbert Dick, verbal communication. Presidial troops were not regularly stationed in the Chama Valley, but La Caseta may have been at one time a station for the local militia.

14. Minge, 1963: 37-38.

15. In the record of a 1731 dispute between Juana Lopez and Diego Torres concerning an abandoned grant in Chama (Chamita), Torres said that Juana had not effectively occupied the grant she inherited from her husband because she only maintained a jacal for sheepherders. Juana retorted that the herder was her son, hence she was a bonafide settler (NMLG Reel 48, PLC 140: Juan José Lobato). Another document refers to a "jacal customarily used for the shelter of the said herders," described in 1737 as a house made of stones chinked with adobe. It was apparently no more than six feet in height and width, hence was truly a hut (SANM I: #1242).

16. SANM I: #571. Bainbridge Bunting writes: "Near the mountains, where timber was more readily available, logs were sometimes employed. The logs were frequently cut flush with the end walls and the surfaces were often plastered with mud to resemble regular adobe masonry" (1964: 6).

17. The Candelarias' *casa fuerte* (hand-adzed and notched log fort, which could be rapidly assembled and disassembled) is the first such structure of record in the San Juan Basin. The second is Rubio Gallegos' log cabin, which was still standing in the early 1960's. Many such structures have been destroyed by fire over the years.

18. SANM I: #655; Bunting, 1964: 3-4.

19. By 1793 the population had risen to 1,558, of whom only 156 (mainly the Genízaros of Abiquiu) were designated as Indians. The remaining 1,402 were described as Spaniards and "people of other classes"— mestizos, mulattos, and coyotes (AASF, Loose Doc. 1795, #13).

20. SANM I: #561. This section is derived from the 1789-1790 census as given in Crocchiola, n.d. (1960), amplified and corrected through reference to AASF, B-10, Box 8 and M-1, Box 4.

21. The nine plazas which apparently existed in that year were, from east to west: Tierra Azul, San Ygnacio, La Puente (the first Santa Rosa), La Capilla, Plaza Colorada, Santo Tomás (Town of Abiquiu), San José del Barranco, San Antonio Vallecito, and Cañones.

22. MANM #809. A Mexican-period census of the El Rito demarcation, undated but apparently made in the 1830's, lists a population of 1,466 with 297 household heads. The settlements of El Rito were scattered into at least five plazas. One hundred and twelve households, according to shared surnames of contiguous residences, appear to be linked in forty seven associations. Thus, the total number of household compounds would have been 232, or an average of 46 units per plaza. However, at least half the households were listed at *El Poblazón* (El Rito proper), which included at least two more placitas: El Cañon (cluster of Trujillo households near the mouth of El Rito Canyon) and *El Llano* (probably the original placita of the García de Noriegas). Taking into account that El Poblazón was growing into a village, the average population of each placita would still be thirty-three units of associated or independent households, much like the pattern at Abiquiu.

23. U.S. census, 1870 and 1880, New Mexico: Río Arriba County.

24. It is fortunate that the 1829 will of Petrona Gonzales, widow of José Ygnacio Martín Serrano, lists the names of her children; this document proves the existence of the younger José Ygnacio and establishes that he was the brother of the petitioner for the Tierra Amarilla Grant (NMLG Reel 48, PLC 140, Exhibit 3).

Heirship documents, land documents, and church records help to untangle the dense web of kinship among contemporaries and between generations. The fact that José Ygnacio Martín, Sr. and Gerónimo Martín received joint title to a grant suggests that they were close relatives. Other documents suggest that Gerónimo Martín may have been a brother or cousin of Severino and Antonio José Martinez (father and uncle, respectively, of the famous Father Martinez of the nineteenth century). The Martín Serranos repeatedly selected one another and various Salazars as baptismal and wedding sponsors (AASF, B-10, Box 8 and M-1, Box 4).

The task of analyzing the historical record is complicated by the high mortality rate and other factors. Loss of spouses led to second and even third marriages. With a high percentage of Martín Serranos in the population, some contemporaries had the same given name and are hard to distinguish from one another. Some infants were given the same baptismal name as a recently deceased sibling; at the same time, some infants appear to have been baptized more than once.

25. Robert Pehrson (1954: 200-1) has noted that postmarital residence among the reindeer herders of Lapland is determined by the ratio of herd size to labor force.

26. NMSRC Maria G. Durán Collection, 12/20/1785.

27. NMLG Reel 52, PLC 227: Juan Antonio Quintana.

28. NMLG Reel 41, PLC 68: Baltazar Cisneros.

29. SANM I: #28, #36, #571, #650, #655, #656, #976. Juan José Lobato was the officiating alcalde in the bestowal of several considerable land grants within the territory later claimed as part of his grant and so confirmed by the Court of Private Land Claims, thus disinheriting families which had been in continuous residence over generations. (See SANM I: #347, #538; NMLG SG Report 149, File 85; PLC 97; PLC 131, File 124; PLC 140; PLC 141.)

30. In colonial and Mexican times, the only professional doctor was one assigned to the Sante Fe presidio. There were also a few "barbers," mainly residents of Santa Fe, who performed simple surgery (see Chavez, 1954a: 122).

31. Schulman-Smith ms., 1962: 253-54. An instance of how much it was taken for granted that a woman returned to her parents' home in late pregnancy and remained through the early lactation period is provided by the record of a dispute in 1754. Gerónimo Martín claimed that the lands near Abiquiu which Francisco Quintana was purchasing from him were forfeit to him because Quintana had deserted them. Quintana showed that he had placed renters on these lands but Martín replied that Quintana had only appeared in person when bringing his wife to stay with her parents. Somewhat as an afterthought, he mentioned the birth of a baby (SANM II: #529). The truth of the matter seems to be that Quintana had the older children under his parents' care in Santa Cruz and had to go there to support them. It seems inconceivable that he would have brought his pregnant wife to Abiquiu and then fled for his own safety.

32. Adams and Chavez, 1956: 126.

33. Gregorio Quintana sold five male and four female captives to Filomeno Sanchez of Manzano, and a little later in 1808 purchased that portion of the García de Noriega Grant which constitutes much of the present village of El Rito (Hurt, 1941: 47; NMLG Reel 27, SG 151: Town of El Rito). After the United States conquest, the number of Navajo captives in the homes of the Chama and San Luis Valleys rose sharply. In addition to the Indians who were household servants, vecinos who were of recent predominantly Indian or casta ancestry tended to occupy a position of social subordination, readily canceled by the acquisition of land and/or moving to a new community.

34. The will of Severino Martinez of Taos states the following after naming all his children: " . . . all of whom I placed in the estate of matrimony with the exception of the youngest, Juan Pascual, who consequently will be rewarded proportionately out of the common" (Minge, 1963:40).

35. In Navarre, Aragon, and Catalonia the "Compañia Gallega" is an institution in which "married sons with their children continued to live in the family home and to work for the common good in forms which have been compared with the Slavic *zadruga*." Under this system, each child received a dowry at marriage, but one child, whether male or female, received the parents' house and balance of the inheritance at their death

on condition of remaining with them during their lifetime, eating from *una sola mesa y manteles* (the same table and table linens) and taking back and maintaining any married sister who might find herself without means of support (Foster, 1960: 153-54, 164).

36. In New Mexico, legend extols but also pokes fun at the dutiful child. "El Grande Casías" was a man who never married because his parents lived over a hundred years; as they grew bald and senile, they quarreled so fiercely at night that he was obliged to build an oversize bed and sleep between them to prevent bloodshed. His self-denying life brought its own reward, however, for El Grande Casías became a very rich man. There are stories about El Grande Casías all over the Rio Arriba country; this version was provided by Elmer Shupe.

37. *Campanilismo* has been noted both for Spain and Latin America by George Foster (1960: 35).

38. Julian Pitt-Rivers has thoroughly described the social function of nicknames as a means of imposing sanctions for deviations from the norm in Alcalá de la Sierra, a community of Andalusia (1961: 161-69).

39. The Moaches continued to visit the Taos area, despite considerable antagonism toward the settlers, arising from the 1844 massacre in Santa Fe. Principal stimulus for the visits was the distilled liquor made at Turley's Mill at Arroyo Hondo, which was known as Taos Lightning. Moaches continued to harass the Rio Colorado Grant settlers at Cuesta and to bar settlement of the Sangre de Cristo Grant at the east end of the San Luis Valley until 1851.

Ute interest in alcoholic beverages was a direct outgrowth of Spanish colonial policy. In 1786, the viceroy of New Spain, Bernardo de Galvez, wrote the following instructions to his administrators:

> The Nations of the North have a fondness for intoxicating liquors, while the Apaches are not acquainted with them, but it will be convenient to incline the latter to the use of brandy or mescal wherever its manufacture may be permitted. With a little effort and in a short time they will acquire a taste for these drinks, in which case it will become with them the most valuable trade, and the one which will allow the greatest profit to our merchants engaged in barter with the Indians. . . . After all, the supplying of drink to the Indians will be a means of gaining their goodwill, discovering their secrets, calming them so they will think less often of conceiving and executing their hostilities, and creating for them a new necessity which will oblige them to recognize their dependence upon us more directly (Galvez, 1951:46-47).

40. Statement, 8/11/1874, quoted in *Rio Grande Sun*, 11/8/1962, Section B: 16.

41. The rate of decline of Hispanic villages in northern New Mexico has been and continues to be uneven. The Tewa Basin Study of Spanish American Villages recorded for the mid-1930's "marked and interesting differences between the people of the different villages. This might be explained by the fact that, even in recent years, the little communities are more or less isolated from each other" (USDA, 1939: iii). At that time the

villages where the greatest extremes of wealth and poverty were present had the strongest manifestations of political *caciquismo* (bossism) and the greatest degree of social disorganization (USDA, 1939: viii).

In the 1930's, El Rito was still thriving. One hundred and eighty five families out of 210 in the village owned some farmland, and 65 families had small grazing permits (USDA, 1939: 132-33). A disastrous blizzard in the late 1930's plunged the families into ruin because they lost all their sheep and were unable to pay their store debts. Ever since, most of the people of El Rito have been forced to seek wage work outside the community and demoralization has been growing (observations of the late George Martin of El Rito).

42. The Mano Negra was a vigilante movement of rural anarchists of Andalusia, Spain, in the late nineteenth and early twentieth centuries. The movement developed after the anarchists were forced underground and after community control of land and government had been obliterated. The concern of this movement was with "justice and the just cause of the people" and to restore the authority vested in the community, "the natural unit of society" (Pitt-Rivers, 1961: 220-22).

During this period of stress in Spain, there was steady migration of Spanish miners, herders, and common laborers from Spain to the New World. Some of these exiles came to New Mexico and the Tierra Amarilla area. While the night riders of the Gorras Blancas appear to have adopted some features of the contemporaneous Anglo-American Ku Klux Klan, the Mano Negra movement may have direct roots in Spain.

43. In October 1966, land grant heirs from many grants, some coming from as far away as California, occupied the Echo Amphitheater Campground in Carson National Forest, in the name of the San Joaquin del Rio Chama Grant, within whose boundaries the campground is located. During the occupation the campers regulated their activities by all the provisions of long-remembered legal codes of which their grandparents had spoken. Many expressed a renewed consciousness of the values which formerly pervaded the social institutions of New Mexico (see Swadesh, 1968: 170-71).

8. FRONTIER HISPANIC SOCIAL RELATIONS

1. Antonio de Escudero, a lawyer from Chihuahua who had visited New Mexico in 1827, recalled his observations of economic and social classes as follows: "It can be asserted that there were no paupers in New Mexico at that time nor could there be any. At the same time, there were no large scale stockmen who could pay wages or make any expenditure whatever in order to preserve and increase their wealth in this branch of agriculture." Escudero described how young men entered into partidario contracts in order to obtain the means to marry. He concluded: "Consequently, even in the homes of the poorest New Mexicans, there is never a

dearth of the means to satisfy the necessities of life and even to afford the comfort and luxuries of the wealthiest class in the country" (Carroll and Haggard, 1942: 40-42). Escudero's recollections may have been idealized, and in the period he described, the rico class of Santa Fe Trail merchants was emerging. Still, the distribution of resources and the social flexibility of New Mexico provided opportunities that were foreclosed in other Mexican states and territories. The poorest Genízaro of Abiquiu, with a little luck in hunting, trading, or raiding, could acquire an abundant supply of deer and buffalo meat, livestock, dressed hides and captive Indian children, and thereby become a rico.

2. SANM II: #434. Another way to increase one's livestock holdings was to declare less than the full number for tithing purposes. In 1820 Fray Teodoro Alcina of Abiquiu asked for an investigation into the true number of sheep subject to tithing. Inquiry was made of sheep owned by Miguel F. Quintana, because Alcina thought that Quintana had not declared the full increase of his flocks. Cristobal Chavez, a partidario of Quintana, testified that a year and a half previously he had taken out 567 of Quintana's sheep, including six newborns belonging to his brother, Juan Cristobal Quintana. Twenty sheep had been turned in for tithing and one hundred were declared to have died in three epidemics of "La Pelotita," sixteen heads of the dead sheep having been carried back to Abiquiu as evidence. Chavez testified that Quintana had separated out sixty breeding ewes and had taken them he knew not where (SANM II: #3041). The resentment of the more affluent Chama Valley citizens was aroused by Alcina's investigation. In short order, petitions came from both Abiquiu and Ojo Caliente for the replacement of the priest (SANM II: #2909, #2920, #2926, #2934).

3. SANM I: #606, #612.

4. NMSRC, Maria G. Durán Collection.

5. SANM II: #402.

6. Schroeder, 1965: 58-59; SANM II: #409, #482.

7. Schroeder, 1965: 57-61.

8. Bolton, 1950: 159-61.

9. MANM #7823, 9/1/1844. The Sabuaganas apparently camped on what used to be called Sabuaganas (or Chaguaguas) Creek, later called Chihuahueños or Pedernales Creek. The Capotes were camped on the *Vega de Riaño* (Riaño Meadow) near the mouth of Cañones Creek, when they fled from Santa Fe after the September 1844 massacre by the guards of Governor Martinez y Lejanza. Both of these campsites were near the old San Miguel Plaza of the Piedra Lumbre-Polvadera settlers. Perhaps the large population of this plaza in 1789 was owing to the attractions of unsupervised trade with the Utes.

10. Schroeder, 1965: 61.

11. SANM II: #414.

12. SANM II: #429.

13. SANM II: #740.

14. SANM II: #855.

15. The regional military commander, stationed in Chihuahua.

16. SANM I: #1333. This important set of colonial administrative records was misfiled among the series on land grants and transfers.

17. SANM II: #920.

18. SANM II: #1393.

19. SANM II: #1592.

20. SANM II: #2511.

21. SANM II: #2894.

22. AASF Loose Doc. 1754, #3: baptism, 8/16/1759. If all the baptismal books of colonial New Mexico and Nueva Vizcaya could be checked for entries of "Yutas," "naciones gentiles" (nomadic tribesmen), or "párvulos de los indios" (Indian children—almost surely captives), we might have a better estimate of the volume of trade in Indian captives, including those obtained by purchase from Ute, Comanche, and Apache captors.

The question of correct procedures in evangelizing nomadic Indians continued to pit civil authorities against the clergy as late as the nineteenth century. An exchange of increasingly irate letters between Governor Joaquín Real del Alencaster, Custos José Prada stationed at Abiquiu, Comandante General Salcedo, and Bishop F. Gabriel de Olivares y Benito in Durango, concerning the "inopportune" baptism of two Navajo girls purchased from the Utes, provides much information on this type of conflict in 1805-1806. In this instance, the victory went to Custos Prada and the Abiquiu master-godfathers (SANM II: #1876, #1877, #1881, #1979).

23. Carroll and Haggard, 1942: 88. Paul Horgan (1954: 458) states that before the market for beaver collapsed in the 1830's, annual shipment of pelts from Abiquiu and Taos was worth $200,000. Crocchiola states that during the same period Jacob Leese ran a trading store at Abiquiu for Céran St Vrain (Crocchiola, n.d. (1960): 11). Although no references have been provided to document these statements, there is no doubt that Abiquiu's commerce expanded in the 1820's and 1830's.

24. Simmons, 1968, gives details on administrative changes in late colonial times.

25. The tensions which developed in Abiquiu whenever civil, church, or military authorities tried to force changes upon the settlers are illuminated by Julian Pitt-Rivers' historical survey of the Andalusian town of Alcalá de la Sierra and George Foster's study of the export of Spanish culture to the New World. Foster observes that democratically formulated codes for all kinds of procedures are constantly modified in the New World by "an effective working relationship with the right people" and that, despite pervasive respect for authority, "laws and regulations are often considered things to be avoided" (1960: 4-6). Pitt-Rivers writes: " I have postulated that this tension (between the authority of the state and the morality of the town, F.L.S.) stands in relation to the divergence in values and the degree of contact between the central government and the

community, in the sense that the greater the difference in culture and values between state and community on the one hand, and on the other the shorter the effective spatial distance and the greater the political pressure exerted by the state, the more this tension increases. For tension implies, by definition, first of all a basis of difference and secondly a ground of common contact" (1961: 213).

26. SANM I: #847.

27. SANM II: #2778.

28. SANM II: #3052.

29. SANM II: #3062.

30. NMSRC, Twitchell Collection: #34.

31. NMSRC, Twitchell Collection: #221, #222, #225, #229-233, #236.

32. Trujillo ms., 1934.

33. SANM II: #2894.

34. In Tzintzuntzan, Mexico, siblings who are compadres continue to address one another as *tu* (Foster, 1964: 121).

35. Pitt-Rivers reports that in Alcalá de la Sierra, use of the term "cousin" has an ambiguous meaning, potentially insulting: "The cousin is the prototype of the mug, for he puts his faith in the strength of kinship and is soon deceived" (1961: 105). The same meaning attaches to *primo* in Mexican urban life but the Hispanic society of New Mexico continues to put its total faith in the strength of kinship.

36. In Alcalá, kinship is not associated with political structure, locality, or economic production, hence the extensions of the elementary family are endowed with no structural importance (Pitt-Rivers, 1961: 103). In New Mexico, especially in the northern villages, the reverse is true. Divergent use of the honorific *don* is parallel to other terminology which diverges from usage in other regions. In a south Texas town, "don" is used as a term of address reflecting social stratification in a non-familial context. The term is applied to the patrón "as the source of employment and security; to the Mexican consul, as the rallying point for patriotic fervor, and to wealthy politicians who can furnish help in times of need" (Romano, 1960:974-75). In the San Juan Basin, however, the author was rebuked for addressing an elderly man as "Don ---." He commented that the deepest respect and friendship could only prevail between people who behaved and felt as equals, who addressed one another as "Señor" and "Señora." In Tzintzuntzan, mestizos address Tarascan Indian neighbors as "don," connoting social distance without true respect (Foster, 1964: 114-15). In the San Juan Basin, to the contrary, Utes are never addressed as "don" but sometimes as "señor," if there is a relationship of respect.

37. The courage and toughness of Hispanic women of the New Mexican frontier communities is legendary. Reference has been made to their work in the fields and occasional armed defense of the community in colonial times. In Chamisal, a community of the Santa Barbara Grant in the Peñasco Valley, there is a tradition that the eight-mile-long diversion

canal for irrigation was first dug by a woman settler, practically with her bare hands. She worked without help for several years because nobody believed that water could be brought over the high hill between the river valley and the community; construction of the canal took eleven years to complete. In the San Juan Basin, the near-legendary Doña Candelaria Mestas, who lived well beyond a hundred years, carried the mail on horseback in the 1890's from Arboles to Rosa, fording the San Juan River and losing several toes to frostbite one freezing day. In her seventies, she journeyed some miles on snowshoes to bring help to her dying lover of previous years, whose children by another woman she had raised.

38. Reviewing a compendium of field studies of northern New Mexico villages, Margaret Mead states: "Although there is a clear distinction between men's and women's work, women will do men's work around the place when the men are away. Men who are off herding or working in towns live together and share the tasks of minimum housekeeping without embarassment. Boys will watch their mother at work in the kitchen and become acquainted with her methods. Farmers are ready to cook for their motherless children, if there is no one else to do this" (Mead, 1955: 164).

39. From the time children of both sexes enter school until they have entered adolescence, they are referred to in the San Juan Basin as *La Plebe* (literally: the common folk). It is during this age span that parental discipline is most severe, although many parents of the San Juan Basin refrain from physical punishment. Adults recalling their own childhood recall a stern parental reproof as a sufficient deterrent to misbehavior during their plebe years. Munro Edmonson delineates different age-status patterns for a Hispanic village south of Gallup, New Mexico. According to him, the term *plebe* refers to boys' gangs. At all age levels, he describes superordination of males over females (1957: 24-27). In the San Juan Basin, there were no boys' gangs (the term for "gang" in northern New Mexico is *gavilla*) and superordination by virtue of sex was minimal.

40. The importance of maintaining the value system within the community was such that people who violated the norms were ordered to leave. In 1909 a resident of Rosa denounced his wife in court for bringing her lover into the home; the wife retorted that, since her husband did nothing to support the family, he was no husband. The justice of the peace ruled that both accused and accuser were disorderly people. Husband, wife and lover were ordered to leave Rosa for six months and only return then if they maintained decorum (Rosa J.P., Book 250: 81-84).

41. See Pitt-Rivers, 1961: Chapter 8; Mead, 1955: 170.

42. The observation concerning the relationship of vergüenza to business practices was discussed by Facundo Valdez in a teachers' seminar under sponsorship of the Colorado College in Santa Fe, 7/8/1970.

43. Wilder and Breitenbach, 1945: description of Plate XVIII.

44. One of the most ironic stories about marital deviance concerns a man who became betrothed somewhat late in life, only to discover after the wedding that his wife was already pregnant by her sister's husband. He

acknowledged the child as his own but thereafter refused to have relations with his wife, instead having children by the aggrieved sister and, in later years, a younger sister. Most of these children were raised in his home, with his wife serving as the mother figure. In reporting this bizarre story of connubial vengeance, narrators tempered their mirth with the observation that at least these children were not deprived of a father.

45. In the San Juan riverine communities and elsewhere in northern New Mexico, dances customarily were held in private homes and no strangers attended. A *bastonero* (a man with a rod of authority, later replaced by an appointed constable, charged with keeping order) called the dances and maintained decorum. If anyone became drunk and disorderly, his kinsmen would escort him to the fields to cool off. The pattern of private dances was first breached in Taos, where the Mountain Men, as invited guests, started brawls. As late as 1947 in Rosa, a man who refused to remove his hat when entering a dance at the Rosa Merc and who insulted the constable with improper language and obscene gestures was promptly arrested. He resisted arrest and defended himself with a poker but was seized and placed under $500 bond, a princely sum in those days (Rosa J.P., Book 250: 11-13).

The only violent actions which were approved in the San Juan Basin were those in defense of the honor of one's family. Provided that insult came from a Ute or Hispanic source, retaliation was instant. Heavy handed jokes made by Anglos, outrageously insulting by the Hispanic code, were usually met with stony silence or a pained smile; the cross-cultural gap and subordinate social status made it difficult to meet these gibes on Hispanic terms. Repressed humiliations caused by Anglo dominance still fan the flames very fast in fights among Hispanos.

46. Rendón, 1963: 12. The word *cojones* (literally, testicles, used to cover all aspects of virility and male dominance in Spain and Mexico; see Pitt-Rivers, 1961: 90) is not in use in northern New Mexico, nor is there an equivalent expression. However, terminology and gestures which downgrade a man's virility are favorite insults.

9. PATHS OF CHANGE

1. This study was based on the baptismal and marriage records of Sacred Heart Parish, Durango (1881-1960); the Parish of Our Lady of Guadalupe, Conejos (1860-1882); the Parish of San Juan Nepomuceno, El Rito (1869-1883); and the Parish of Saint Joseph, Parkview (1883-1910). The records of several other parishes could have been studied with benefit, especially because Rosa, during its eighty-three years of existence, was assigned to a succession of parishes. Incomplete as the data were, however, the selected sample included ancestors of about two-thirds of the 1960 population of the San Juan Basin communities included in the study.

2. Carroll and Haggard, 1942: 51. Young people were rarely espoused absolutely against their will, but in many cases the couple had little opportunity of getting acquainted prior to marriage.

3. Jaramillo, 1941: 31.

4. Pitt-Rivers, 1961: 104-6. The author notes that in Alcalá and other Andalusian towns, cousin and sibling-exchange marriages are rare.

5. Arensberg and Kimball, 1940: 57-65.

6. See Romero, 1928, for an interesting review of Father Martinez' views. Today in New Mexico a fresh controversy has arisen between young Hispanic priests and the hierarchy over the issue of priestly celibacy; some priests have chosen to marry despite consequent expulsion from the priesthood.

7. The enactments of Emperor Justinian in the sixth century A.D. banned marriage between spiritual relatives. Between 1300 and 1600 A.D., marriage between persons within seven degrees of kinship was also banned, effectively eliminating all people identifiably related by blood (Mintz and Wolf, 1950: 344-47). Canon Law no. 769 revoked in 1919 the ban on marriage between compadres.

8. Foster, 1953b: 4-10, 20-25.

9. Foster, 1953b: 4-5.

10. There are disadvantages in a selected sample. Many of the characteristics which can be analyzed out from it may be peculiar to a minority of the population. For genealogical tracking, however, it was imperative to select a lineage that could be traced over several generations. The conclusions drawn from the selected sample were checked against results from random samples in the same communities, with shallow pedigree data (Van Arsdale, communication, 1964) and the same patterns were found in both. The selected sample analyzed here had a larger Penitente representation than their percentage in the total population, because the Durango parish books furnished a more complete record for Cañada Bonita than for Rosa. In the Van Arsdale contemporary sample, selection of mother's parents to baptize the first child and of father's parents to baptize the second child is sufficiently high to demonstrate a clear-cut preference, although not a rule.

11. Pitt-Rivers, 1961: 106.

12. UNM Microfilm 73-12, 7/16/1833.

13. Jaramillo, 1941: 76.

14. An eyewitness account of a wake and burial at La Posta is given in Bryce, 1961: 194. This account largely accords with recollections of past proceedings and of occasional wakes held in recent years of which the author heard.

15. The Unión Protectiva is found in a number of communities of northern New Mexico, the center in Santa Fe being the first to be founded, in 1916. It is now a large and prosperous organization. Originally it sought to set up branches in other communities but later desisted. All

informants deny that this lay religious burial society was at any time sponsored by the Church and are at a loss to explain how it was founded in so many places within a few years.

16. For an extraordinarily perceptive analysis of the Pueblo world view, see Ortiz, 1969.

17. Juan de Oñate was descended from Montezuma. Antonio de Salazar of the Corral de Piedra Grant was a grandson of one of Oñate's soldiers and his Zuñi Pueblo wife.

18. The Matachine Dance is performed at Taos Pueblo at Christmas time, to the accompaniment of guitar and fiddle music played by Hispano musicians. At Picurís Pueblo, Hispano neighbors are usually among the dancers. Matachines are performed in the Hispano villages of Chimayó and Ranchos de Taos, former site of a Genízaro settlement. For a good description of the Matachine dance at San Juan Pueblo, see Kurath, 1970: 257-78.

19. Social enclavement, as Morton Freed has pointed out (1957), is the self-protective reaction of a small ethnic group which feels that its way of life is threatened by acculturative pressures. Freed gives as examples the Jewish *shtetl* (pale of settlement) of Eastern Europe before World War I and the Old Order Amish of Pennsylvania. The physical isolation of northern New Mexico used to be the principal perpetuating force for enclavement. Since the extension of the highway network and tourism into remote areas of the state, the Spanish language and a distinctive philosophical outlook continue to act as effective border maintaining mechanisms. See also Hawley and Senter, 1946.

20. Loomis and Grisham, 1943.

21. See chapter 1. See also Blawis, 1971, chapters 1 and 2.

22. Sanchez, 1940.

23. Trujillo ms., 1934.

Bibliography

AASF: Archives of the Archdiocese of Santa Fé, as indexed in Fray
Angélico Chaves, 1957, *Archives of the Archdiocese of Santa Fé,
1678-1900*. Washington, D.C.: Academy of American Franciscan
History.

Abel, Annie Heloise, ed., 1915. *The Official Correspondence of James C.
Calhoun*. Washington, D.C.: Government Printing Office.

Abel, Annie Heloise, 1916. The Journal of John Greiner. *Old Santa Fe*
3/2: 189-243.

Abel, Annie Heloise, 1941. From the Journal of John Ward. *New Mexico
Historical Review* 16: 206-232.

Abert, Lt. J.W., 1962. *Abert's New Mexico Report, 1846-1847*. Albuquerque: Horn and Wallace.

Adams, Eleanor B., ed., 1954. *Bishop Tamaron's Visitation of New Mexico, 1760*. Historical Society of New Mexico, Publications in History, 15.

Adams, Eleanor B. and Fray Angélico Chavez, 1956. *The Missions of New
Mexico, 1776*. Albuquerque: University of New Mexico Press.

AGN: *Archivo General de la Nación*. Originals stored in Mexico, D.F.

Alarid Leblanc, María del Refugio, 1873-1907. Correspondence with her
brother, J.M.H. Alarid, and other relatives. Letters loaned from
collection of family correspondence by Miss Josephine Silva of Del
Norte, Colorado.

Apodaca, Anacleto, 1952. Corn and Custom, in *Human Problems in
Technological Change*, Edward H. Spicer, ed. New York: John Wiley
and Sons, Inc.

Arensberg, Conrad M. and Solon T. Kimball, 1940. *Family and Community in Ireland*. Cambridge: Harvard University Press.

239

Bancroft, Hubert Howe, 1889. *History of North Mexican States and Texas* 2. San Francisco: The History Company, Publ.

Bancroft, Hubert Howe, 1889. *History of Arizona and New Mexico.* San Francisco: The History Company, Publ.

Blawis, Patricia Bell, 1971. *Tijerina and the Land Grants.* New York: International Publishers.

Bloom, Reverend Lansing Bartlett, 1913. Table of Missions, a ms. of New Mexico Archives in the Library of Congress. *Old Santa Fe* 1/1: 28.

Bolton, Herbert E., 1950. *Pageant in the Wilderness.* Salt Lake City: Utah Spanish Historical Society.

Borhegyi, Stephen F. de, 1956. *El Santuario de Chimayó.* Pamphlet of the Spanish Colonial Arts Society, Inc.

Boyd, E., 1957. Troubles at Ojo Caliente. *El Palacio* 64: 347-360.

Brayer, Herbert O., 1949. *William Blackmore: The Spanish-Mexican Land Grants of New Mexico and Colorado, 1863-1878,* 1. Denver: Bradford-Robinson.

Bryce, Mrs. John, 1961. A Lost Cemetery, in *Pioneers of the San Juan Country.* Sarah Platt Decker Chapter, N.S.D.A.R., vol. 4: 93-94. Denver: Bradford-Robinson.

Bunting, Bainbridge, 1964. *Taos Adobes.* Fort Burgwin Research Center, publ. no. 2. Santa Fe: Museum of New Mexico Press.

Burma, John and David E. Williams, 1961. *An Economic, Social and Educational Survey of Rio Arriba and Taos Counties.* Prepared for Northern New Mexico College, El Rito, ms.

Carroll, H. Bailey and J. Villasana Haggard, ed. and trans., 1942. *Three New Mexico Chronicles.* Quivira Society, 11. Albuquerque: University of New Mexico Press.

Chavez, Fray Angélico, 1954a. *Origins of New Mexico Families.* Santa Fe: Historical Society of New Mexico.

Chavez, Fray Angélico, 1954b. The Penitentes of New Mexico. *New Mexico Historical Review* 29: 97-123.

Chavez, Fray Angélico, 1955. José Gonzales, Genízaro Governor. *New Mexico Historical Review* 30: 190-194.

Chavez, Fray Angélico, 1967. Pohe-Yemo's Representative and the Revolt of 1680. *New Mexico Historical Review* 42: 85-126.

Cornelius, Olive Frazier, 1961. San Juan County Pioneers, in *Pioneers of the San Juan Country.* Sarah Platt Decker Chapter, N.S.D.A.R., vol 4: 151-157. Denver: Bradford-Robinson.

Crocchiola, Father Stanley, (n.d.). *The Abiquiu Story.* Private Publ.

Darley, Alex M., 1893. *Penitentes of the Southwest.* Pueblo, Colorado: Private Publ.

Di Peso, Charles, 1968. Casas Grandes and the Gran Chichimeca. *El Palacio* 75/4: 45-61.

Dozier, Edward, 1970. *The Pueblo Indians of North America.* New York: Holt, Rinehart, and Winston, Inc.

Edmonson, Munro, 1957. *Los Manitos: A Study of Institutional Values.*

Middle American Research Institute, publ. 25. New Orleans: Tulane University.

El Reino de Dios. Antonito, Colorado: Parish Bulletin. June 1934, "A la Parroquia de Conejos en sus Bodas de Diamante."

Espinosa, J.M., transl., introd., notes, 1940. *First Expedition of De Vargas into New Mexico, 1692.* Albuquerque: Coronado Historical Series, 10.

Forbes, Jack, 1960. *Apache, Navajo and Spaniard.* Norman: University of Oklahoma Press.

Foster, George M., 1953a. What is Folk Culture? *American Anthropologist* 55: 59-173.

Foster, George M., 1953b. Cofradia and Compadrazgo in Spain and Spanish America. *Southwestern Journal of Anthropology* 9: 1-28.

Foster, George M., 1960. *Culture and Conquest.* Viking Fund Publications in Anthropology, no. 27.

Foster, George M., 1960-1961. Interpersonal Relations in Peasant Society. *Human Organization* 19: 174-187.

Foster, George M., 1964. Speech Forms and Perceptions of Social Distance in a Spanish-Speaking Mexican Village. *Southwestern Journal of Anthropology* 20: 107-122.

Francis, E.K., 1956. Padre Martinez: A New Mexico Myth. *New Mexico Historical Review* 31: 265-289.

FRC: Federal Records Center, Denver, Colorado. Records of Southern Ute Agency, 1877-1952, as indexed by Frances L. Swadesh in Omer C. Stewart, *Ethnohistorical Bibliography of the Ute Indians of Colorado.* Boulder: University of Colorado Press, 1971, appendix A.

Freed, Stanley A., 1957. Suggested Type Societies in Acculturation Studies. *American Anthropologist* 59: 55-68.

Galvez, Bernardo de, 1951. *Instructions For Governing the Interior Provinces of New Spain, 1786.* Transl. and ed. by Donald E. Worcester. Berkeley: The Quivira Society, 12.

Gibson, Charles, 1952. *Tlaxcala in the 16th Century.* New Haven: Yale University Press.

Gilpin, William, 1862. Annual Report of Superintendent of Indian Affairs for Colorado Territory, in *Annual Report of Commissioner of Indian Affairs, 1861:* 712-713. Washington, D.C.: Government Printing Office.

Gill, Mario, 1964. *Nuestros Buenos Vecinos.* Mexico, D.F.: Editorial Azteca.

Grubbs, Frank, 1960-1962. Frank Bond: Gentleman Sheepherder of Northern New Mexico, 1883-1915. *New Mexico Historical Review* 35: 169-199 (part 1) and 37: 43-71 (conclusion).

Gunnerson, Dolores A., 1956. The Southern Athabascans: Their Arrival in the Southwest. *El Palacio* 63: 346-365.

Gunnerson, James H., 1969. Apache Archeology in Northeastern New Mexico. *American Antiquity* 34/1: 32-39.

Gunnerson, James H. and Dolores A., 1970. Evidence of Apaches at Pecos. *El Palacio* 76/3: 1-6.

Hackett, Charles W., ed. and transl., 1937. *Historical Documents Relating to New Mexico, Nueva Vizcaya and Approaches Thereto*, 3. Washington, D.C.: Carnegie Institute, publ. no. 33.

Hackett, Charles W. and C.C. Shelby, 1942. *Revolt of the Pueblo Indians and Otermin's Attempted Reconquest 1680-1682.* Albuquerque: Coronado Historical Series 8-9.

Hafen, Leroy R. and Ann W., 1954. *Old Spanish Trail: Santa Fe to Los Angeles.* Glendale, California: The Arthur H. Clark Company.

Haines, Francis, 1938a. Where Did the Plains Indians Get Their Horses. *American Anthropologist* 40/1: 112-117.

Haines, Francis, 1938b. The Northward Spread of Horses Among the Plains Indians. *American Anthropologist* 40/3: 429-437.

Hall, Edward T., 1944. Recent Clues to Athabascan Prehistory in the Southwest. *American Anthropologist* 46:98-105.

Haring, Clarence H., 1947. *The Spanish Empire in America*, New York and Burlingame: Harcourt, Brace, and World, Inc. (Harbinger Books ed., 1963).

Harper, Allan G., Andrew Cordova and Kalervo Oberg, 1943. *Man and Resources in the Middle Rio Grande Valley.* Inter-American Studies 2. Albuquerque: University of New Mexico Press.

Haury, Emil, 1967. The Hohokam, First Masters of the American Desert. *National Geographic* 70-695.

Hawley, Florence and Donovan Senter, 1946. Group-Designated Behavior in Two Acculturating Groups. *Southwestern Journal of Anthropology* 2: 133-151.

Hefferan, Vioalle Clark, 1940. *Thomas Benton Catron.* Unpublished M.A. Thesis, University of New Mexico.

Henderson, Alice Corbin, 1937. *Brothers of Light.* New York: Harcourt, Brace and Company (reprinted, 1962, Chicago: The Rio Grande Press, Inc.).

Hibben, Frank, 1951. Sites of the Paleo-Indian in the Middle Rio Grande Valley. *American Antiquity* 17/1: 41-46.

Horgan, Paul, 1954. *Great River: The Rio Grande in North American History.* New York-Toronto: Rhinehart and Company, Inc.

Hurt, Wesley R., 1941. *Manzano, a Study of Community Disorganization.* Unpublished Ph.D. Thesis, University of New Mexico.

Jaramillo, María Cliofes M. de, 1941. *Shadows of the Past.* Santa Fe: The Seton Village Press.

Jennings, Jesse D., 1964. The Desert Southwest, in *Prehistoric Man in the New World*, J.D. Jennings and E. Norbeck, eds. Chicago: University of Chicago Press.

Jones, Oakah L., 1966. *Pueblo Warriors and Spanish Conquest.* Norman: University of Oklahoma Press.

Keleher, William A., 1957. *Violence in Lincoln County.* Albuquerque: University of New Mexico Press.

Keleher, William A., 1962. *The Fabulous Frontier.* Albuquerque: University of New Mexico Press, revised edition.

Knowlton, Clark S., 1964. One Approach to the Economic and Social Problems of New Mexico. *New Mexico Business* 3: 15-22.

Kurath, Gertrude P., 1970. *Music and Dance of the Tewa Pueblos.* Santa Fe: Museum of New Mexico Press.

Lange, Charles and Carroll Riley, eds., 1966. *The Southwestern Journals of Adolph Bandelier, 1880-1882.* Albuquerque: University of New Mexico Press.

Larson, Robert W., 1962. Statehood for New Mexico, 1888-1912. *New Mexico Historical Review* 37: 161-200.

Lowie, Robert, 1963. *Indians of the Plains.* Garden City, New York: The Natural History Press.

Maloney, Thomas J., 1964. Recent Demographic and Economic Changes in Northern New Mexico. *New Mexico Business* 3: 4-14.

MANM: *Mexican Archives of New Mexico, 1822-1846.* New Mexico State Records Center, Santa Fe. Microfilm.

McCarty, Frankie, 1969. *Land Grant Problems in New Mexico.* Albuquerque Journal Pamphlet.

McClellan, Ella, 1961. History of the Sacred Heart Church, in *Pioneers of the San Juan Country.* Sarah Platt Decker Chapter N.S.D.A.R., vol. 4:112-114. Denver: Bradford-Robinson.

McCulloch, Mary B., 1961. Pioneering the Ute Strip, in *Pioneers of the San Juan Country.* Sarah Platt Decker Chapter N.S.D.A.R., vol. 4:195-197. Denver: Bradford-Robinson.

Mead, Margaret, ed., 1954. The Spanish Americans of New Mexico in *Cultural Patterns and Technical Change.* New York: A Mentor Book (by arrangement with UNESCO).

Minge, Ward Alan, 1963. The Last Will and Testament of Don Severino Martinez. *New Mexican Quarterly* 33/1: 33-56.

Minge, Ward Alan, 1965. *Frontier Problems in New Mexico Preceding the Mexican War, 1840-1845.* Unpublished Ph.D. Thesis, University of New Mexico.

Mintz, Sidney W. and Eric R. Wolf, 1950. An Analysis of Ritual Co-Parenthood (Compadrazgo). *Southwestern Journal of Anthropology* 6: 341-368.

Moorhead, Max L., 1958. *New Mexico's Royal Road: Trade and Travel on the Chihuahua Trail.* Norman: University of Oklahoma Press.

NMLG: New Mexico Land Grants, as indexed in *A Guide to the Microfilm of Papers Relating to New Mexico Land Grants,* by Albert James Diaz. Albuquerque: University of New Mexico Press. (63 microfilm reels in Bureau of Land Management, Santa Fe, and elsewhere). SG refers to the case numbers of land claims adjudicated by the Surveyor General and to the file numbers of unadjudicated land claims in the years 1854-1890. PLC refers to land claims adjudicated by the Court of Private Land Claims in the years 1891-1904.

NMT: *New Mexico Territorial Archives.* New Mexico State Records Center, Santa Fe.

NMSRC: *New Mexico State Records Center.* Archives, Special Collections, referred to by name of collector: *Maria G. Duran, Fiske, Silviano, Salazar, Twitchell.* Also, *miscellaneous documents,* referred to as *NMSRC Misc.*

Ortiz, Alfonso, 1969. *The Tewa World.* Chicago: University of Chicago Press.

Parish Records: *San Juan Nepomuceno,* El Rito, New Mexico, 1869-1882; *Saint Joseph,* Parkview, New Mexico, 1883-1900; *Our Lady of Guadalupe,* Conejos, Colorado, 1860-1884; *Sacred Heart,* Durango, Colorado, 1881-1960.

Pehrson, Robert N., 1954. Bilateral Kin Groupings as a Structural Type: A Preliminary Statement. *Journal of East Asiatic Studies* 3: 199-202. (Bobbs-Merrill Reprint No. A-181).

Pitt-Rivers, Julian A., 1961. *People of the Sierra.* Chicago and London: University of Chicago Press (A Phoenix Book).

Price, Glen W., 1967. *Origins of the War With Mexico.* Austin: University of Texas Press.

Quintana, J.V. and Sons, *Store Records,* 1905-1919, 2 vols. Microfilmed for Tri-Ethnic Project and donated by Miguel F. Quintana to Western History Collection, University of Colorado Library.

Rasch, Philip, 1965. Feuding at Farmington. *New Mexico Historical Review* 60: 215-232.

Read, Benjamin M., 1912. *Illustrated History of New Mexico.* Santa Fe: Santa Fe New Mexican Printing Company.

Reeve, Frank D., 1937. *The Federal Indian Policy in New Mexico, 1858-1880.* Unpublished Ph.D. Thesis, University of Texas. (Published, 1938, in *New Mexico Historical Review.*)

Rendon, Gabino, 1963. *Hand on My Shoulder,* New York: Board of National Missions, Presbyterian Church in the U.S.A. (revised edition).

Richie, Eleanor Louise, 1932. *Spanish Relations with the Yuta Indians.* Unpublished M.A. Thesis, University of Denver.

Río Grande County School Bulletin 10/1962. Del Norte, Colorado.

Río Grande Sun, Special Historical Edition, 11/8/1962, Española, New Mexico.

Romano V., Octavio Ignacio, 1960. Donship in a Mexican-American Community in Texas. *American Anthropologist* 62: 966-976.

Romero, Cecil V., transl., 1928. Apologia of Antonio José Martinez, 1838. *New Mexico Historical Review* 3: 325-346.

Rosa J.P. Court Records, 1889-1947 (partial), Book No. 5, Book No. 250.

Sanchez, George I., 1940. *Forgotten People, A Study of New Mexicans.* Albuquerque: University of New Mexico Press.

Sanford, Albert B., 1933. Recollections of a Trip to San Luis Valley in 1877. *Colorado Magazine* 10: 176.

SANM: Spanish Archives of New Mexico, as indexed and described by Ralph Emerson Twitchell in *Spanish Archives of New Mexico.* Cedar Rapids, Iowa: The Torch Press, 1914. Volume 1: Wills and Land Transfers, originals in vaults of Bureau of Land Management, Santa Fé and microfilmed for NMLG. Volume 2: Judicial and Military Documents, originals in Archives, New Mexico State Records Center, Santa Fé.

Schulman, Sam and Anne M. Smith, 1962. *Health and Disease in Northern New Mexico.* Unpublished monograph, Institute of Behavioral Science, University of Colorado.

Scholes, France V., 1942. *Troublous Times in New Mexico, 1659-1670.* Historical Society of New Mexico, Publications in History, 2.

Schroeder, Albert H., 1965. A Brief History of the Southern Utes. *Southwestern Lore* 30: 53-78.

Simmons, Marc, 1964. Tlaxcalans in the Spanish Borderlands. *New Mexico Historical Review* 39/2: 101-110.

Simmons, Marc, 1968. *Spanish Government in New Mexico.* Albuquerque: University of New Mexico Press.

Spicer, Edward H., 1962. *Cycles of Conquest.* Tucson: University of Arizona Press.

Swadesh, Frances Leon, 1962. *The Southern Utes and Their Neighbors, 1877-1926.* Unpublished M.A. Thesis, University of Colorado.

Swadesh, Frances Leon, 1965. Property and Kinship in Northern New Mexico. *Rocky Mountain Social Science Journal* 2/1: 209-214.

Swadesh, Frances Leon, 1966. *Hispanic Americans of the Ute Frontier.* Unpublished Ph.D. Thesis, University of Colorado.

Swadesh, Frances Leon, 1968. The Alianza Movement: Catalyst for Social Change in New Mexico. *Proceedings of the 1968 Annual Spring Meeting of the American Ethnological Society:* 162-177.

Swadesh, Frances Leon. The Alianza Movement: The Interplay of Social Change and Public Commentary, in *Minorities and Politics,* Henry J. Tobias and Charles Woodhouse, eds., 53-84. Albuquerque: University of New Mexico Press.

TAG: *Abstract of Title to the Tierra Amarilla Grant* in the County of Rio Arriba, New Mexico, known as the "Old Hernandez Abstract."

Tate Gallery, 1970. *Guadalupe Hidalgo Treaty of Peace, 1848, and the Gadsden Treaty with Mexico, 1853.* Española: the Rio Grande Sun Press.

Taylor, John W., 1933-1934. *Interviews with, and Letters to Leroy Hafen.* State Historical Museum Library Collection, Denver, Colorado.

TEP: *Tri-Ethnic Project Records* (1960 Community Census, field diaries and interview notes, microfilm record of historical documents). University of Colorado.

Thomas, Alfred B., 1932. *Forgotten Frontiers.* Norman: University of Oklahoma Press.

Trujillo, José E., 1934. *History of Atanacio Trujillo,* as originally written in 1866 by his son, Luis Rafael Trujillo. Translated by Frances Leon Swadesh from microfilm in the historical records of the Tri-Ethnic Project; original is in the collection of the Colorado Writers' Project, State Historical Museum Library Collection, Denver, Colorado.

Turley, J., 1935. *Motion for Leave to File Petition to Appear as Amicus Curiae,* Supreme Court of the United States, October Term, 1935, No. 15. Original, State of Texas, Complainant vs. State of New Mexico, Defendant.

Twitchell, Ralph Emerson, 1911-1912. *Leading Facts of New Mexico History,* 1 (1911), 2 (1912). Cedar Rapids, Iowa: The Torch Press.

Twitchell, Ralph Emerson, 1925. *Old Santa Fe.* Reprinted, 1963. Chicago: The Rio Grande Press, Inc.

United States Census Reports: Rio Arriba County, New Mexico, 1870, especially Tierra Amarilla; Rio Arriba County, New Mexico, 1880, especially San Juan Precincts; Conejos, Huérfano and Animas Counties, Colorado, 1870; Conejos County, Colorado, 1880.

University of New Mexico Microfilm, No. 73-12: Baptismal Records of Abiquiu, 1832-1861.

USDA: *United States Department of Agriculture,* Soil Conservation Service, Region 8, Albuquerque, New Mexico, Regional Studies.

  1936 *Reconnaissance Survey of Human Dependency on Resources in the Rio Grande Watershed,* Regional Bulletin No. 33.

  1937 *Notes on Community-Owned Land Grants in New Mexico,* Section of Human Surveys.

  1939 *Tewa Basin Study, Vol. 2: The Spanish-American Villages.*

Van Arsdale, Minor, 1964. Communication concerning a partial study of a random sample of marriage and godparent choices among Hispanos and Utes of the Tri-Ethnic Community.

Velasquez, Jesus María, n.d. *Testimony on the 1854 settlement of the Guadalupe Colony,* in collection of Colorado Writers' Project. State Historical Museum Library, Denver, Colorado.

Velasquez, José, 1912-1913. *Correspondence with the Office of Indian Affairs and Affidavits* in relation to charges brought against him by Superintendent Stephen Abbot. Documents loaned by Mrs. María Perfecta S. de Velasquez and microfilmed for the historical collection of the Tri-Ethnic Project.

Waldrip, William M., 1953. New Mexico During the Civil War. *New Mexico Historical Review* 28: 251-290.

Warner, Louis H., 1931. Conveyance of Property, the Spanish or Mexican Way. *New Mexico Historical Review* 6: 334-359.

Westphall, Victor, 1965. *The Public Domain in New Mexico, 1854-1891.*
 Albuquerque: University of New Mexico Press.
Wilder, Mitchell A. and Edgar Breitenbach, 1943. *Santos.* Colorado
 Springs: The Taylor Museum of Colorado Springs Fine Arts Center.
Woodward, Dorothy, 1935. *The Penitentes of New Mexico.* Unpublished
 Ph.D. Thesis, Yale University.

Index

249

dians, 7-8; proposal for Utes and Comanches, 38-39; among 16th century Pueblos, 9; on San Joaquin grant, 49; on Tierra Amarilla grant, 82-83; on Ute lands on shares, 98. *See also* Irrigation
Farmington, N.M., 89-90, 94
Fergusson, H. B., 112
Fernando VII, King of Spain, 50
Forfeiture. *See Realengo*
Fort Garland: troops attack *Penitentes*, 76
Fort Lewis, Colo., 90
Fort Lowell, N.M., 82
Fort Sumner, N.M., 65
Frances Creek: Stollsteimer-Piedra confluence, 103, 121; tributary of San Juan River, 105
Franciscans: at Abiquiu, 44; forcible evangelization by, forbidden, 15; mission founded at Abiquiu, 39; during Pueblo Revolt, 14; in 17th century, 13; Third Order of, 75. *See also* Evangelization; Priests
Freeman, J. M., 87
Frontier: 18th century way of life on, 41-42, 153; rate of change, 150-51; settlement of, 72, 94-95
Frost, Max, 90, 94

Gallegos families: J. Pablo, 83; Pedro Ygnacio, 50; Rubio, 121
Gallina, N.M., 70
Gamboa, Juan de, 33
García families: Filomena, 119; Jacobo, 220 n. 3; Juan Manuel, 119; Lagos, 169
García de la Mora families: José, 49; Juan, 163; Manuel, 168, 210 n. 11
García de Noriega family: Juan Cristobal, 174; Juan Estevan, 34, 48; Joaquin, 48, 54; Mateo, 168
Genízaros, 23, 38, 40, 213 n. 17, 214 n. 20; citizenship and political activity of, 23, 53, 54; in 1837 rebellion, 58-59; and land, 38, 39-40, 42, 54-58; lifestyle, 41-46; pottery-making, 41; pov-

erty of, 58, 59-60; Pueblo Indians as, 40; and religion, 41; and social mobility, 42-43, 45-46, 160; surnames in Abiquiu, 40-41
Gilpin, William, 79
Girón, Vicente, 33
Given, Isaac, 60
Gobernador, N.M., 105
Godparents. *See* Baptism
Gold rush, 64, 67
Gomez family, 65
Gonzales families: Anastasio, 222 n. 9; Andrea, 228 n. 24; José, 58; Petrona, 228 n. 24
Gossip, 155
Governors (New Mexico): Anza, Juan Bautista de, 40, 166; Armijo, Manuel, 55, 58, 59, 69; Arny, William (acting), 69; Chacon, Fernando de, 168; Codallos y Rabal, Juan, 36; Cruzat y Góngora, Gervasio, 33; Gonzales, José, 58; Martinez y Lejanza, Mariano, 62, 232 n. 9; Melgares, Facundo, 53, 172, 174; Mendinueta, Pedro Fermín de, 134-135, 165, 226 n. 4; Olavide y Michelena, Enrique de, 165; Paez Hurtado, Juan, 33, 215 n. 30; Perez, Albino, 58; Pile, William, 69; Real Alencaster, Joaquin del, 43, 233 n. 22; Trebol Navarro, Francisco, 165-67; Veles Cachupin, Tomás, 35-36, 39, 42, 137
Grant, Henry, 218 n. 32
Greiner, John, 78
Griego family: Juan Domingo, 149; Mariana, 220 n. 6; origins of, 215 n. 28
Guadalupe, Colo., 72, 78
Guadalupe Hidalgo, Treaty of, 28-29, 69, 71, 204
Gurule family: Juan Roman, 122, 221 n. 6; origins, 215 n. 28

Haines, William B., 90-91
Hayes, Rutherford B., 71
Head, Lafayette (Rafael Cabeza),